C++ High Performance

Boost and optimize the performance of your C++17 code

Viktor Sehr
Björn Andrist

BIRMINGHAM - MUMBAI

C++ High Performance

Commissioning Editors: Aaron Lazar
Acquisition Editor: Denim Pinto
Content Development Editors: Nikhil Borkar
Technical Editor: Jijo Maliyekal
Copy Editor: Safis Editing
Project Coordinator: Vaidehi Sawant
Proofreader: Safis Editing
Indexers: Rekha Nair
Graphics: Tania Dutta
Production Coordinator: Arvindkumar Gupta

First published: January 2018

Production reference: 1300118

Published by Packt Publishing Ltd.
Livery Place
35 Livery Street
Birmingham
B3 2PB, UK.

ISBN 978-1-78712-095-2

www.packtpub.com

Mapt

Foreword

C++ stepped onto the stage in 1983 and hasn't stopped reinventing itself for a single year since. It has gone from a single frontend language on top of C to a first-class citizen of the compiler world. Each new C++ standard has added substantial functionality, sometimes to excess. In the words of Stroustrup, "Within C++, there is a much smaller and cleaner language struggling to get out."

The problem, of course, is that the "smaller and cleaner language" to be found within C++ changes with situation. Mastering C++ is akin to mastering a multitude of domain-specific languages, each tailored to a specific use. The dialect that makes sense for embedded system is nonsensical for large enterprise applications, and the phrasing that powers a game engine is unbearable when applied to a word processor.

C++ High Performance teaches you a C++ dialect for rapidly developing high-performance code. From C++11 onward, there have been a vast array of features in both the C++ language and the C++ STL that let you spend more time writing your application and less time handling implementation details. This is the focus of the book and where it shines.

Each topic is framed in the larger context of application development and computer science. For the reader who needs to get up to speed with the latest C++ techniques on a short notice, this information provides the necessary landmarks to stay oriented. Specific examples, recipes, and logical progressions take you from a basic use of auto and <algorithm> all the way up to using Boost to transparently run your algorithms on the GPU via OpenCL. Fundamental issues around modern C++ (memory management and ownership, considerations of time and space, advance template usage, and others) are explained step by step so that, by the later chapters, the readers proceed into advanced territory with confidence.

I have worked on a wide variety of projects—large and small, low level and managed, and some even in custom languages I designed and built—but C++ holds a special place in my heart. My first full-time job was writing C++ code for a game technology company in the early 2000s. I loved it, not least of all because a big part of the technology revolved around the reflection of the C++ code base into the editor and scripting language. Someone once described C++ as an octopus made by nailing extra legs onto a dog, and I spent a lot of time with a hammer making our code base do things that C++ was never intended to do. Yet, the octopus we ended up with was, in its own way, beautiful and very effective.

C++ has evolved tremendously since those days, and it is my privilege to open the door for you as you walk into an exciting new world of possibilities. Viktor and Björn are brilliant and experienced developers with a remarkable pedigree, and they have a lot of great things in store for you.

Ben Garney
CEO, The Engine Company

Contributors

About the authors

Viktor Sehr is the main developer at Toppluva, working with a highly-optimized graphics engine aimed for mobile hardware.
He has 10 years of professional experience using C++, with real-time graphics, audio, and architectural design as his focus areas. Through his career, he has developed medical visualization software at Mentice and Raysearch Laboratories as well as real-time audio applications at Propellerhead Software. Viktor holds an M.S. in media science from Linköping University.

I would like to acknowledge the colleagues who have broadened my knowledge in programming during my carrier (in alphabetical order); Andreas Brinck, Peter Forsberg, Rickard Holmberg, Sigfred Håvardssen, Tobias Kruseborn, Philippe Peirano, Johan Riddersporre, Marcus Sonestedt, and Mattias Unger. Additionally, I would like to thank our technical reviewers Louis E. Mauget, and especially, Sergey Gomon. Lastly, my Hanna, for your love and support.

Björn Andrist is a freelance software consultant currently focusing on audio applications. For more than 10 years, he has been working professionally with C++ in projects ranging from Unix server applications to real-time audio applications on desktop and mobile. In the past, he has also taught courses in algorithms and data structures, concurrent programming, and programming methodologies. Björn holds a BS in computer engineering and an MS in computer science from KTH Royal Institute of Technology.

First I would like to thank the team at Packt Publishing who helped and contributed to make this book possible. Thank you Louis E. Mauget for reviewing the book and providing me with insights, knowledge, and encouragement. A special thanks goes to Sergey Gomon, who has done an outstanding job reviewing the book and working with the code examples. Last, and most of all, I must thank my family for their support and for understanding my many hours at the computer - thank you Aleida, Agnes, and Clarence.

About the reviewers

Sergey Gomon started his journey in IT 10 years ago in Belarus State University of Informatics and Radioelectronics in the artificial intelligence department. He has about 8 years of industrial programming experience using C++ in several fields, such as network programming, information security, and image processing. In his free time, he likes reading, traveling, and studying something new.

He currently works at Regula and SolarWinds MSP, and is an activist of the CoreHard C++ community.

> *I want to say thanks to my friend Artem Lapitsky who is always ready to share his wisdom with me.*

Louis E. Mauget never saw the ENIAC but coded in those languages, adding several modern languages and frameworks. C++ continues to evolve, and Lou evolves with it. Interested in reactive functional programming, containers, and deep learning, he blogs about software technology for Keyhole Software, where he works as a senior software engineer. A coauthor of three computer books, he also wrote IBM developerWorks tutorials and a WebSphere Journal two-part LDAP tutorial. He cowrote several J2EE certification tests for IBM and has been a reviewer for Packt Publishing and others.

Packt is searching for authors like you

Table of Contents

Preface

C++ of today provides programmers the ability to write expressive and robust code while still having the ability to target almost any hardware platform or real-time requirements. This makes C++ a unique language. Over the last few years, C++ has turned into a modern language that is more fun to use and with better defaults.

This book aims to give the reader a solid foundation to write efficient applications as well as an insight into strategies for implementing libraries in modern C++. We have tried to take a practical approach to explain how C++ works today, where C++14/C++17 features are a natural part of the language, rather than looking at C++ historically.

This book has been written by us, Viktor and Björn, collaboratively. However, the drafts of each chapter were written individually, and after that, we have worked together to improve the chapters and assemble them into a complete book. Viktor is the main author of chapter 1, 2, 5, 8, 9, and 11. Björn is the main author of chapter 3, 4, 7, and 10. We have worked hard to attain a consistent style throughout the book, and we think that it has been a big advantage to write this book together. Many subjects have been debated and processed for the better.

Who this book is for

This book expects you to have a basic knowledge of C++ and computer architecture and a genuine interest in evolving your skills. Hopefully, by the time you finish this book, you will have gained a few insights into how you can improve your C++ applications, both performance-wise and syntactically. On top of that, we also hope that you will have a few aha moments.

What this book covers

`Chapter 1`, *A Brief Introduction to C++*, introduces some important properties of C++ such as zero-cost abstractions, value semantics, const correctness, explicit ownership, and error handling. It also discusses the drawbacks of C++.

`Chapter 2`, *Modern C++ Concepts,* outlines automatic type deduction using `auto`, lambda functions, move semantics, `std::optional`, and `std::any`.

`Chapter 3`, *Measuring Performance,* discusses asymptotic complexity and big O notation, practical performance testing, and how to profile your code to find hotspots.

`Chapter 4`, *Data Structures,* takes you through the importance of structuring the data so that it can be accessed quickly. STL containers such as `std::vector`, `std::list`, `std::unordered_map`, and `std::priority_queue` are introduced. Finally, we describe how to iterate over parallel arrays.

`Chapter 5`, *A Deeper Look at Iterators,* dives into the concept of iterators, and shows how iterators can go beyond just referring to objects in containers.

`Chapter 6`, *STL Algorithms and Beyond,* shows the obvious, and the not so obvious, advantages of STL algorithms over hand rolled for loops. It also takes a look at the limitations of STL algorithms and how the new Ranges library overcomes these limits.

`Chapter 7`, *Memory Management,* focuses on safe and efficient memory management. This includes memory ownership, RAII, smart pointers, stack memory, dynamic memory, and custom memory allocators.

`Chapter 8`, *Metaprogramming and Compile-Time Evaluation,* explains metaprogramming concepts such as `constexpr`, heterogeneous containers, `type_traits`, `std::enable_if`, and `std::is_detected`. It also gives practical examples of metaprogramming use cases, such as reflection.

`Chapter 9`, *Proxy Objects and Lazy Evaluation,* explores how proxy objects can be used to perform under-the-hood optimizations while preserving clean syntax. Additionally, some creative uses of operator-overloading are demonstrated.

`Chapter 10`, *Concurrency,* covers the fundamentals of concurrent programming, including parallel execution, shared memory, data races, and deadlocks. It also includes an introduction to the C++ thread support library, the atomic library, and the C++ memory model.

`Chapter 11`, *Parallel STL,* starts by showing the complexity of writing parallel algorithms. It then demonstrates how to utilize STL algorithms in a parallel context using the parallel extensions for STL and Boost Compute.

To get the most out of this book

To get the most out of this book, you need to have a basic knowledge of C++. It's preferable if you have already been facing problems related to performance and are now looking for new tools and practices to have ready the next time you need to work with performance and C++.

There are a lot of code examples in this book. Some are taken from the real world, but most of them are artificial or vastly simplified examples to prove a concept rather than providing you with production-ready code. We have put all the code examples in source files divided by chapter so that it is fairly easy to find the examples you want to experiment with. If you open up the source code files, you will note that we have replaced most of the `main()` functions from the examples with test cases written with Google Test framework. We hope that this will help you rather than confuse you. It allowed us to write helpful descriptions for each example, and it also makes it easier to run all the examples from one chapter at once.

In order to compile and run the examples, you will need the following:

- A computer
- An operation system (we have verified the examples on Windows and macOS)
- A compiler (we have been using Clang, GCC, and Microsoft Visual C++)
- CMake

The CMake script provided with the example code will download and install further dependencies such as Boost, OpenCL, and Google Test.

During the writing of this book, it has been of great help for us to use Compiler Explorer, which is available at `https://godbolt.org/`. Compiler Explorer is an online compiler service that lets you try various compilers and versions. Try it out if you haven't already!

Download the example code files

You can download the example code files for this book from your account at `www.packtpub.com`. If you purchased this book elsewhere, you can visit `www.packtpub.com/support` and register to have the files emailed directly to you.

You can download the code files by following these steps:

1. Log in or register at `www.packtpub.com`.
2. Select the **SUPPORT** tab.
3. Click on **Code Downloads & Errata**.
4. Enter the name of the book in the **Search** box and follow the onscreen instructions.

Once the file is downloaded, please make sure that you unzip or extract the folder using the latest version of:

- WinRAR/7-Zip for Windows
- Zipeg/iZip/UnRarX for Mac
- 7-Zip/PeaZip for Linux

The code bundle for the book is also hosted on GitHub at `https://github.com/PacktPublishing/Cpp-High-Performance`. We also have other code bundles from our rich catalog of books and videos available at `https://github.com/PacktPublishing/`. Check them out!

Conventions used

There are a number of text conventions used throughout this book.

`CodeInText`: Indicates code words in text, folder names, filenames, file extensions, dummy URLs, and user input. Here is an example: "The keyword `constexpr` was introduced in C++11."

A block of code is set as follows:

```
#include <iostream>

auto main() -> int {
  std::cout << "High Performance C++\n";
}
```

When we wish to draw your attention to a particular part of a code block, the relevant lines or items are set in bold:

```
#include <iostream>

auto main() -> int {
  std::cout << "High Performance C++\n";
}
```

Any command-line input or output is written as follows:

```
$ clang++ -std=c++17 high_performance.cpp
$ ./a.out
$ High Performance C++
```

Bold: Indicates a new term, an important word, or words that you see onscreen. For example, words in menus or dialog boxes appear in the text like this. Here is an example: "Select **System info** from the **Administration** panel."

Warnings or important notes appear like this.

Tips and tricks appear like this.

Get in touch

Feedback from our readers is always welcome.

General feedback: Email `feedback@packtpub.com` and mention the book title in the subject of your message. If you have questions about any aspect of this book, please email us at `questions@packtpub.com`.

Errata: Although we have taken every care to ensure the accuracy of our content, mistakes do happen. If you have found a mistake in this book, we would be grateful if you would report this to us. Please visit `www.packtpub.com/submit-errata`, selecting your book, clicking on the Errata Submission Form link, and entering the details.

Piracy: If you come across any illegal copies of our works in any form on the Internet, we would be grateful if you would provide us with the location address or website name. Please contact us at `copyright@packtpub.com` with a link to the material.

If you are interested in becoming an author: If there is a topic that you have expertise in and you are interested in either writing or contributing to a book, please visit `authors.packtpub.com`.

Reviews

Please leave a review. Once you have read and used this book, why not leave a review on the site that you purchased it from? Potential readers can then see and use your unbiased opinion to make purchase decisions, we at Packt can understand what you think about our products, and our authors can see your feedback on their book. Thank you!

For more information about Packt, please visit `packtpub.com`.

1

A Brief Introduction to C++

This chapter will introduce some of the features of C++ that we think are important for writing robust and high performance applications. We will also discuss advantages and disadvantages of C++ over languages based upon a garbage collector. Last, we will look at some examples of how to handle exceptions and resources.

Why C++?

We begin this book by exploring some of the reasons for using C++ today. In short, C++ is a highly portable language which offers zero-cost abstractions. Furthermore, we believe that C++ provides programmers with the ability to write and manage large, expressive, and robust code bases. Let's explore the meaning of each of these properties.

Zero-cost abstractions

Active code bases grow. The more developers working on a code base, the larger the code base becomes. We need abstractions such as functions, classes, data structures, layers and so on in order to manage the complexity of a large-scale code base. But constantly adding abstractions and new levels of indirection comes at a price — efficiency. This is where zero-cost abstractions plays its role. A lot of the abstractions offered by C++ comes at a very low price. At a minimum, C++ offers efficient alternatives at hot spots where performance really is a concern.

With C++ you are free to talk about memory addresses and other computer related low-level terms when needed. However, in a large-scale software project it is desirable to express code in terms that deals with whatever the application is doing, and let the libraries handle the computer related terminology. The source code of a graphics application may deal with pencils, colors, and filters, whereas a game may deal with mascots, castles, and mushrooms. Low-level computer-related terms such as memory addresses can stay hidden in C++ library code where performance is critical.

By library code, we refer to code whose concepts are not strictly related to the application. The line between library code and application code can be blurry though, and libraries are often built upon other libraries. An example could be the container algorithms provided in the **Standard Template Library (STL)** of C++ or a general-purpose math library.

Programming languages and machine code abstractions

In order to relieve programmers from dealing with computer-related terms, modern programming languages use abstractions so that a list of strings, for example, can be handled and thought of as a list of strings rather than a list of addresses that we may easily lose track of if we make the slightest typo. Not only do the abstractions relieve the programmers from bugs, they also make the code more expressive by using concepts from the domain of the application. In other words, the code is expressed in terms that are closer to a spoken language than if expressed with abstract programming keywords.

C++ and C are nowadays two completely different languages. Still, C++ is highly compatible with C and has inherited a lot of its syntax and idioms from C. To give you some examples of C++ abstractions we will here show how a problem can be solved in both C and C++.

Take a look at the following C/C++ code snippets, which correspond to the question: "How many copies of *Hamlet* is in the list of books?". We begin with the C version:

```
// C version
struct string_elem_t { const char* str_; string_elem_t* next_; };
int num_hamlet(string_elem_t* books) {
  const char* hamlet = "Hamlet";
  int n = 0;
  string_elem_t* b;
  for (b = books; b != 0; b = b->next_)
    if (strcmp(b->str_, hamlet) == 0)
      ++n;
  return n;
}
```

The equivalent version using C++ would look something like this:

```
// C++ version
int num_hamlet(const std::list<std::string>& books) {
  return std::count(books.begin(), books.end(), "Hamlet");
}
```

Although the C++ version is still more of a robot language than a human language, a lot of programming lingo is gone. Here are some of the noticeable differences between the preceding two code snippets:

- The pointers to raw memory addresses are not visible at all
- The `std::list<std::string>` container is an abstraction of `string_elem_t`
- The `std::count()` method is an abstraction of both the `for` loop and the `if` condition
- The `std::string` class is (among other things) an abstraction of `char*` and `strcmp`

Basically, both versions of `num_hamlet()` translate to roughly the same machine code, but the language features of C++ makes it possible to let the libraries hide computer related terminology such as pointers. Many of the modern C++ language features can be seen as abstractions of basic C functionality and, on top of that, basic C++ functionality:

- C++ classes are abstractions of C-structs and regular functions
- C++ polymorphism is the abstraction of function pointers

On top of that, some recent C++ features are abstractions of former C++ features:

- C++ lambda functions are abstractions of C++ classes
- Templates are abstractions of generating C++ code

Abstractions in other languages

Most programming languages are based on abstractions, which are transformed into machine code to be executed by the CPU. C++ has evolved into a highly expressive language just like many of the other popular programming languages of today. What distinguishes C++ from most other languages is that, while the other languages have implemented these abstractions at the cost of runtime performance, C++ has always strived to implement its abstractions at zero cost at runtime. This doesn't mean that an application written in C++ is by default faster than the equivalent in, say, C#. Rather, it means that by using C++, you'll have explicit control of the emitted machine code instructions and memory footprint if needed.

To be fair, optimal performance is very rarely required today and compromising performance for lower compilation times, garbage collection, or safety, like other languages do, is in many cases more reasonable.

Portability

C++ has been a popular and comprehensive language for a long time. It's highly compatible with C and very little has been deprecated in the language, for better or worse. The history and design of C++ has made it to a highly portable language, and the evolution of modern C++ has ensured that it will stay that way for a long time to come. C++ is a living language and compiler vendors are currently doing a remarkable job to implement new language features rapidly.

Robustness

In addition to performance, expressiveness, and portability, C++ offers a set of language features that gives the programmer the ability to write robust code.

In our experience, robustness does not refer to strength in the programming language itself – it's possible to write robust code in any language. However, strict ownership of resources, const correctness, value semantics, type safety, and deterministic destruction of objects are some of the features offered by C++ that makes it easier to write robust code. That is, the ability to write functions, classes, and libraries that are easy to use and hard to misuse.

C++ of today

To sum it up, C++ of today provides programmers the ability to write an expressive and robust code base while still having the ability to target almost any hardware platform or real-time requirements. Of the most commonly used languages today, C++ is the only one that gives all of these properties.

The aim of this book

This book aims to give the reader a solid foundation to write efficient applications as well as an insight into strategies for implementing the libraries in modern C++. We have tried to take a practical approach to explain how C++ works today where C++14/C++17 features are a natural part of the language, rather than looking at C++ historically.

Expected knowledge of the reader

This book expects you to have a basic knowledge of C++ and computer architecture, and a genuine interest in evolving your skills. Hopefully, by the time you finish this book, you will have gained a few insights into how you can improve your C++ applications, both performance-wise and syntactically. On top of that, we also hope that you will have a few *aha* moments.

C++ compared with other languages

A multitude of application types, platforms, and programming languages have emerged since C++ was first released. Still, C++ is a widely used language, and its compilers are available for most platforms. The major exception, as of today, is the web platform, where JavaScript and its related technologies are the foundation. However, the web platform is evolving into being able to execute what was previously only possible in desktop applications, and in that context C++ has found its way into web applications using technologies such as Emscripten/`asm.js` and web assembly.

Competing languages and performance

In order to understand how C++ achieves its performance compared to other programming languages, we'd like to discuss some fundamental differences between C++ and most other modern programming languages.

For simplicity, this section will focus on comparing C++ to Java, although the comparisons for most parts also apply to other programming language based upon a garbage collector, such as C# and JavaScript.

Firstly, Java compile to bytecode, which is then compiled to machine code while the application is executing, whereas C++ directly compiles the source code to machine code. Although bytecode and just-in-time compilers may theoretically be able to achieve the same (or theoretically, even better) performance than precompiled machine code, as of today, they simply do not. To be fair though, they perform well enough for most cases.

Secondly, Java handle dynamic memory in a completely different manner from C++. In Java, memory is automatically deallocated by a garbage collector, whereas a C++ program handles memory deallocations by itself. The garbage collector does prevent memory leaks, but at the cost of performance and predictability.

Thirdly, Java places all its objects in separate heap allocations, whereas C++ allows the programmer to place objects both on the stack and on the heap. In C++ it's also possible to create multiple objects in one single heap allocation. This can be a huge performance gain for two reasons: objects can be created without always allocating dynamic memory, and multiple related objects can be placed adjacent to one another in memory.

Take a look at how memory is allocated in the following example. The C++ function uses the stack for both objects and integers; Java places the objects on the heap:

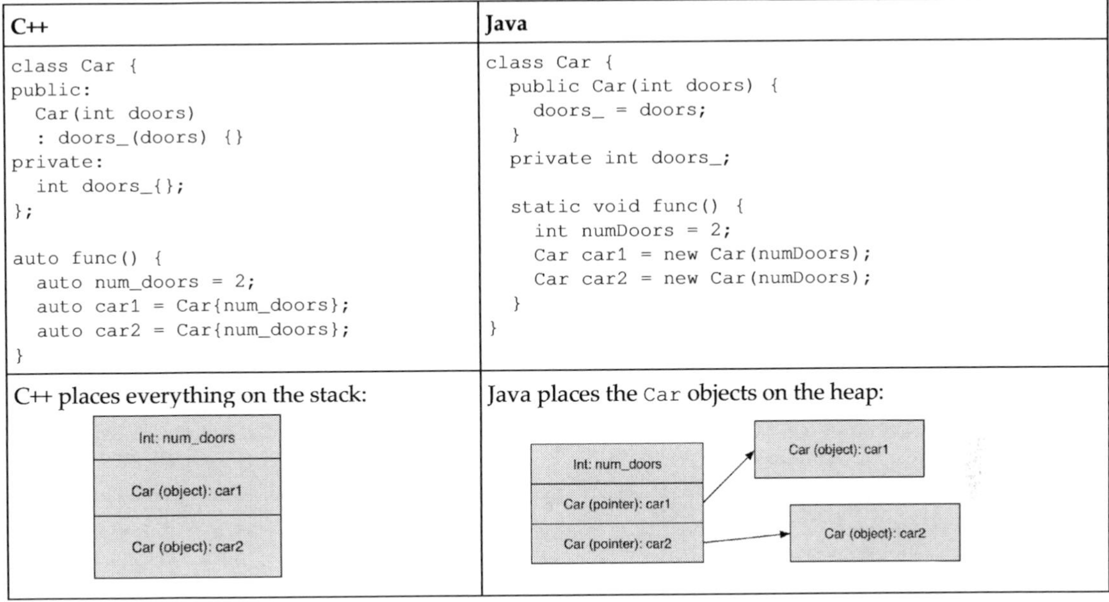

C++

```
class Car {
public:
  Car(int doors)
  : doors_(doors) {}
private:
  int doors_{};
};

auto func() {
  auto num_doors = 2;
  auto car1 = Car{num_doors};
  auto car2 = Car{num_doors};
}
```

C++ places everything on the stack:

Java

```
class Car {
  public Car(int doors) {
    doors_ = doors;
  }
  private int doors_;

  static void func() {
    int numDoors = 2;
    Car car1 = new Car(numDoors);
    Car car2 = new Car(numDoors);
  }
}
```

Java places the `Car` objects on the heap:

Now take a look at the next example and see how an array of `Car` objects are placed in memory when using C++ and Java respectively:

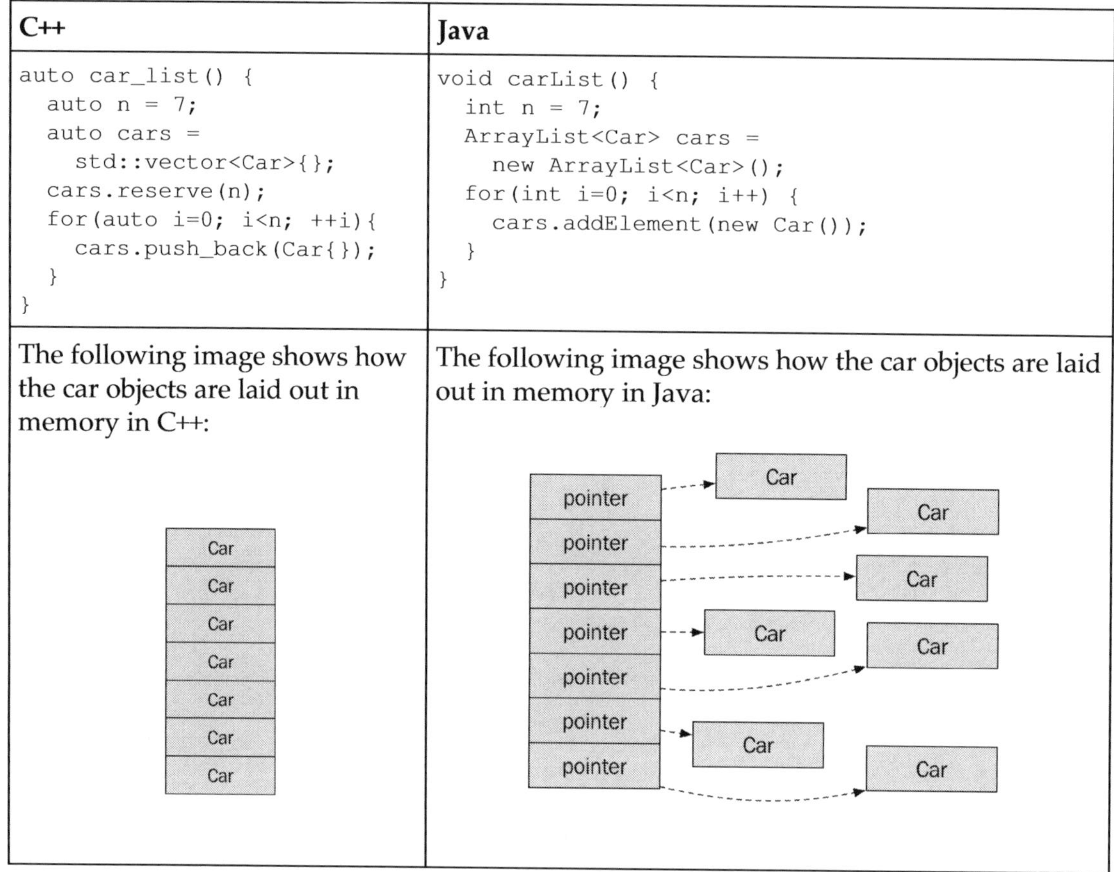

C++

```cpp
auto car_list() {
  auto n = 7;
  auto cars =
    std::vector<Car>{};
  cars.reserve(n);
  for(auto i=0; i<n; ++i){
    cars.push_back(Car{});
  }
}
```

The following image shows how the car objects are laid out in memory in C++:

Java

```java
void carList() {
  int n = 7;
  ArrayList<Car> cars =
    new ArrayList<Car>();
  for(int i=0; i<n; i++) {
    cars.addElement(new Car());
  }
}
```

The following image shows how the car objects are laid out in memory in Java:

The C++ vector contains the actual `Car` objects placed in one contiguous memory block, whereas the equivalent in Java is a contiguous memory block of *references* to `Car` objects. In Java, the objects has been allocated separately, which means that they can be located anywhere in the heap.

This affects the performance as Java has to execute seven allocations instead of one. It also means that whenever the application iterates the list, there is a performance win for C++, since accessing nearby memory locations is faster than accessing several random spots in memory.

Non-performance-related C++ language features

In some discussions about C++ versus other languages, it's concluded that C++ should only be used if performance is a major concern. Otherwise, it's said to just increase the complexity of the code base due to manual memory handling, which may result in memory leaks and hard-to-track bugs.

This may have been true several C++ versions ago, but a modern C++ programmer relies on the provided containers and smart pointer types, which are part of the STL.

We would here like to highlight two powerful features of C++ related to robustness rather than performance, that we think are easily overlooked: value semantics and const correctness.

Value semantics

C++ supports both value semantics and reference semantics. Value semantics lets us pass objects by value instead of just passing references to objects. In C++, value semantics is the default, which means that when you pass an instance of a class or struct, it behaves in the same way as passing an `int`, `float`, or any other fundamental type. To use reference semantics, we need to explicitly use references or pointers.

The C++ type system gives us the ability to explicitly state the ownership of an object. Compare the following implementations of a simple class in C++ and Java. We start with the C++ version:

```
// C++
class Bagel {
public:
  Bagel(const std::set<std::string>& ts) : toppings_(ts) {}
private:
  std::set<std::string> toppings_;
};
```

The corresponding implementation in Java could look like this:

```
// Java
class Bagel {
  public Bagel(ArrayList<String> ts) { toppings_ = ts; }
  private ArrayList<String> toppings_;
}
```

In the C++ version, the programmer states that the `toppings` are completely encapsulated by the `Bagel` class. Had the programmer intended the topping list to be shared among several bagels, it would have been declared as a pointer of some kind: `std::shared_ptr`, if the ownership is shared among several bagels, or a `std::weak_ptr`, if someone else owns the topping list and is supposed to modify it as the program executes.

In Java, objects references each other with shared ownership. Therefore, it's not possible to distinguish whether the topping list is intended to be shared among several bagels or not, or whether it is handled somewhere else or if it is, as in most cases, completely owned by the `Bagel` class.

Compare the following functions; as every object is shared by default in Java (and most other languages), programmers have to take precautions for subtle bugs such as this:

<table>
<tr><th>C++</th><th>Java</th></tr>
<tr><td>Note how the bagels do not share toppings:

<pre>auto t = std::set<std::string>{};
t.insert("salt");
auto a = Bagel{t};

// 'a' is not affected
// when adding pepper
t.insert("pepper");

// 'a' will have salt
// 'b' will have salt & pepper
auto b = Bagel{t};

// No bagel is affected
t.insert("oregano");</pre></td><td>Note how both the bagels subtly share toppings:

<pre>TreeSet<String> t = new
  TreeSet<String>();
t.add("salt");
Bagel a = new Bagel(t);

// Now 'a' will subtly
// also have pepper
t.add("pepper");

// 'a' and 'b' share the
// toppings in 't'
Bagel b = new Bagel(t);

// Both bagels subtly
// also have "oregano"
toppings.add("oregano");</pre></td></tr>
</table>

Const correctness

Another powerful feature of C++, that Java and many other languages lack, is the ability to write const correct code. Const correctness means that each member function signature of a class explicitly tells the caller whether the object will be modified or not; and it will not compile if the caller tries to modify an object declared `const`.

Here follows an example of how we can use `const` member functions to prevent unintentional modifications of objects. In the following `Person` class, the member function `age()` is declared `const` and is therefore not allowed to mutate the `Person` object; whereas `set_age()` mutates the object and *cannot* be declared `const`:

```
class Person {
public:
  auto age() const { return age_; }
  auto set_age(int age) { age_ = age; }
private:
  int age_{};
};
```

It's also possible to distinguish between returning mutable and immutable references to members. In the following `Team` class, the member function `leader() const` returns an immutable `Person`; whereas `leader()` returns a `Person` object that may be mutated:

```
class Team {
public:
  auto& leader() const { return leader_; }
  auto& leader() { return leader_; }
private:
  Person leader_{};
};
```

Now let's see how the compiler can help us find errors when we try to mutate immutable objects. In the following example, the function argument `teams` is declared `const`, explicitly showing that this function is not allowed to modify them:

```
auto nonmutating_func(const std::vector<Team>& teams) {
  auto tot_age = int{0};
  // Compiles, both leader() and age() are declared const
  for (const auto& team: teams)
    tot_age += team.leader().age();

  // Will not compile, set_age() requires a mutable object
  for (auto& team: teams)
    team.leader().set_age(20);
}
```

If we want to write a function which *can* mutate the `teams` object we simply remove `const`. This signals to the caller that this function may mutate the `teams`:

```
auto mutating_func(std::vector<Team>& teams) {
  auto tot_age = int{0};
  // Compiles, const functions can be called on mutable objects
  for (const auto& team: teams)
    tot_age += team.leader().age();

  // Compiles, teams is a mutable variable
  for (auto& team: teams)
    team.leader().set_age(20);
}
```

Object ownership and garbage collection in C++

Except in very rare situations, a C++ programmer should leave the memory handling to containers and smart pointers and never have to rely on manual memory handling.

To put it clearly, the garbage collection model in Java could almost be emulated in C++ by using `std::shared_ptr` for every object. Note that garbage-collecting languages don't use the same algorithm for allocation tracking as `std::shared_ptr`. The `std::shared_ptr` is a smart pointer based on a reference-counting algorithm that will leak memory if objects have cyclic dependencies. Garbage-collecting languages have more sophisticated methods that can handle and free cyclic dependent objects.

However, rather than relying on a garbage collector, forcing a strict ownership delicately avoids subtle bugs that may result from sharing objects by default, as in the case of Java.

If a programmer minimize shared ownership in C++, the resulting code is easier to use and harder to abuse, as it can force the user of the class to use it as it is intended.

Avoiding null objects using C++ references

In addition to strict ownership, C++ also has the concept of references, which is different from references in Java. Internally, a reference is a pointer which is not allowed to be null or repointed; therefore no copying is involved when passing it to a function.

As a result, a function signature in C++ can explicitly restrict the programmer from passing a null object as a parameter. In Java the programmer must use documentation or annotations to indicate non-null parameters.

Take a look at these two Java functions for computing the volume of a sphere. The first one throws a runtime exception if a null object is passed to it; whereas the second one silently ignores null objects.

This first implementation in Java throws a runtime exception if passed a null object:

```
// Java
float getVolume1(Sphere s) {
  float cube = Math.pow(s.radius(), 3);
  return (Math.PI * 4 / 3) * cube;
}
```

This second implementation in Java silently handles null objects:

```
// Java
float getVolume2(Sphere s) {
  float rad = a == null ? 0.0f : s.radius();
  float cube = Math.pow(rad, 3);
  return (Math.PI * 4 / 3) * cube;
}
```

In both function implemented in Java, the caller of the function has to inspect the implementation of the function in order to determine whether null objects are allowed or not.

In C++, the first function signature explicitly accepts only initialized objects by using references which cannot be null. The second version using pointers as arguments, explicitly shows that null objects are handled.

C++ arguments passed as references indicates that null values are not allowed:

```
auto get_volume1(const Sphere& s) {
  auto cube = std::pow(s.radius(), 3);
  auto pi = 3.14f;
  return (pi * 4 / 3) * cube;
}
```

C++ arguments passed as pointers indicates that null values are being handled:

```
auto get_volume2(const Sphere* s) {
  auto rad = s ? s->radius() : 0.0f;
  auto cube = std::pow(rad, 3);
  auto pi = 3.14f;
  return (pi * 4 / 3) * cube;
}
```

Being able to use references or values as arguments in C++ instantly informs the C++ programmer how the function is intended to be used. Conversely, in Java, the user must inspect the implementation of the function, as objects are always passed as pointers, and there's a possibility that they could be null.

Drawbacks of C++

Comparing C++ with other programming languages wouldn't be fair without mentioning some of its drawbacks. As mentioned earlier, C++ has more concepts to learn, and is therefore harder to use correctly and to its full potential. However, if a programmer can master C++, the higher complexity turns into an advantage and the code base becomes more robust and performs better.

There are, nonetheless, some shortcomings of C++, which are simply just shortcomings. The most severe of those shortcomings are long compilation times, the reliance on the manual handling of forward declarations, header/source files, and the complexity of importing libraries.

This is mainly a result of C++ relying on an outdated import system where imported headers are simply pasted into whatever includes them. At the time of writing this book, a modern module-based import system is up for standardization, but until the standardized C++ version becomes available, project management remains very tedious.

Another apparent drawback of C++ is the lack of provided libraries. While other languages usually come with all the libraries needed for most applications, such as graphics, user interfaces, networking, threading, resource handling, and so on, C++ provides, more or less, nothing more than the bare minimum of algorithms, threads, and, as of C++17, file system handling. For everything else, programmers have to rely on external libraries.

To summarize, although C++ has a steeper learning curve than most other languages, if used correctly, the robustness of C++ is an advantage compared to many other languages. So, despite the outdated import/library system of C++, we believe that C++ is a well suited language for large-scale projects, even for projects where performance is not the highest priority.

Class interfaces and exceptions

Before diving deeper into the concepts of C++ high performance, we would like to emphasize some concepts that you should not compromise on when writing C++ code.

Strict class interfaces

A fundamental guideline when writing classes, is to relieve the user of the class from dealing with the internal state by exposing a strict interface. In C++, the copy-semantics of a class is part of the interface, and shall therefore also be as strict as necessary.

Classes should either behave as deep-copied or should fail to compile when copied. Copying a class should not have side effects where the resulting copied class can modify the original class. This may sound obvious, but there are many circumstances when, for example, a class requires a heap-allocated object accessed by a pointer member variable of some sort, for example `std::shared_ptr`, as follows:

```
class Engine {
public:
  auto set_oil_amount(float v) { oil_ = v; }
  auto get_oil_amount() const { return oil_; }
private:
  float oil_{};
};
class YamahaEngine : public Engine {
  //...
};
```

The programmer of the `Boat` class has left a rather loose interface without any precautions regarding copy semantics:

```
class Boat {
public:
  Boat(std::shared_ptr<Engine> e, float l)
  : engine_{e}
  , length_{l}
  {}
  auto set_length(float l) { length_ = l; }
  auto& get_engine() { return engine_; }
private:
  // Being a derivable class, engine_ has to be heap allocated
  std::shared_ptr<Engine> engine_;
  float length_{};
};
```

Later, another programmer uses the `Boat` class and expects correct copy behavior:

```
auto boat0 = Boat{std::make_shared<YamahaEngine>(), 6.7f};
auto boat1 = boat0;
// ... and does not realize that the oil amount applies to both boats
boat1.set_length(8.56f);
boat1.get_engine()->set_oil_amount(3.4f);
```

This could have been prevented if the `Boat` class interface were made stricter by preventing copying. Now, the second programmer will have to rethink the design of the algorithm handling boats, but she won't accidentally introduce any subtle bugs:

```
class Boat {
private:
  Boat(const Boat& b) = delete; // Noncopyable
  auto operator=(const Boat& b) -> Boat& = delete; // Noncopyable
public:
  Boat(std::shared_ptr<Engine> e, float l) : engine_{e}, length_{l} {}
  auto set_length(float l) { length_ = l; }
  auto& get_engine() { return engine_; }
private:
  float length_{};
  std::shared_ptr<Engine> engine_;
};

// When the other programmer tries to copy a Boat object...
auto boat0 = Boat{std::make_shared<YamahaEngine>(), 6.7f};
// ...won't compile, the second programmer will have to find
// another solution compliant with the limitations of the Boat
auto boat1 = boat0;
```

Error handling and resource acquisition

In our experience, exceptions are being used in many different ways in different C++ code bases. (To be fair, this also applies to other languages which supports exceptions.) One reason is that distinct applications can have vastly different requirements when dealing with runtime errors. With some applications, such as a pacemaker or a power plant control system, which may have a severe impact if they crash, we may have to deal with every possible exceptional circumstance, such as running out of memory, and keep the application in a running state. Some applications even completely stay away from using the heap memory as the heap introduces an uncontrollable uncertainty as mechanics of allocating new memory is out of the applications control.

In most applications, though, these circumstances could be considered so exceptional that it's perfectly okay to save the current state and quit gracefully. By exceptional, we mean that they are thrown due to environmental circumstances, such as running out of memory or disk space. Exceptions should not be used as an escape route for buggy code or as some sort of signal system.

Preserving the valid state

Take a look at the following example. If the `branches_ = ot.branches_` operation throws an exception due to being out of memory (`branches_` might be a very big member variable), the `tree0` method will be left in an invalid state containing a copy of `leafs_` from `tree1` and `branches_` that it had before:

```
struct Leaf { /* ... */ };
struct Branch { /* ... */ };

class OakTree {
public:
  auto& operator=(const OakTree& other) {
    leafs_ = other.leafs_;
    // If copying the branches throws, only the leafs has been
    // copied and the OakTree is left in an invalid state
    branches_ = other.branches_;
    *this;
  }
  std::vector<Leaf> leafs_;
  std::vector<Branch> branches_;
};
auto save_to_disk(const std::vector<OakTree>& trees) {
  // Persist all trees ...
}

auto oaktree_func() {
  auto tree0 = OakTree{std::vector<Leaf>{1000}, std::vector<Branch>{100}};
  auto tree1 = OakTree{std::vector<Leaf>{50}, std::vector<Branch>{5}}
  try {
    tree0 = tree1;
  }
  catch(const std::exception& e) {
    // tree0 might be broken
    save_to_disk({tree0, tree1});
  }
}
```

We want the operation to preserve the valid state of `tree0` that it had before the assignment operation so that we can save all our oak trees (pretend we are creating an oak tree generator application) and quit.

This can be fixed by using an idiom called copy-and-swap, which means that we perform the operations that might throw exceptions before we let the application's state be modified by non-throwing `swap` functions:

```
class OakTree {
public:
  auto& operator=(const OakTree& other) {
    // First create local copies without modifying the OakTree objects.
    // Copying may throw, but this OakTree will still be in a valid state
    auto leafs = other.leafs_;
    auto branches = other.branches_;

    // No exceptions thrown, we can now safely modify
    // the state of this object by non-throwing swap
    std::swap(leads_, leafs);
    std::swap(branches_, branches);
    return *this;
  }
  std::vector<Leaf> leafs_;
  std::vector<Branch> branches_;
};
```

Resource acquisition

Note that the destructors of all the local variables are still executed, meaning that any resources (in this case, memory) allocated by `leafs` and `branches` will be released. The destruction of C++ objects is predictable, meaning that we have full control over when, and in what order, resources that we have acquired are being released. This is further illustrated in the following example, where the mutex variable `m` is always unlocked when exiting the function as the lock guard releases it when we exit the scope, regardless of how and where we exit:

```
auto func(std::mutex& m, int val, bool b) {
  auto guard = std::lock_guard<std::mutex>{m}; // The mutex is locked
  if (b) {
    // The guard automatically releases the mutex at early exit
    return;
  }
  if (val == 313) {
    // The guard automatically releases if an exception is thrown
```

```
        throw std::exception{};
    }
    // The guard automatically releases the mutex at function exit
}
```

Ownership, lifetime of objects, and resource acquisition are fundamental concepts in C++ which we will cover later on in this book.

Exceptions versus error codes

In the mid 2000s, using exceptions in C++ affected performance negatively, even if they weren't thrown. Performance-critical code was often written using error code return values to indicate exceptions. Bloating the code base with returning error codes and error code handling was simply the only way of writing performance-critical and exception-safe code.

In modern C++ compilers, exceptions only affect the performance when thrown. Considering all the thrown exceptions are rare enough to quit the current process, we can safely use exceptions even in performance-critical systems and benefit from all the advantages of using exceptions instead of error codes.

Libraries used in this book

As mentioned earlier, C++ does not provide more than the bare necessities in terms of libraries. In this book, we will, therefore, have to rely on external libraries where necessary. The most commonly used library in the world of C++ is probably the Boost library (`http://www.boost.org`). In order to keep the number of used libraries low, we will use the Boost library for hardware-dependent optimizations such as SIMD and GPU.

Throughout this book, we will use the Boost library where the standard C++ library is not enough. Many upcoming parts of the C++ standard are available today in Boost (`filesystem`, `any`, `optional`, and `variant`), and we will not avoid any libraries planned for inclusion in the C++ standard. We will only use the header-only parts of the Boost library, which means that using them yourself does not require any specific build setup; rather, you just have to include the specified header file.

Summary

In this chapter we have highlighted some features and drawbacks of C++ and how it evolved to the state it is in today.

Further, we discussed the advantages and disadvantages of C++ compared with other languages, both from the perspective of performance and robustness. Hopefully, some myths about C++ and exceptions were dispelled.

You also learned the importance of strict interfaces, resource acquisition, and correct exception handling.

2

Modern C++ Concepts

In this chapter, we will take an in-depth look at some modern C++ concepts such as move-semantics, forwarding references, `std::optional`, `std::any`, and lambda functions. Some of these concepts still confuse even experienced C++ programmers and therefore we will look into both their use cases and how they work under the hood.

Automatic type deduction with the auto keyword

Since the introduction of the `auto` keyword in C++11, there has been a lot of confusion in the C++ community about how to use the different flavors of `auto`, such as `const auto&`, `auto&`, and `auto&&`.

Using auto in function signatures

Although discouraged by some C++ programmers, in our experience the use of `auto` in function signatures vastly increases readability when browsing and viewing header files.

Here is how the new `auto` syntax looks compared to the old syntax with explicit types:

Old syntax with explicit type:	New syntax with auto:

<pre>struct Foo {
  int val() const {
    return m_;
  }
  const int& cref() const {
    return m_;
  }
  int& mref() {
    return m_;
  }
  int m_{};
};</pre>
	<pre>struct Foo {
	  auto val() const {
	    return m_;
	  }
	  auto& cref() const {
	    return m_;
	  }
	  auto& mref() {
	    return m_;
	  }
	  int m_{};
	};</pre>

The `auto` syntax can be used both with and without trailing return type. The trailing return is necessary if you put the function definition in the `.cpp` file instead of in the header declaration.

Note that the `auto` syntax can also be used with free functions:

Return type	Syntactic variants (all of a, b, and c corresponds to the same result):

Value	`auto val() const // a) auto, deduced type`
	`auto val() const -> int // b) auto with type`
	`int val() const // c) explicite type`

Const reference	`auto& cref() const // a) auto, deduced type`
	`auto cref() const -> const int& // b) auto, trailing type`
	`const int& cref() const // c) explicite type`

Mutable reference	`auto& mref() // a) auto, deduced type`
	`auto mref() -> int& // b) auto, trailing type`
	`int& mref() // c) explicite type`

Using auto for variables

The introduction of the `auto` keyword in C++11 has initiated quite a debate among C++ programmers. Many people think it reduces readability, or even that it makes C++ similar to a dynamically typed language. Even if we tend to not participate in those debates, our personal opinion is that you should (almost) always use `auto` as, in our experience, it makes the code safer and less littered with clutter.

We prefer to use auto for local variables using the left-to-right initialization style. This means that we keep the variable on the left, followed by an equal sign, and then the type on the right side, like this:

```
auto i = 0;
auto x = Foo{};
auto y = create_object();
auto z = std::mutex{};
```

With copy elision guarantees introduced in C++17, the statement `auto x = Foo{}` is identical to `Foo x{}`. That is, the language guarantees that there is no temporary object that needs to be moved or copied in this case. This means that we can now use the left-to-right initialization style without worrying about performance and we can also use it for non-moveable/non-copyable types.

Using `auto` help us using the correct type for our variables. What we still need to do though, is to express how we intent to use a variable by specifying if we need a reference or a copy, and if we want to modify the variable or just read from it.

Const reference

A const reference, denoted `const auto&`, has the ability to bind to anything. The created variable is always immutable. We believe that the const reference should be the default choice for variables you don't want to modify.

If the const reference is bound to a temporary object, the lifetime of the temporary will be extended to the lifetime of the reference. This is demonstrated in the following example:

```
auto func(const std::string& a, const std::string& b) {
   const auto& str = a + b;  // a + b returns a temporary
   ...
} // str goes out of scope, temporary will be destroyed
```

It's also possible to end up with a const reference by using `auto&`. This can be seen in the following example:

```
auto func() {
   auto foo = Foo{};
   auto& cref = foo.cref(); // cref is a const reference
   auto& mref = foo.mref(); // mref is a mutable reference
}
```

Even though this is perfectly valid, we prefer to always explicitly express that we are dealing with a const references by using `const auto&`, and more important, we leave `auto&` to **only** denote mutable references.

Mutable reference

In contrast to a const reference, a mutable reference cannot bind to a temporary. We use `auto&` to denote mutable references. Use mutable references only when you intent to change the object it references.

Forwarding reference

`auto&&` is called a forwarding reference (also referred to as a *universal reference*). It can bind to anything which makes it useful for certain cases. Forwarding references will, just like const references, extend the lifetime of a temporary. But in contrast to the const reference, `auto&&` allows you to mutate objects it references, temporaries included.

Use `auto&&` for variables that you only forward to some other code. In those forwarding cases you rarely care about whether the variable is a const or a mutable, you just want to pass it to some code that actually going to use the variable.

It's important to note that only `auto&&` and `T&&` in a template method are forwarding references. Using the `&&` syntax with an explicit type, for example `std::string&&` is an r-value and does not have the properties of a forwarding reference (r-values and move-semantics will be discussed later in this chapter).

Conclusion

Although this is our own personal opinion, we strongly recommend to always use `const auto&` when possible, this communicates that you simply just want to fetch a value and that nothing fishy is going on. This should be the case to the majority of the variable declaration in a C++ code base.

`auto&` and `auto` should only be used when you require the behavior of a mutable reference or an explicit copy; this communicates to the reader of the code that those variables are important as they either mutate another variable, or they might mutate another variable if not copied. Finally, use `auto&&` for forwarding code only.

Following these rules makes your code base easier to read, debug, and reason about.

It might seem odd that while we recommend using `const auto&` for most variable declarations, we tend to use a simple `auto` throughout the book. The only reason we use plain `auto` is the limited space the format of a book provides.

The lambda function

The lambda function, introduced in C++11 and further enhanced with polymorphic capabilities in C++14, is one of the most useful features in modern C++. Its versatility comes not only from easily passing functions to algorithms but it can also be used in a lot of circumstances where you need to pass the code around, especially as you can store a lambda function in `std::function`.

Although the lambda function made these programming techniques vastly simpler to work with, everything here is possible to perform without them by making classes with `operator()` overloaded.

We will explore the lambda function's similarities to these kind of classes later, but first let's introduce the lambda function in a simple use case.

Basic syntax of a C++ lambda function

In a nutshell, the lambda function capability enables programmers to pass functions to regular functions, just as easily as a variable is passed.

Let's compare passing a lambda function to an algorithm with passing a variable:

```
// Prerequisite
auto vals = std::vector<int>{1, 3, 2, 5, 4};

// Look for number three
auto three = 3;
auto num_threes = std::count(vals.begin(), vals.end(), three);
// num_threes is 1

// Look for a numbers which is larger than three
auto is_above_3 = [](int v){ return v > 3; };
auto num_above_3 = std::count_if(vals.begin(), vals.end(), is_above_3);
// num_above_3 is 2
```

Notice how we pass a variable to search for with `std::count()` in the first case, and a function to search for with `std::count_if()` in the latter case. This is a typical use case for lambda functions: we pass a function to be evaluated many times to another function (in this case, `std::count_if`).

Also, the lambda does not need to be tied to a variable; just as we can put a variable right into an expression, we can do the same with a lambda function:

```
auto num_3 = std::count(vals.begin(), vals.end(), 3);
auto num_above_3 = std::count_if(vals.begin(), vals.end(), [](int v){
  return v > 3;
});
```

The capture block

Let's make this a little more advanced. In the previous example, we hard coded the value we wanted to count numbers above. What if we want to use an external variable inside the lambda instead? What we do is capture the external variables by putting them in the capture block, that is, the `[]` part of the lambda:

```
auto count_value_above(const std::vector<int>& vals, int th) {
  auto is_above = [th](int v) { return v > th; };
  return std::count_if(vals.begin(), vals.end(), is_above);
}
```

In this example, we captured the `th` variable by copying it into the lambda function, if we want to declare the `th` as a reference, we put a `&` at the beginning like this:

```
auto is_above = [&th](int v) { return v > th; };
```

The variable is now merely a reference to the outer `th` variable, just like a regular reference variable in C++.

Capture by reference versus capture by value

Using the capture block for referencing and copying variables works just like regular variables. To see the difference, take a look at these two examples and see if you can spot the difference:

Capture by value	**Capture by reference**

`auto func() {`
`  auto vals = {1,2,3,4,5,6};`
`  auto th = 3;`
`  auto is_above=[th](int v){`
`    return v > th;`
`  };`
`  th = 4;`
`  auto count_b=std::count_if(`
`    vals.begin(),`
`    vals.end(),`
`    is_above`
`  );`
`  // count_b equals 3`
`}`
	`auto func() {`
	`  auto vals = {1,2,3,4,5,6};`
	`  auto th = 3;`
	`  auto is_above=[&th](int v){`
	`    return v > th;`
	`  };`
	`  th = 4;`
	`  auto count_b=std::count_if(`
	`    vals.begin(),`
	`    vals.end(),`
	`    is_above`
	`  );`
	`  // count_b equals 2`
	`}`

In the first example, the threshold was copied into the lambda functions and is therefore not affected when `th` was mutated, therefore `std::count_if()` counts the number of values above 3.

In the second example, `th` is captured by reference, and therefore `std::count_if()` counts the number of values above 4 instead.

Similarities between a Lambda and a class

To understand what the lambda function consists of, one can view it as a regular class with restrictions:

- The class only consists of one member function.
- The capture block is a combination of the class's member variables and its constructor.
- Each lambda function has its own unique type. Even if two lambda functions are plain clones of each other, they still have their own unique type.

The following table shows a simple lambda function, `is_above`, and a class which corresponds to the lambda function. The left column uses *capture by value* and the right column shows *capture by reference.*

Lambda with capture by value...	**Lambda with capture by reference...**

`auto th = 3;`
`auto is_above = [th](int v) {`
` return v > th;`
`};`
`auto test = is_above(5);`
`// test equals true`
	`auto th = 3;`
	`auto is_above = [&th](int v) {`
	` return v > th;`
	`};`
	`auto test = is_above(5);`
	`// test equals true`

...corresponds to this class:	**...corresponds to this class:**

`auto th = 3;`
`class IsAbove {`
`public:`
` IsAbove(int th) : th{th} {}`
` // The only member function`
` auto operator()(int v)const{`
`   return v > th;`
` }`
`private:`
` int th{}; // Members`
`};`
`auto is_above = IsAbove{th};`
`auto test = is_above(5);`
`// test equals true`
	`auto th = 3;`
	`class IsAbove{`
	`public:`
	` IsAbove(int& th) : th{th} {}`
	` // The only member function`
	` auto operator()(int v)const{`
	`   return v > th;`
	` }`
	`private:`
	` int& th; // Members`
	`};`
	`auto is_above = IsAbove{th};`
	`auto test = is_above(5);`
	`// test equals true`

Initializing variables in capture

As seen in the previous example, the capture scope initializes member variables in the corresponding class. This means that we can also initialize member variables inside a lambda, which are only visible from inside the lambda:

<table>
<tr><th>Lambda function...</th><th>...corresponding class:</th></tr>
<tr><td><pre>auto func = [c=std::list<int>{4,2}]() {
  for(auto v : c)
    std::cout << v;
};
func();
// Output: 42</pre></td><td><pre>class Func {
public:
 Func() : c{4, 2} {}
 auto operator()()const->void{
  for(auto v : c)
    std::cout << v;
 }
private:
 std::list<int> c;
};
auto func = Func{};
func();
// Output: 42</pre></td></tr>
</table>

Mutating lambda member variables

As the lambda function works just like a class with member variables, it can also mutate them. In the following example, the lambda mutates the threshold variable every time it is invoked.

In order to allow the lambda to mutate its members, we need to specify `mutable` when declaring the lambda. The `mutable` modifier on a lambda function works like the inverse for a `const` modifier for a regular class member function; in contrast to a class member function, a lambda function is `const` by default, and therefore a mutating lambda must be explicitly specified:

<table>
<tr><th>Capture by value</th><th>Capture by reference</th></tr>
<tr><td><pre>auto func() {
  auto v = 7;
  auto lambda = [v]() mutable {
    std::cout << v << " ";
    ++v;
  };
  assert(v == 7);
  lambda();
  lambda();
  assert(v == 7);
  std::cout << v;
}</pre></td><td><pre>auto func() {
  auto v = 7;
  auto lambda = [&v]() {
    std::cout << v << " ";
    ++v;
  };
  assert(v == 7);
  lambda();
  lambda();
  assert(v == 9);
  std::cout << v;
}</pre></td></tr>
<tr><td>Output: <code>7 8 7</code></td><td>Output: <code>7 8 9</code></td></tr>
</table>

If we want to capture the `v` by reference instead, we do not have to specify the `mutable` keyword as the lambda itself doesn't mutate. Instead, the original `v` in `func` will mutate, meaning that we have a different output.

Mutating member variables from the compiler's perspective

To understand what's going in the above example, take a look at how the compiler sees the previous lambda objects:

Capture by value case	**Capture by reference case**

`class MutatingLambda {`
`public:`
` MutatingLambda(int m)`
` : v{m} {}`
` auto operator()() {`
`   std::cout<< v <<" ";`
`   ++v;`
` }`
`private:`
`  int v{};`
`};`
	`class MutatingLambda {`
	`public:`
	` MutatingLambda(int& m)`
	` : v{m} {}`
	` auto operator()()const{`
	`   std::cout<< v <<" ";`
	`   ++v;`
	` }`
	`private:`
	` int& v;`
	`};`

As you can see, the first case corresponds to a class with a regular member, whereas the capture by reference case simply corresponds to a class where the member variable is a reference.

You might have noticed that we add the modifier `const` on the `operator()` member function of the capture by reference class, and we also do not specify mutable on the corresponding lambda. The reason this class is still considered `const` is that we do not mutate anything inside the actual class/lambda; the actual mutation applies to the referenced value, and therefore the function is still considered `const`.

Capture all

In addition to capturing variables one by one, all variables in the scope can be captured by simply writing `[=]` or `[&]`.

Using `[=]` means that every variable will be captured by value, whereas `[&]` captures all variables by reference.

If inside a class, it is also possible to capture the class member variables by reference using `[this]` and by copy by writing `[*this]`:

```
class Foo {
public:
 auto member_function() {
   auto a = 0;
```

```
        auto b = 1.0f;
        // Capture all variables by copy
        auto lambda_0 = [=]() { std::cout << a << b << m_; };
        // Capture all variables by reference
        auto lambda_1 = [&]() { std::cout << a << b << m_; };
        // Capture member variables by reference
        auto lambda_2 = [this]() { std::cout << m_; };
        // Capture member variables by copy
        auto lambda_3 = [*this]() { std::cout << m_; };
    }
  private:
   int m_{};
  };
```

Note that using `[=]` does not mean that all variables in the scope are copied into the lambda, only the variables actually utilized are copied.

Although it is convenient to capture all variables with `[&]` or `[=]`, we recommend capturing variables one by one, as it improves the readability of the code by clarifying exactly which variables are used inside the lambda scope.

When capturing all variables by value, you can specify variables to be captured by reference (and vice versa). The following table shows the result of different combination in the capture block:

Capture block	**Resulting capture types**
`int a, b, c;` `auto func = [=](){};`	Capture `a, b, c` by value.
`int a, b, c;` `auto func = [&](){};`	Capture `a, b, c` by reference.
`int a, b, c;` `auto func = [=, &c](){};`	Capture `a, b` by value. Capture `c` by reference.
`int a, b, c;` `auto func = [&, c](){};`	Capture `a, b` by reference. Capture `c` by value.

Assigning C function pointers to lambdas

Let's say you are using a C library, or an older C++ library, which uses a callback function as a parameter. For convenience, you would like to use a lambda function like this:

```
external void download_webpage(
  const char* url, void (*callback)(int, const char*));
```

The callback here is a return code and the web page HTML. If you want to invoke this with a lambda, you have to use a plus in front of the lambda in order to convert it into a regular function pointer:

```
auto func() {
  auto lambda = +[](int result, const char* str) {};
  download_webpage("http://www.packt.com", lambda);
}
```

This way, the lambda is converted into a regular function pointer. Note that the lambda cannot have any captures at all in order to use this functionality.

Lambdas and std::function

As mentioned before, every lambda function has its own type, even if they have the same signature (and even if they are identical).

The signature of a `std::function` is defined as follows:

```
std::function< return_type ( parameter0, parameter1...) >
```

So, a `std::function` returning nothing and having no parameters is defined like this...

```
auto func = std::function<void(void)>{};
```

A `std::function` returning a `bool` and having an `int` and a `std::string` as parameters is defined like this:

```
auto func = std::function<bool(int, std::string)>{};
```

Assigning lambdas to std::functions

As mentioned earlier, every lambda function has its own type, and therefore cannot be assigned to other lambda functions, even if they look exactly the same. However, a `std::function` can hold any lambda function which has the same signature, that is, it has the same parameters and the same return value. A `std::function` can also be reassigned at run time. This makes `std::function` the type to use if you want a variable to hold a lambda function.

What is important here is that what is captured by the lambda does not affect its signature, and therefore both lambdas with and without captures can be assigned to the same `std::function`.

The following code block shows how different lambdas are assigned the same `std::function` object:

```
// Create an unassigned std::function object
auto func = std::function<void(int)>{};
// Assign a lambda without capture to the std::function object
func = [](int v) { std::cout << v; };
func(12); // Prints 12

// Assign a lambda with capture to the same std::function object
auto forty_two = 42;
func = [forty_two](int v) { std::cout << (v + forty_two); };
func(12); // Prints 54
```

Implementing a simple Button class with std::function

Let's put the `std::function` to use in something that resembles a real-world example. If we create a `Button` class, we can use the `std::function` to store the action corresponding to clicking the buttons, so that when we call the `on_click()` member function, the corresponding code is executed.

We can declare the `Button` class like this:

```
class Button {
public:
  Button(std::function<void(void)> click) : on_click_{click} {}
  auto on_click() const { on_click_(); }
private:
  std::function<void(void)> on_click_{};
};
```

We can then use it to create a multitude of buttons with different actions. As each button still has the same type, they can also be stored in a container:

```
auto make_buttons() {
  auto beep_button = Button([beep_count = 0]() mutable {
    std::cout << "Beep:" << beep_count << "! ";
    ++beep_count;
  });
  auto bop_button = Button([]{ std::cout << "Bop. "; });
  auto silent_button = Button([]{});
  auto buttons = std::vector<Button>{
    beep_button,
    bop_button,
    silent_button
  };
  return buttons;
}
```

Iterating the list by executing the `on_click()` on each button will execute the corresponding function:

```
auto buttons = make_buttons();
for(const auto& b: buttons) {
  b.on_click();
}
buttons.front().on_click();
// Output: "Beep: 0! Bop. Beep: 1!"
```

As you can see, the `on_click()` member function is a const function, yet it is mutating the member variable `on_click_` by increasing the `beep_count_`. This might seem like it breaks const correctness rules, as a const member function of `Button` is allowed to call a mutating function on one of its class members. The reason it is allowed is the same reason that member pointers are allowed to mutate their pointed-to value in a const context. Later on in this chapter we will discuss how to propagate constness for pointer data members.

Performance consideration of std::function

A `std::function` has a few performance losses compared to a lambda function, which we'll discuss in the subsequent sections.

An std::function cannot be inlined

When it comes to lambda functions, the compiler has the ability to inline the function call, that is, the overhead of the function call is eliminated. The flexible design of `std::function` make it nearly impossible for the compiler to inline a function wrapped in a `std::function`. This overhead can have an impact on the performance if small functions wrapped in `std::function` are being called very frequently.

An std::function heap allocates and captures variables

If a lambda function with captured variables/references is assigned to a `std::function`, the `std::function` will, in most cases, allocate space on the heap to store the captured variables (note that some implementations of `std::function` do not heap-allocate if the size of the captured variable is less than a specific threshold).

This means that not only is there a slight performance penalty due to heap allocation and the execution of `std::function` but also that it is slower, as heap allocation implies cache misses (more about cache misses in `Chapter 4`, *Data Structures*).

Invoking an std::function requires a few more operations than a lambda

Calling a `std::function` is generally a bit slower than executing a lambda as a little more code is involved, for example, executing 1 million function calls for a `std::vector` of the explicit lambda type versus a `std::vector` of a corresponding `std::function` as follows.

Benchmark invocation without capture of lambda vs std::function:

Lambda	std::function

`auto test_direct_lambda() {`
`  auto lbd = [](int v) {`
`    return v * 3;`
`  };`
`  using L = decltype(lbd);`
`  auto fs = std::vector<L>{};`
`  fs.resize(1'000'000, lbd);`
`  auto res = int{0};`
`  for (const auto& f: fs) {`
`    res = f(res);`
`  }`
`  return res;`
`}`
	`auto test_std_function() {`
	`  auto lbd = [](int v) {`
	`    return v * 3;`
	`  };`
	`  using F = std::function<int(int)>;`
	`  auto fs = std::vector<F>{};`
	`  fs.resize(1'000'000, lbd);`
	`  auto res = int{0};`
	`  for (const auto& f: fs) {`
	`    res = f(res);`
	`  }`
	`  return res;`
	`}`

The first version, using the lambda directly, executes at roughly one-fourth of the time compared to the second version, where we instead use a vector of `std::function`.

The polymorphic lambda

Although having a complex-sounding name, a polymorphic lambda is simply a lambda accepting `auto` as a parameter, making it possible to invoke it with any type. It works just like a regular lambda, but the `operator()` has been defined as a member function template.

Only the parameters are template variables, not the captured values. In other words, the captured value `v` in the following example will stay as an integer.

So, if you define a polymorphic lambda like this:

```
auto v = 3;
auto lambda = [v](auto v0, auto v1){ return v + v0*v1; };
```

If we translate the above lambda to a class, it would correspond to something like this:

```
class Lambda {
public:
  Lambda(int v) : v_{v} {}
  template <typename T0, typename T1>
  auto operator()(T0 v0, T1 v1) const { return v_ + v0*v1; }
private:
```

```
  int v_{};
};
auto v = 3;
auto lambda = Lambda{v};
```

This means that, just like the templated version, the compiler won't generate the actual function until the lambda is invoked.

So, we can invoke the previous lambda like this:

```
auto res_int = lambda(1, 2);
auto res_float = lambda(1.0f, 2.0f);
```

The compiler will generate something similar to the following lambdas:

```
auto lambda_int = [v](int v0, const int v1) { return v + v0*v1; };
auto lambda_float = [v](float v0, float v1) { return v + v0*v1; };
auto res_int = lambda_int(1, 2);
auto res_float = lambda_float(1.0f, 2.0f);
```

As you might have figured, these versions are further handled just like regular lambdas.

Creating reusable polymorphic lambdas

Here are two vectors, one resembling a farm with the number of animals, and the other one mapping countries to their corresponding continent:

```
auto farm = std::vector<std::pair<std::string, int>>{
  {"Bear", 5},
  {"Deer", 0},
  {"Pig", 4}
};

enum class Continent { Europe, Asia, America };
auto countries = std::vector<std::pair<std::string, Continent>>{
  {"Sweden", Continent::Europe},
  {"India", Continent::Asia},
  {"Belarus", Continent::Europe},
  {"Mexico", Continent::America}
};
```

Let's say we want to sort the animals in order of how many the farm contains, and the countries in order of the continent they belong to. Speaking in code, we want to sort the vectors according to the `std::pair::second` member. As the vectors contain different value types, we use a polymorphic lambda. In order to avoid code duplication, we tie the lambda to a variable, and the lambda can be used for sorting both vectors:

```
auto less_by_second = [](const auto& a, const auto& b) {
  return a.second < b.second;
};
// Both vectors can be sorted with the same lambda
std::sort(farm.begin(), farm.end(), less_by_second);
std::sort(countries.begin(), countries.end(), less_by_second);
```

Creating a reusable lambda for sorting like this is straightforward as we don't require any captures. However, what do we do if we want to make a reusable lambda which requires a capture?

For example, let's say we want to count the number of animals we have five of, or the number of countries in Europe. What we have to do is to wrap the capture into a function like this:

```
template <typename T>
auto is_second_equal(const T& x) {
  // A lambda capturing x is returned
  return [&x](const auto& p) { return p.second == x; };
}

auto missing_animals = std::count_if(farm.begin(), farm.end(),
is_second_equal(0));
// missing_animals equals 1 as there are no deers in the farm

auto num_european_countries = std::count_if(
  countries.begin(),
  countries.end(),
  is_second_equal(Continent::Europe)
);
// num_european_countries is two as Sweden and Belarus are in Europe
```

As you see, the template function `is_second_equal` is utilized as a proxy to make the capture type a template. Then, the returned polymorphic lambda does not need to know about the full type of the pair. The actual lambda function isn't generated until the `std::count_if` is invoked.

So, the compiler stumbles upon the following line:

```
auto lambda = is_second_equal(5);
```

It then starts by generating a function which returns a polymorphic lambda where `x` is an `int` like this:

```
auto is_second_equal_int(const int& x) {
  return [&x](const auto& p) { return p.second == x; };
}
```

When that function is generated, the compiler goes on and generates a class similar to this:

```
class Lambda {
public:
  Lambda(const int& x) : x_{x} {}
  template <typename T>
  auto operator()(const T& p) const { return p.second == x_; }
  int x_{};
};
```

Then, an object of this `Lambda` class is constructed and passed to the algorithm like this:

```
auto missing_animals = std::count_if(farm.begin(), farm.end(), Lambda{0});
```

The template `operator()` member function of the `Lambda` class is further converted to the following function:

```
auto operator()(const std::pair<std::string, int>& p) const {
  return p.second == x_;
}
```

Const propagation for pointers

A common mistake when writing const-correct code in C++ is that a const initialized object can still manipulate the values that member pointers points at. The following example illustrates the problem:

```
class Foo {
public:
  Foo(int* ptr) : ptr_{ptr} {}
  auto set_ptr_val(int v) const {
    *ptr_ = v; // Compiles despite function being declared const!
  }
private:
```

```
  int* ptr_{};
};

auto main() -> int {
  const auto foo = Foo{};
  foo.set_ptr_val(42);
}
```

Although the function `set_ptr_val()` is mutating the `int` value, it's valid to declared it `const` since the pointer `ptr_` itself is not mutated, only the `int` object that the pointer is pointing at.

In order to prevent this in a readable way, a wrapper called `std::experimental::propagate_const` has been added to the `std` library extensions (included in, as of the time of writing this, the latest versions of Clang and GCC). Using `propagate_const`, the function `set_ptr_val()` will not compile. Note that `propagate_const` only applies to pointers, and pointer-like classes such as `std::shared_ptr` and `std::unique_ptr`, not `std::function`.

Here is a usage example:

```
namespace exp = std::experimental;
class Foo {
public:
  auto set_ptr(int* p) const {
    ptr_ = p;  // Will not compile, as expected
  }
  auto set_val(int v) const {
    val_ = v;  // Will not compile, as expected
  }
  auto set_ptr_val(int v) const {
    *ptr_ = v; // Will not compile, const is propagated
  }
private:
  exp::propagate_const<int*> ptr_ = nullptr;
  int val_{};
};
```

Move semantics explained

Move semantics is a concept introduced in C++11 which, in our experience, is quite hard to grasp even by experienced programmers. Therefore, we will try to give you an in-depth explanation of how it works, when the compiler utilizes it, and, most importantly, why it is needed.

Essentially, the reason C++ even has the concept of move semantics, whereas most other languages don't, is a result of being a value-based language as discussed in `Chapter 1`, *A Brief Introduction to C++*. If C++ did not have move semantics built in, the advantages of value-based semantics would get lost in many cases and programmers would have to perform one of the following trade-offs:

- Performing redundant deep-cloning operations with high performance costs
- Using pointers for objects like Java do, losing the robustness of value semantics
- Performing error-prone swapping operations at the cost of readability

We do not want either of these, so let's have a look at how move semantics helps us.

Copy-construction, swap, and move

Before we go into the details of move, we first explain and illustrate the differences between copy-constructing and object, swapping two objects, and move-constructing an object.

Copy-constructing an object

When copying an object handling a resource, a new resource needs to be allocated, and the resource from the source object needs to be copied so that the two objects are completely separated. The resource allocations of copy construction in the following code block is illustrated as follows:

```
auto a = Object{};
auto b = a; // Copy-construction
```

The following image illustrates the process:

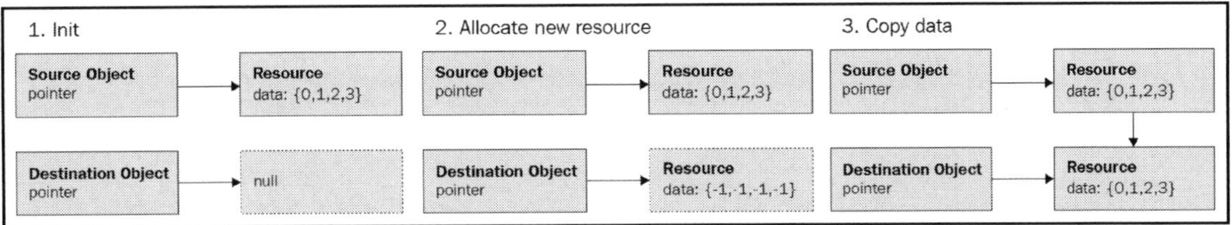

Copying an object with resources

The allocation and copying is slow and, in many cases, the source object isn't needed anymore. With move semantics, the compiler detects cases like these where the old object is not tied to a variable, and instead performs a move operation. This will be explained in the following detail.

Swapping two objects

Before move semantics were added in C++11, swapping the content of two objects was a common way to transfer data without allocating and copying. The objects simply swaps the content with each other:

```
auto a = Object{};
auto b = Object{};
std::swap(a, b);
```

The following image illustrates the process:

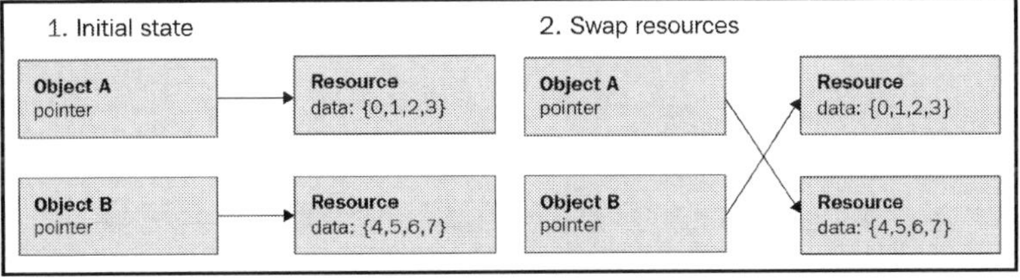

Swapping resources between two objects

Move-constructing an object

When moving an object, the destination object steals the resource straight from the source object, and the source object is reset, as illustrated in the following image. As you can see, it is very similar to swapping, except that the *moved-from* object does not have to receive the resources from the *moved-to* object:

```
auto a = Object{};
auto b = std::move(a); // Tell the compiler to move the resource into b
```

The following image illustrates the process:

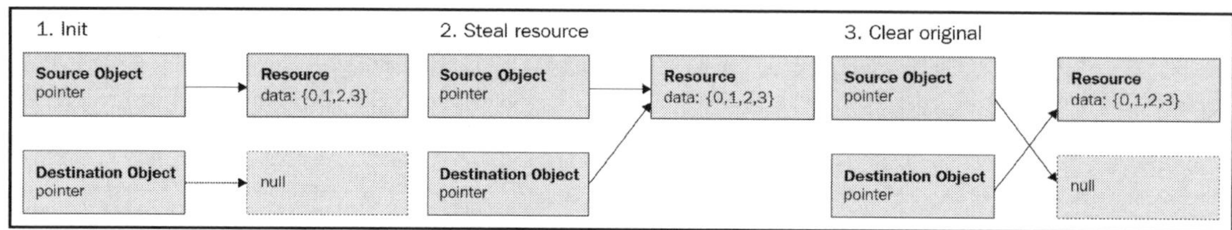

Moving resources from one object to another

Moving objects only makes sense if the object type owns a resource of some sort (the most common case being heap-allocated memory). If all data is contained within the object, the most efficient way to move an object is to just copy.

Resource acquisition and the rule of three

Now that you have a handle on what is going on, let's go into detail.

To fully understand move semantics, we need to go back to the basics of classes and resource acquisition in C++. One of the basic concepts of classes and resource acquisition in C++ is that a class should completely handle its resources.

This means that when a class is copied, assigned, or destructed, the class should make sure its resources are also copied, assigned and destructed. The necessity of implementing these three functions is commonly referred to as *the rule of three*.

The rule of three is such an obvious part of C++ and STL that there is a chance that you are using it without thinking about it. But if we take a look at a simple function which copies a `std::vector<int>`, there are quite a few things that actually go on under the hood:

```
0. auto func() {
1.   // Prerequisite
2.   const auto a0 = std::vector<int>{1,2,3,4,5,6};
3.   const auto a1 = std::vector<int>{7,8,9};
4.   // Copy-construct
5.   auto b = a0;
6.   // Copy-assign
7.   b = a1;
8. }
```

The allocated data in `a0` is copy-constructed into `b` to a new allocation in vector `b` at line 5 and the data of `a1` is copy-assigned into `b1` at line 7. When the function exits, the allocations held by `a0`, `a1`, and `b` are automatically freed up by their destructors.

Implementing the rule of three

Prior to C++11, automatic resource acquisition in C++ was implemented using a guideline called *the rule of three,* where the *three* refers to the special member functions: *copy-constructor, copy-assignment* and *destructor*. The rule says that if you are handling resources in any of these three functions, you most likely need to do it in all three of them.

Let's have a look at how the rule of three can be implemented in a class handling an allocated resource. In the `Buffer` class defined in the following code snippet, the allocated resource is an array of floats pointed at by the raw pointer `ptr_`. Note how the rule of three handles the resource by allocating and deallocating the `float` array:

```
class Buffer {
public:
  // Constructor
  Buffer(const std::initializer_list<float>& values)
  : size_{values.size()} {
    ptr_ = new float[values.size()];
    std::copy(values.begin(), values.end(), ptr_);
  }
  // 1. Copy constructor
  Buffer(const Buffer& other) : size_{other.size_} {
    ptr_ = new float[size_];
    std::copy(other.ptr_, other.ptr_ + size_, ptr_);
  }
  // 2. Copy assignment
```

```
  auto& operator=(const Buffer& other) {
    delete [] ptr_;
    ptr_ = new float[other.size_];
    size_ = other.size_;
    std::copy(other.ptr_, other.ptr_ + size_, ptr_);
    return *this;
  }
  // 3. Destructor
  ~Buffer() {
    delete [] ptr_; // Note, it is valid to delete a nullptr
    ptr_ = nullptr;
  }
  // Iterators for accessing the data
  auto begin() const { return ptr_; }
  auto end() const { return ptr_ + size_; }
private:
  size_t size_{0};
  float* ptr_{nullptr};
};
```

In this case, the handled resource is a block of allocated memory. Allocated memory is probably the most common resource for classes to handle, but remember that a resource can be so much more: a mutex, a handle for a texture on the graphics card, a thread handle, and so on.

Constructor

We can construct a `Buffer` object like this:

```
auto float_array = Buffer({0.0f, 0.5f, 1.0f, 1.5f});
```

The actual object will then look like this in computer memory:

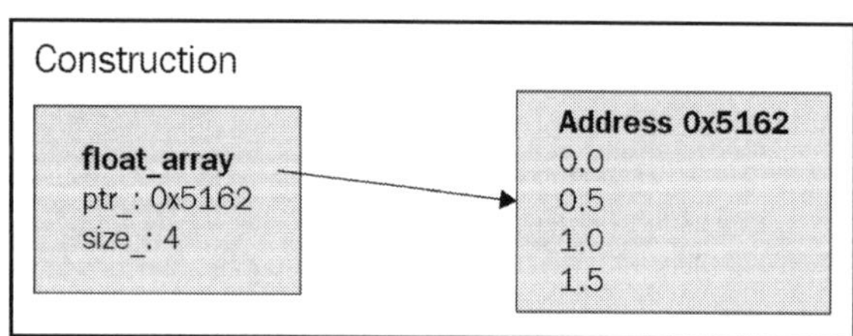

The copy-constructor, copy-assignment, and destructor are invoked in the following cases:

```
auto func() {
  // Construct
  auto b0 = Buffer({0.0f, 0.5f, 1.0f, 1.5f});
  // 1. Copy-construct
  auto b1 = b0;
  // 2. Copy-assignment as b0 is already initialized
  b0 = b1;
  // 3. When the function exits, the destructors are automatically invoked
}
```

Limitations of the rule of three

Although a correct implementation of the rule of three is all that is required for a class to handle its internal resources, two problems arise:

- **Resources which cannot be copied**: In the `Buffer` class example, our resource can be copied, but there are other types of resources where a copy wouldn't make sense. For example, the resource contained in a class might be a `std::thread`, a network connection, or something else which it is not possible to copy. In these cases, it is simply not possible to pass around the object.
- **Unnecessary copies**: If we return our `Buffer` class from a function, the entire array needs to be copied.

The following example shows how a `Buffer` object created inside `make_buffer()` is fully copied from `local_buffer` to `buffer` when returned from a function:

```
auto make_buffer() {
  auto local_buffer = Buffer({2.0f, 4.0f, 6.0f, 8.0f});
  return local_buffer;
}

auto buffer = make_buffer();
```

If we would add move-semantics to our `Buffer` class, this copy will be omitted as the compiler sees that `local_buffer` is not used any more.

Avoiding copies without move semantics

Without move semantics, these problems were usually avoided by allocating via a pointer, and passing around the pointer instead of the actual class. In this case, we utilize an old-fashioned raw pointer for clarity, although some sort of smart pointer is probably the most used case (such as `shared_ptr`, `unique_ptr`, or the old, deprecated `auto_ptr`):

```
auto make_buffer() -> Buffer* {
  auto buffer = new Buffer({2.0, 4.0, 6.0, 8.0});
  return buffer;
}

// The actual Buffer object isn't copied, just the pointer
auto buffer = make_buffer(); // buffer is Buffer*
```

This has several disadvantages:

- The advantage of value semantics in C++ is lost: the programmer is not relieved from handling pointers manually
- The code gets bloated with pointers which are simply only used for the sake of optimization
- More heap allocations are required, leading to potentially slower code due to cache misses and an increase in allocations

Introducing move semantics

In order to get rid of these problems, *the rule of three* was expanded to *the rule of five*.

To be specific, in addition to the copy-constructor and copy-assignment, we now also have move-constructor and move-assignment.

Instead of taking a const reference as a parameter, the move versions accept a `Buffer&&` object.

The `&&` modifier indicates that the parameter is an object which we intend to move from instead of copying it. Speaking in C++ terms, this is called an r-value and we will talk a little bit more about those later.

Whereas the copy functions copy an object, the move equivalents are intended to move resources from one object to another, freeing the moved-from object from the resource.

It's important to notice that the moved-from object still has to remain in a valid state; the moved-from object must still be able to execute it's destructor or reassigned a new value.

This is how we would extend our `Buffer` class with move-constructor and move-assignment. As you can see, these functions will not throw an exception and can therefore be marked as `noexcept`. This is because, as opposed to the copy-constructor/copy-assignment, they do not allocate or do something which might throw exceptions:

```
class Buffer {
  ...
  Buffer(Buffer&& other) noexcept
  : ptr_{other.ptr_}
  , size_{other.size_} {
    other.ptr_ = nullptr;
    other.size_ = 0;
  }
  auto& operator=(Buffer&& other) noexcept {
    ptr_ = other.ptr_;
    size_ = other.size_;
    other.ptr_ = nullptr;
    other.size_ = 0;
    return *this;
  }
  ...
};
```

Now, when the compiler detects that we perform what seems to be a copy, such as returning a `Buffer` from a function, but the copied-from value isn't used anymore, it will utilize the no-throw move-constructor/move-assignment instead of copying.

This is pretty sweet: the interface remains as clear as when copying but, under the hood, the compiler has performed a simple move. Thus, the programmer does not need to use any esoteric pointers or out-parameters in order to avoid a copy; as the class has move-semantics implemented, the compiler handles this automatically.

Do not forget to mark your move-constructors and move-assignment operators as `noexcept` (unless they might throw an exception, of course). Not marking them `noexcept` prevents STL containers and algorithms from utilizing them and resorts to a regular copy/assignment under certain conditions.

Named variables and r-values

So, when is the compiler allowed to move objects instead of copying? As a short answer, the compiler moves an object when the object can be categorized as an *r-value*. The term *r-value* might sound complicated, but in essence it is just an object which is not tied to a named variable, for either of the following reasons:

- It's coming straight out of a function
- We make a variable an r-value by using `std::move(...)`

The following example demonstrates both of these scenarios:

```
// Below, the object coming out of make_buffer is not tied to a variable
// Therefore moved to x
auto x = make_buffer();

// Below, "x" is passed into std::move(...)
// Therefore move-assigned to y
auto y = std::move(x);
```

Let's make this a little bit more advanced by setting a member variable of type `std::string` in a class.

Let's look at a few cases of copying in detail, given the following prerequisite:

```
class Bird {
public:
  Bird() {}
  auto set_song(const std::string& s) { song_ = s; }
  auto set_song(std::string&& s) { song_ = std::move(s); }
  std::string song_;
};
auto bird = Bird{};
```

Case 1: `Bird::song_` is **copy-assigned** as the song is tied to the variable `cuckoo_a`.

```
auto cuckoo_a = std::string{"I'm a Cuckoo"};
bird.set_song(cuckoo_a);
```

Case 2: `Bird::song_` is **move-assigned** as the `cuckoo_b` variable is passed through `std::move()`.

```
auto cuckoo_b = std::string{"I'm a Cuckoo"};
bird.set_song(std::move(cuckoo_b));
```

Case 3: `Bird::song_` is **move-assigned** as the song string is coming straight out of a function.
`auto make_roast_song() { return std::string{"I'm a Roast"}; }`
`bird.set_song(make_roast_song());`

Case 4: `Bird::song_` is **copy-assigned** as the song string is held by the`roast_song_a` variable.
`auto roast_song_a = make_roast_song();`
`bird.set_song(roast_song_a);`

Case 5: `Bird::song_` is **copy-assigned** as `roast_song_b` is declared **const**, and thus not allowed to mutate.
`const auto roast_song_b = make_roast_song();`
`bird.set_song(std::move(roast_song_b));`

As you can see, determining whether an object is moved or copied is quite simple. If it has a variable name, it is copied; otherwise, it is moved.

Accept arguments by move when applicable

Consider a function which converts a `std::string` to lower case. In order to use the move-constructor where applicable, and the copy-constructor otherwise, it may seem like two functions are required:

```
// Argument, s, is a const reference
auto str_to_lower(const std::string& s) -> std::string {
  auto clone = s;
  for(auto& c: clone) c = std::tolower(c);
  return clone;
}
// Argument, s, is an r-value
auto str_to_lower(std::string&& s) -> std::string {
  for(auto& c: s) c = std::tolower(c);
  return s;
}
```

However, by taking the `std::string` by value instead, we can write one function which covers both cases:

```
auto str_to_lower(std::string s) -> std::string {
  for(auto& c: s)
    c = std::tolower(c);
  return s;
}
```

Let's see why this implementation of `str_to_lower()` avoids unnecessary copying where possible.

When passed a regular variable, shown as follows, the content of `str` is **copy-constructed** into `s` prior to the function call, and then move-assigned back to `str` when the functions returns.

```
auto str = std::string{"ABC"};
str = str_to_lower(str);
```

When passed an r-value, shown as follows, the content of `str` is **move-constructed** into `s` prior to the function call, and then move-assigned back to `str` when the function returns. Therefore, no copy was made through the function call.

```
auto str = std::string{"ABC"};
str = str_to_lower(std::move(str));
```

Default move semantics and the rule of zero

This section discusses automatically generated copy-assignment operators, it's important to know that the generated function does not have strong exception guarantees. Therefore, if an exception is thrown during the copy-assignment, the object might end up in a state where it is only partially copied.

As with the copy-constructor and copy-assignment, the move-constructor and move-assignment can be generated by the compiler. Although some compilers allow themselves to automatically generate these functions under certain conditions (more about this later), we can simply force the compiler to generate them by using the `default` keyword.

In the case of the `Bird` class, we simply extend it like this:

```
class Bird {
...
  // Copy-constructor/copy-assignment
  Bird(const Bird&) = default;
  auto operator=(const Bird&) -> Bird& = default;
  // Move-constructor/move-assignment
  Bird(Bird&&) noexcept = default;
  auto operator=(Bird&&) noexcept -> Bird& = default;
  // Destructor
  ~Bird() = default;
  ...
};
```

To make it even simpler, if you do not declare any custom *copy-constructor/copy-assignment* or *destructor*, the *move-constructors/move-assignments* are implicitly declared, meaning that the first `Bird` class actually handles everything:

```
class Bird {
...
// Nothing here, the compiler generates everything automatically!
...
};
```

In other words, adding just a custom destructor, shown as follows:

```
class Bird {
public:
  Bird() {}
  ~Bird() { std::cout << "Bird is dead." << '\n'; }
  auto set_song(const std::string& song) { song_ = song; }
  auto set_song(std::string&& song) { song_ = std::move(song); }
private:
  std::string song_;
};
```

If we do this, the move operators are not generated, and the class will always be copied.

Rule of zero in a real code base

In practice, the cases where you have to write your own *copy/move-constructors* and *copy/move-assignments* should be very few. If you create a class in your application code base which requires these to be custom written, these parts should probably be moved to some library in your code base.

Writing your classes so that they do not require any explicitly written *copy-constructor, copy-assignment, move-constructor, move-assignment,* or *destructor* is often referred to as the rule of zero. This means that if a class in the application code base is required to have any of these function written explicitly, that piece of code would probably be better off in the library part of your code base.

Later on in this chapter we will discuss `std::optional` , which is a handy utility class for dealing with optional members when applying the rule of zero.

A note on empty destructors

Note that writing an empty destructor prevents the compiler from implementing certain optimizations. As you can see in the following table, copying an array of a trivial class with an empty destructor yields the same, non-optimized, assembler code as copying with a handcrafted for loop:

<table>
<tr><th>Empty destructor and std::copy</th><th>Copy by handwritten for-loop</th></tr>
<tr><td><pre>struct Point {
 int x, y;
 ~Point(){}
};
auto copy(Point* src, Point* dst) {
 std::copy(src, src+64, dst);
}</pre></td><td><pre>struct Point {
  int x, y;
};
auto copy(Point* src, Point* dst) {
  const auto end = src + 64;
  for(; src != end; ++src, ++dst) {
    *dst = *src;
  }
}</pre></td></tr>
</table>

This generates the following x86 assembler:

```
 xor eax, eax
.L2:
 mov rdx, QWORD PTR [rdi+rax]
 mov QWORD PTR [rsi+rax], rdx
 add rax, 8
 cmp rax, 512
 jne .L2
 rep ret
```

However, if we remove or declare the destructor default, the compiler optimize `std::copy` to utilize `memmove` instead of a loop. The assembler is generated using GCC 7.1 in *Compiler Explorer* available at `https://godbolt.org/`.

No destructor and std::copy	Explicit default destructor and std::copy

`struct Point {`
`  int x, y;`
`};`
`auto copy(Point* src, Point* dst) {`
`  std::copy(src, src+64, dst);`
`}`
	`struct Point {`
	`  int x, y;`
	`  ~Point() = default;`
	`};`
	`auto copy(Point* src, Point* dst) {`
	`  std::copy(src, src+64, dst);`
	`}`

This generated the following x86 assembler, with memmove optimization!

```
mov rax, rdi
mov edx, 512
mov rdi, rsi
mov rsi, rax
jmp memmove
```

To summarize, use default destructors in favor of empty destructors to squeeze a little bit more performance of your application.

A common pitfall - moving non-resources

There is one common pitfall when using default created move-assignments: classes which mix simple types with more advanced types. As opposed to more advanced types, simple types such as integers, Booleans, and such are simply copied when moved as they don't handle any resources.

When a simple type is mixed with a resource-owning type, the move-assignment becomes a mixture of move and copy.

Here is an example of a class which will fail:

```
class TowerList {
public:
  TowerList() : max_height_idx_{1}, tower_heights_{25.0f, 44.0f, 12.0f} {}
  auto get_max_tower_height() const {
    return max_height_idx_ >= 0 ?
      tower_heights_[max_height_idx_] : 0.0f;
  }
  std::vector<float> tower_heights_{};
  int max_height_idx_{-1};
};
```

The `TowerList` class will have undefined behavior if it is handled like this:

```
auto a = TowerList{};
auto b = std::move(a);
auto max_height = a.get_max_tower_height();
```

The undefined behavior happens as the `tower_heights_` vector is moved and is therefore empty. The `max_height_idx_`, on the other hand, is copied, and therefore still has the value `2` in the moved-from object `a`. When the `get_max_tower_height()` is called, the function will try to access `tower_heights_` at index `2` and the program will crash.

In these cases, the move-constructor/assignment is better implemented by simply swapping the members like this:

```
TowerList(TowerList&& tl) noexcept {
  std::swap(tower_heights_, tl.tower_heights_);
  std::swap(max_height_idx_, tl.max_height_idx_);
}
auto& operator=(TowerList&& tl) noexcept {
  std::swap(tower_heights_, tl.tower_heights_);
  std::swap(max_height_idx_, tl.max_height_idx_);
  return *this;
}
```

This way, the `TowerList` class can be safely moved while still preserving the no exception guaranteed. Later in this book, in `Chapter 8`, *Metaprogramming and Compile-Time Evaluation*, you will learn how to take advantage of reflection techniques in C++ in order to automate the process of creating *move-constructor/assignment* functions which swap the elements.

Applying the && modifier to class member functions

In addition to being applied to objects, you can also add the `&&` modifier to a member function of a class, just as you can apply a `const` modifier to a member function. As in the case with the `const` modifier, a member function which has the && modifier is only permitted to be executed on an r-value.

```
struct Foo {
  auto func() && {}
};
auto a = Foo{};
a.func(); // Does not compile, 'a' is not an r-value
std::move(a).func(); // Compiles
Foo{}.func(); // Compiles
```

It might seem odd that one would ever want this behavior, but there are cases. We will investigate one of those cases in `Chapter 9`, *Proxy Objects and Lazy* Evaluation.

Representing optional values with std::optional

Although quite a minor feature in C++17, `std::optional` is a neat addition to the STL library which simplifies a common case which couldn't be expressed in a clean straightforward syntax prior to `std::optional`. In a nutshell, it is a small wrapper for any type where the wrapped type can be both initialized and uninitialized.

To put it in C++ lingo, `std::optional` is a *stack-allocated container with a max size of one*.

Note that the *Boost Libraries* has had an equivalent of `std::optional`, named `boost::optional` for many years.

Optional return values

Before the introduction of `std::optional`, there was no clear way to define functions which may not return a defined value, such as the intersection point of two line segments. With the introduction of `std::optional`, such optional return values can be clearly expressed. Following is an implementation of a function which returns an optional intersection between two lines:

```
// Prerequisite
class Point {...}; class Line {...};
external auto is_intersecting(Line a, Line b) -> bool {...}
external auto get_intersection(Line a, Line b) -> Point {...}

auto get_intersection_point(const Line& a, const Line& b)
-> std::optional<Point> {
  return is_intersection(a, b) ?
    std::make_optional(get_intersection(a, b)):
    std::optional<Point>{};
}
```

The syntax of `std::optional` resembles that of a pointer, the value is accessed by `operator*` or `operator->`. If trying to access the value of an empty optional, the `std::optional` throws an exception. Following is a simple usage example of a returned `std::optional`:

```
// Prerequisite
auto line0 = Line{...};
auto line1 = Line{...};
external auto set_magic_point(Point p);

// Get optional intersection
auto intersection = get_intersection_point(line0, line1);
if(intersection.has_value()) {
  // std::optional throws an exception if intersection is empty
  set_magic_point(*intersection);
}
```

The object held by a `std::optional` is always stack allocated, and the memory overhead of a `std::optional<T>` compared to `T` is the size of one bool (usually one byte), plus possible padding.

Optional member variables

Let's say we have a class which represents a human head. The head can have a hat of some sort, or no hat at all. By using `std::optional` to represent the hat member variable the implementation is as expressive as can be.

```
struct Hat {...}
class Head {
public:
  Head() { assert(!hat_); } // hat_ is empty by default
  auto set_hat(const Hat& h){ hat_ = h; }
  auto has_hat() const { return hat_.has_value(); }
  auto& get_hat() const { assert(hat_.has_value()); return *hat_; }
  auto remove_hat() { hat_ = {}; } // Hat is cleared by assigning to {}
private:
  std::optional<Hat> hat_;
};
```

Without `std::optional`, representing an optional member variable would rely on, for example, a pointer or an extra bool member variable. Both having disadvantages such as allocating on the heap, or accidentally accessing an optional considered empty without a warning.

Sorting and comparing std::optional

The `std::optional` is both equally comparable and sortable, using the following rules as shown in the following table:

Two **empty** optional's are considered equal.
`auto a = std::optional<int>{};`
`auto b = std::optional<int>{};`
`auto c = std::optional<int>{4};`
`assert(a == b);`
`assert(b != c);`
	An empty optional is considered **less** than a non-empty.
	`auto a = std::optional<int>{};`
	`auto b = std::optional<int>{4};`
	`auto c = std::optional<int>{5};`
	`assert(a < b);`
	`assert(b < c);`

Therefore, if you sort a container of `std::optional<T>`, the empty optional's would end up at the beginning of the container, whereas the non-empty optional's are sorted as usual, shown as follows:

```
auto c = std::vector<std::optional<int>>{{3}, {}, {1}, {}, {2}};
std::sort(c.begin(), c.end());
// c is {}, {}, {1}, {2}, {3}
```

Representing dynamic values with std::any

Just like `std::optional`, `std::any` can store an optional single value, but with the difference that it can store any type at runtime, just like a dynamically typed}language. As the `std::any` can withhold any type, you need to explicitly specify the type using the global function `std::any_cast` when reading the held object.

If the `std::any` is empty or withholds another type than the specified type, an exception is thrown.

Here is an example of how it works:

```
// Initialize an empty std::any
auto a = std::any{};
// Put a string in it
a = std::string{"something"};
// Return a reference to the withheld string
auto& str_ref = std::any_cast<std::string&>(a);
// Copy the withheld string
auto str_copy = std::any_cast<std::string>(a);
// Put a float in the 'any' and read it back
a = 135.246f;
auto flt = std::any_cast<float>(a);
// Copy the any object
auto b = a;
auto is_same =
  (a.type() == b.type()) &&
  (std::any_cast<float>(a) == std::any_cast<float>(b));
// a equals b as they contain the same type and value
```

Asking the `std::any` instance if it contains a type via the `typeid` is quite verbose, but you can easily create a convenience function which checks if the `std::any` contains a specified type like this:

```
template <typename T>
auto is_withheld_type(const std::any& a) -> bool {
  return typeid(T) == a.type();
}

auto a = std::any{32.0};
auto is_int = is_withheld_type<int>(a);
// is_int is false, 'a' contains a double
auto is_double = is_withheld_type<double>(a);
// is_double is true, 'a' contains a double
```

Performance of std::any

In contrast to `std::optional` and `std::variant` (`std::variant` is discussed in Chapter 8, *Meta programming and Compile-Time evaluation*), `std::any` heap-allocates its withheld value (although implementers are encouraged to store small objects inside of the `any`). Also, invoking a `std::any_cast` to retrieve the value is quite slow compared to `std::variant`.

The Boost equivalent of `std::any`, `boost::any`, provides a fast version of `std::any_cast` called `boost::any_cast_unsafe` which can be utilized if you know which type is contained. In contrast to `std::any_cast`, using a `boost::any_cast_unsafe` with the wrong type will result in undefined behavior instead of a thrown exception.

Summary

In this chapter you have learned how to use modern C++ features such as forwarding references, move-semantics, lambda functions, `std::any`, and `std::optional`. In the next chapter we will look into strategies for how to measure performance in C++.

3
Measuring Performance

Since this is a book about writing C++ code that runs efficiently, we need to cover some basics regarding how to measure software performance and estimate algorithmic efficiency. Most of the topics in this chapter are not specific to C++, and can be used whenever you are facing a problem where performance is an issue.

We are going to learn how to estimate algorithmic efficiency using big O notation. This is essential knowledge when choosing algorithms and data structures from STL. If you are new to big O notation, this part might take some time to grasp. But don't give up! This is a very important topic to grasp in order to understand the rest of the book, and, more importantly to become a performance-aware programmer. If you want a more formal or more practical introduction to these concepts, there are plenty of books and online resources dedicated to this topic. On the other hand, if you have already mastered big O notation and know what amortized time complexity is, you could probably skim the next section and go to the later parts of this chapter.

Altogether, this chapter includes:

- Estimating algorithmic efficiency using big O notation
- A suggested workflow when optimizing code so that we don't spend time fine-tuning code without good reasons
- CPU profilers—what they are and why you should use them

Asymptotic complexity and big O notation

There is usually more than one way to solve a problem and if efficiency is a concern, you should first and foremost focus on the high-level optimizations by choosing the right algorithms and data structures. A useful way of evaluating and comparing algorithms is by analyzing their asymptotic computational complexity—that is, analyzing how the running time or memory consumption grows when the size of the input increases. In addition, the C++ **Standard Template Library** (**STL**) specifies the asymptotic complexity for all containers and algorithms, which means that a basic understanding of this topic is a must if you are using STL. If you already have a good understanding of algorithm complexity and the big O notation, you can safely skip this section.

Let's start off with an example. Suppose we want to write an algorithm that returns `true` if it finds a specific key in an array, or `false` otherwise. In order to find out how our algorithm behaves when passed different sizes of the array, we would like to analyze the running time of this algorithm as a function of its input size:

```
auto linear_search(const std::vector<int>& vals, int key) {
  for (const auto& v : vals) {
    if (v == key) {
      return true;
    }
  }
  return false;
}
```

The algorithm is straightforward: It iterates over the elements in the array and compares each element with the key. If we are lucky, we find the key in the beginning of the array and it returns immediately, but we might loop through the entire array without finding the key at all. This would be the worst case for the algorithm, and in general, that is the case we want to analyze. But what happens with the running time when we increase the input size? Say we double the size of the array. Well, in the worst case, we need to compare all elements in the array that would double the running time. There seems to be a linear relationship between the input size and the running time. We call this a linear growth rate:

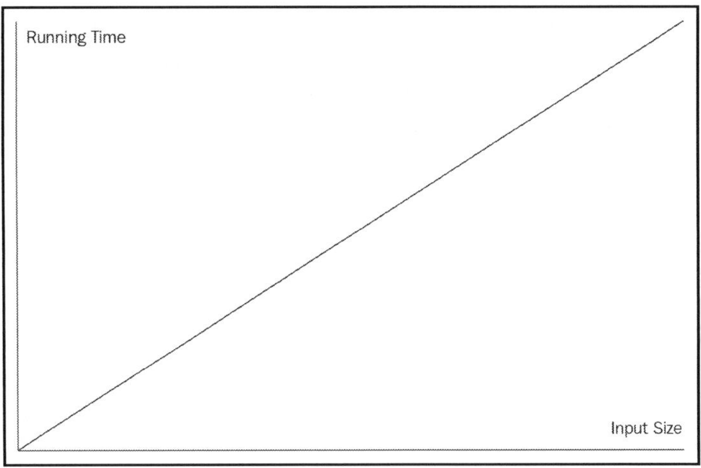

Linear growth rate

How about the following algorithm:

```
struct Point {
  int x{};
  int y{};
};

auto linear_search(const std::vector<Point>& a, const Point& key) {
  for (size_t i = 0; i < a.size(); ++i) {
    if (a[i].x == key.x && a[i].y == key.y) {
      return true;
    }
  }
  return false;
}
```

We are comparing points instead of integers and we are using an index with the subscript operator to access each element. How is the running time affected by these changes? The absolute running time is probably higher compared to the first algorithm since we are doing more work—for example, the comparison of points involves two integers instead of just one for each element in the array. However, at this stage we are interested in the growth rate the algorithm exhibits, and if we plot the running time against the input size, we would still end up with a straight line, as shown in the preceding image.

As the last example of searching for integers, let's see whether we can find a better algorithm if we assume that the elements in the array are sorted. Our first algorithm would work regardless of the order of the elements, but if we know that they are sorted, we can use a binary search. It works by looking at the element in the middle and determines whether it should continue searching in the first or second half of the array:

```
auto binary_search(const std::vector<int>& a, int key) {
  if (a.empty()) {
    return false;
  }
  auto low = size_t{0};
  auto high = a.size() - 1;
  while (low <= high) {
    const auto mid = low + ((high - low) / 2);
    if (a[mid] < key) {
      low = mid + 1;
    }
    else if (a[mid] > key) {
      high = mid - 1;
    }
    else {
      return true;
    }
  }
  return false;
}
```

As you can see, this algorithm is harder to get correct than the simple linear scan. It looks for the specified key by *guessing* that it's in the middle of the array. If it's not, it compares the key with the element in the middle to decide which half of the array should keep looking for the key. So in each iteration it cuts the array in half. Assume we called `binary_search()` with an array containing 64 elements. In the first iteration we reject 32 elements, in the next iteration we reject 16 elements, the next iteration 8 elements, and so on, until there are no more elements to compare or until we find the key. For an input size of 64, there will be at most 7 loop iterations. What if we double the input size to 128? Since we halve the size in each iteration, it means that we only need one more loop iteration. Clearly, the growth rate is no longer linear—it's actually logarithmic. If we measure the running time of `binary_search()`, we will see that the growth rate would look something like the one in the following image:

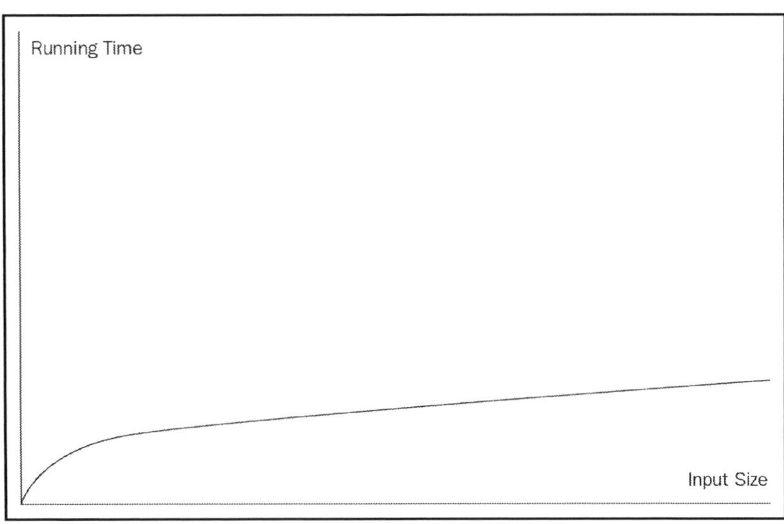

Logarithmic growth rate

On my machine, a quick timing of the three algorithms repeatedly called 10,000 times with various input sizes (*n*) produced the results shown in the following table:

Algorithm	**n = 10**	**n = 1,000**	**n = 1,00,000**
• Linear search with `int`	0.04 ms	4.7 ms	458 ms
• Linear search with `Point`	0.07 ms	6.7 ms	725 ms
• Binary search with `int`	0.03 ms	0.08 ms	0.16 ms

Comparing algorithms **1** and **2**, we can see that comparing points instead of integers takes more time, but they are still in the same order of magnitude even when the input size increases. However, if we compare all three algorithms when the input size increases, what really matters is the growth rate the algorithm exhibits. By exploiting the fact that the array was sorted, we could implement the search function with very few loop iterations. For large arrays, binary search is practically free compared to linearly scanning the array.

Never spend time tuning your code before you are certain that you have chosen the correct algorithms and data structures for your problem.

Wouldn't it be nice if we could express the growth rate of algorithms in a way that would help us decide which algorithm to use? Here is where the big O notation comes in handy. Here follows an informal definition: If $f(n)$ is a function that specifies the running time of an algorithm with input size n, we say that $f(n)$ is $O(g(n))$ if there is a constant k such that $f(n) \leq k * g(n)$. This means that we could say that the time complexity of `linear_search()` is $O(n)$, for both versions with integers and points, whereas the time complexity of `binary_search()` is $O(log\ n)$ or big O of $log\ n$.

In practice, when we want to find the big O of a function, we can do that by eliminating all terms except the one with the largest growth rate and then remove any constant factors. For example, if we have an algorithm with a time complexity described by $f(n) = 4n^2 + 30n + 100$, we would pick out the term with the highest growth rate, $4n^2$. Next, we remove the constant factor of 4 and end up with n^2, which means that we can say that our algorithm runs in $O(n^2)$. Finding the time complexity of an algorithm can be hard, but the more you start thinking of it while writing code, the easier it will get. For the most part, it's enough to keep track of loops and recursive functions.

Here is another example:

```
auto insertion_sort(std::vector<int>& a) {
  for (size_t i = 1; i < a.size(); ++i) {
    auto j = i;
    while (j > 0 && a[j-1] > a[j]) {
      std::swap(a[j], a[j-1]);
      --j;
    }
  }
}
```

The input size is the size of the array. The running time could be estimated approximately by looking at the loops that iterate over all elements. First, there is an outer loop iterating over $n - 1$ elements. The inner loop is different: the first time we reach the `while`-loop, `j` is 1 and the loop only run one iteration. On the next iteration, `j` starts at 2 and decreases to 0. For each iteration in the outer for loop, the inner loop needs to do more and more work. Finally, `j` starts at $n - 1$, which means that we have, in the worst case, executed swap $1 + 2 + 3 + ... + (n - 1)$ times. We can express this in terms of n by noting that this is an arithmetic series. The sum of the series is $1 + 2 + ... + k = (1/2)(k * (k+1))$. So if we set $k = (n - 1)$, we have the complexity as $(1/2)((n-1) * (n-1 + 1)) = (1/2)((n-1) * n) = (1/2)(n^2-n) = (1/2)\ n^2 - (1/2)n$. We can now find the big O of this function by first eliminating all terms except the one with the largest growth rate, which gives us $(1/2)n^2$ left. After that, we remove the constant $1/2$ and conclude that the running time of the sorting algorithm is $O(n^2)$.

Growth rates

As stated previously, the first step in finding the big O of a complexity function is to remove all terms except the one with the highest growth rate. To be able to do that, we must know the growth rate of some common functions. In the following figure, we have plotted some of the most common functions:

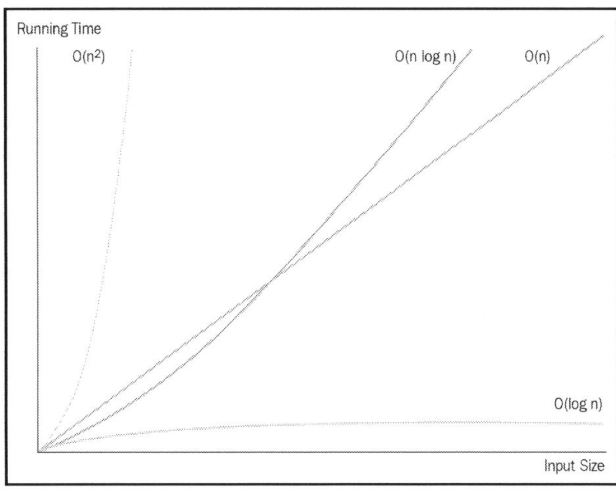

Comparison of growth rate functions

The growth rates are independent of machine or coding style and so on, when the growth rates differ between two algorithms, the one with the slowest growth rate will always win when the input size gets sufficiently large. Let's see what happens with the running time for different growth rates if we assume that it takes *1 ms* to perform *1 unit* of work. The following table lists the growth function, its common name, and different input sizes, *n*:

f(n)	**Name**	**n = 10**	**n = 50**	**n = 1000**
O(1)	Constant	0.001 sec	0.001 sec	0.001 sec
O(log n)	Logarithmic	0.003 sec	0.006 sec	0.01 sec
O(n)	Linear	0.01 sec	0.05 sec	1 sec
O(n log n)	Linearithmic or *n log n*	0.03 sec	0.3 sec	10 sec
O(n^2)	Quadratic	0.1 sec	2.5 sec	16.7 minutes
O(2^n)	Exponential	1 sec	357 centuries	∞

Amortized time complexity

Usually, an algorithm behaves differently with different inputs. Going back to our algorithm that linearly searched an element in an array, we were analyzing the case where the key was not in the array at all. For that algorithm, that was the worst case—that is, it used the *most* resources the algorithm will need. The best case refers to the *least* amount of resources the algorithm will need, whereas the average case states how many resources the algorithm will use on average with different input.

The STL usually refers to the amortized running time of functions that operate on containers. If an algorithm runs in constant amortized time, it means that it will run in *O(1)* in almost all cases, except a very few where it will perform worse. At first sight, amortized running time can be confused with average time, but as we will see, they are not the same.

To understand amortized time complexity, we will spend some time thinking about `std::vector::push_back()`. Let's assume that the vector internally has a fixed size array to store all its elements in. If there is room for more elements in the fixed-size array when calling `push_back()`, the operation will run in constant time, *O(1)*—that is, it's not dependent on how many elements are already in the vector as long as the internal array has room for one more:

```
if (internal_array.size() > size) {
  internal_array[size] = new_element;
  ++size;
}
```

But what happens when the internal array is full? One way to handle the growing of the vector is to create a new empty internal array with a bigger size, and then move all the elements from the old array to the new one. This is obviously not constant time anymore since we need one move per element in the array—that is, *O(n)*. If we considered this the worst case, it would mean that `push_back()` is *O(n)*. However, if we call `push_back()` many times, we know that the expensive `push_back()` can't happen very often, and so it would be pessimistic, and not very useful, to say that `push_back()` is *O(n)* if we know that `push_back()` is called many times in a row. Amortized running time is used for analyzing a sequence of operations rather than a single one. We are still analyzing the worst case, but for a sequence of operations. The amortized running time can be computed by first analyzing the running time of the entire sequence and then dividing that by the length of the sequence. Suppose we are performing a sequence of *m* operations with the total running time *T(m)*:

$$T(m) = t_0 + t_1 + t_2 ... + t_{m-1}$$

Where $t_0 = 1$, $t_1 = n$, $t_2 = 1$, $t_3 = n$, and so on. In other words, half of the operations run in constant time and the other half run in linear time:

$$T(m) = n\frac{m}{2} + \frac{m}{2} = \frac{(n+1)m}{2}$$

The amortized complexity for each operation is the total time divided by the number of operations, which turns out to be *O(n)*:

$$T(m)/m = \frac{(n+1)m}{2m} = \frac{n+1}{2} = O(n)$$

However, if we can guarantee that the expensive operations due to occur orders of magnitude less frequently, we will achieve lower amortized running costs. For example, if we can guarantee that an expensive operation only occurs once in a sequence *T(n)* + *T(1)* + *T(1)* + ..., then the amortized running time is *O(1)*. So depending on the frequency of the expensive operations, the amortized running time changes.

Now, back to `std::vector`. The standard states that `push_back()` needs to run in amortized constant time, *O(1)*. How do the STL vendors achieve this? If the capacity is increased by a fixed number of elements each time the vector becomes full, we will have a case similar to the preceding one where we had a running time of *O(n)*. Even if we use a large constant, the capacity changes would still occur at fixed intervals. The key insight is that the vector needs to grow exponentially in order to get the expensive operations to occur rarely enough. Internally, the vector uses a growth factor such that the capacity of the new array is the current size times the growth factor.

A big growth factor would potentially waste more memory but would make the expensive operation occur less frequently. To simplify the math, let's assume we double the capacity each time the vector needs to grow. We can now estimate how often the expensive calls occur. For a vector of size *n*, we would need to grow the internal array $log_2(n)$ times since we are doubling the size all the time. Each time we grow the array, we need to move all the elements that are currently in the array. The *i:th* time we grow the array there will be 2^i elements to move. So if we perform *m* number of `push_back()` operations, the running time of the entire sequence will be:

$$T(m) = \sum_{i=1}^{log_2(m)} 2^i$$

This is a geometric series and can also be expressed as:

$$\frac{2 - 2^{log_2(m)+1}}{1 - 2} = 2m - 2 = O(m)$$

Dividing this by the length of the sequence, i.e. *m*, we end up with the amortized running time *O(1)*.

As we have already said, amortized time complexity is used a lot in the STL, so it's good to have an understanding of it. Thinking about how `push_back()` could be implemented in amortized constant time has helped me remember the simplified version of amortized constant time: It will run in *O(1)* in almost all cases, except a very few where it will perform worse.

That is all we are going to cover regarding asymptotic complexity. Now we will move on to how you can go ahead and tackle a performance problem and work effectively with optimizing your code.

What to measure?

Optimizations almost always add complexity to your code. High-level optimizations, such as choice of algorithm and data structures, can make the intention of the code clearer, but for the most part, optimizations will make the code harder to read and maintain. We therefore want to be absolutely sure that the optimizations we add have an actual impact on what we are trying to achieve in terms of performance. Do we really need to make the code faster? In what way? Does the code really use too much memory? To understand what optimizations are possible, we need to have a good understanding of the requirements, such as latency, throughput, and memory usage. Optimizing code is fun, but it's also very easy to get lost without any measurable winnings. We start this section by suggesting a workflow to follow when tuning your code:

1. **Define a goal**: It's easier to know how to optimize and when to stop optimizing if you have a well-defined, quantitative goal. For some applications, it's clear from the start what the requirements are, but in many cases it tends to be fuzzier. Even though it might be obvious that the code is running too slow, it's important to know what would be good enough. Each domain has its own limits, so make sure you understand the ones that are relevant to your application. Here are some examples to make it more concrete:

- Response time for user interactive applications 100 ms; refer to `https://www.nngroup.com/articles/response-times-3-important-limits`
- Graphics with 60 **FPS (Frames Per Second)** gives you 16 ms per frame
- Real-time audio with a 128 sample buffer at 44.1 kHz sample rate means slightly less than 3 ms

2. **Measure**: Once we know what to measure and what the limits are, we proceed by measuring how the application is performing right now. From *step 1*, it should be obvious if we are interested in average times, peaks, load, and so on. In this step, we are only concerned with measuring the goal we have set up. Depending on the application, measuring can be anything from using a stopwatch to using highly sophisticated performance analysis tools.
3. **Find the bottlenecks**: Next, we need to find the application's bottlenecks, the parts that are too slow and make the application useless. Don't trust your gut feeling at this point! Maybe you gained some insights by measuring the code at various points in *step 2*—that's fine, but you usually need to profile your code further in order to find the hot spots that matters most.
4. **Make an educated guess**: Come up with a hypothesis for how to improve the performance. Can a lookup table be used? Can we cache data to gain the overall throughput? Can we change the code so that the compiler can vectorize it? Can we decrease the number of allocations in the critical sections by reusing memory? Coming up with ideas is usually not that hard if you know that they are just educated guesses. It's okay to be wrong; we will find out later whether they had an impact or not.
5. **Optimize**: Let's implement the hypothesis we sketched in *step 4*. Don't spend too much time on this step making it perfect before you know that it actually has an effect. Be prepared to reject this optimization. It might not have the desired effect.
6. **Evaluate**: Measure again. Do the exact same test as in *step 2* and compare the results. What did we gain? If we didn't gain anything, reject the code and go back to *step 4*. If the optimization actually had a positive effect, you need to ask yourself whether it's good enough to spend more time on. How complicated is the optimization? Is it worth the effort? Is this a general performance gain or is it highly specific to a certain case/platform? Is it maintainable? Can we encapsulate it or does it spread out all over the code base? If you can't motivate the optimization, go back to *step 4*, otherwise continue to the final step.
7. **Refactor**: If you followed the instructions in *step 5* and didn't spend too much time writing perfect code in the first place, it's time to refactor the optimization to make it cleaner. Optimizations almost always need some comments to explain why we are doing things in an unusual way.

Performance properties

Before you start measuring, you must know what performance properties are important for the application you are writing. In this section, we will explain some of the frequently-used terms when measuring performance. Depending on the application you are writing, some of the properties are more relevant than others. For example, throughput might be a more important property than latency if you are writing an online image converter service, whereas latency is key when writing interactive applications with real-time requirements:

- **Latency/response time**: Depending on the domain, latency and response time might have very precise and different meanings. However, in this book, we mean the time between the request and the response of an operation—for example, the time it takes for an image conversion service to process one image.
- **Throughput**: This refers to the number of transactions (operations, requests, and so on) processed per time unit—for example, the number of images that an image conversion service can process per second.
- **I/O bound or CPU bound**: A task usually spends the majority of its time computing things on the CPU or waiting for I/O (hard drives, networks, and so on). A task is said to be CPU bound if it would run faster if the CPU were faster. it's said to be I/O bound if it would run faster by making the I/O faster. Sometimes you can hear about memory-bound tasks too, which means that the amount or speed of the main memory is the current bottleneck.
- **Power consumption**: This is a very important consideration for code that executes on mobile devices with batteries. In order to decrease the power usage, the application needs to use the hardware more efficiently, just as if we are optimizing for CPU usage, network efficiency, and so on. Other than that, high frequency polling should be avoided since it prevents the CPU from going to sleep.
- **Aggregating data**: This is usually necessary when collecting a lot of samples while measuring performance. Sometimes *mean values* are a good enough indicator of how the program performs, but more often the *median* tells you more about the actual performance since it's more robust against outliers. If you are interested in outliers, you can always measure *min* and *max* values (or the 10th percentile, for example).

Performance testing – best practices

For some reason, it's more common to see regression tests to cover functional requirements than it's to see performance requirements or other nonfunctional requirements. Performance testing is usually more sporadic and, more often than not, way too late in the development process. Our recommendation is to measure early and detect regression as soon as possible by adding performance tests to your nightly builds, and so on.

Choose the algorithms and data structures wisely if they are to handle large inputs, but don't fine-tune code without good reason. It's also important to test your application with realistic test data early on. Ask questions about data sizes early in the project. How many table rows is the application supposed to handle and still be able to scroll smoothly? Don't just try it with 100 elements and hope that your code will scale, test it!

Plotting your data is a very effective way of understanding the data you have collected. There are so many good and easy-to-use plotting tools available today, so there is really no excuse for not plotting. The plot does not have to look pretty in order to be useful. Once you plot your data, you are going to see the outliers and patterns that are usually hard to find in a table full of numbers.

Knowing your code and hot spots

The Pareto principle, or the 80/20 rule, has been applied in various fields since it was first observed by the Italian economist Vilfredo Pareto more than 100 years ago. He was able to show that 20% of the Italian population owned 80% of the land. In computer science, it has been widely used (and maybe even overused). In software optimization, it suggests that 20% of the code is responsible for 80% of the resources that a program uses. This is, of course, only a rule of thumb and shouldn't be taken too literally. Nevertheless, for code that has not been optimized, it's common to find some relatively small hot spots that spend the vast majority of the total resources. As a programmer, this is actually good news because it means that we can write most of our code without tweaking it for performance reasons and instead focus on keeping the code clean. It also means that when doing optimizations, we have a better idea of where to do them; otherwise, there is a good chance we will optimize code that will not have an impact on the overall performance. In this section, we will look at methods and tools for finding the 20% of your code that might be worth optimizing.

Profilers

Using a profiler is usually the most efficient way of finding hot spots in a program. Profilers analyze the execution of a program and output a statistical summary, a profile, of how often the functions or instructions in the program are being called. In addition, profilers usually also output a call graph that shows the relationship between function calls, that is, the callers and callees for each function that was called during the profiling. In the following figure, we can see that the `sort()` function was called from `main()` (the caller) and that `sort()` did call the function `swap()` (the callee):

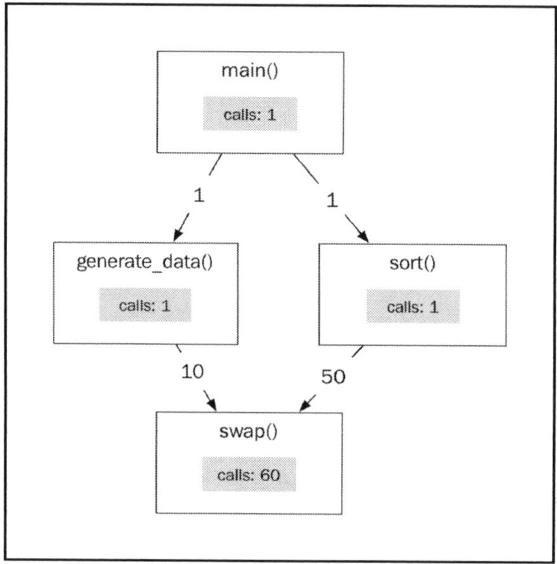

Example of a call graph

There are two main categories of profilers: sampling profilers and instrumentation profilers. There is also a third category mixing both approaches, that is, a hybrid of sampling and instrumentation. `gprof`, the UNIX performance analysis tool, is an example of this third approach.

Instrumentation profilers

By instrumentation, we mean inserting code into the program to be analyzed in order to gather information about how frequently each function is being executed. Typically, the inserted instrumentation code records each entry and exit point. You can write your own primitive instrumentation profiler by inserting the code manually yourself, or you can use a tool that automatically inserts the necessary code as a step in the build process. A naive implementation might be good enough for your purposes, but be aware of the impact that the added code can have on the performance, which can make the profile misleading. Another problem with naive implementations is that they might prevent compiler optimizations or run the risk of being optimized away.

Just to give you an example of an instrumentation profiler, here is a simplified version of a timer class we have used in previous projects:

```
class ScopedTimer {
public:
  using ClockType = std::chrono::steady_clock;

  ScopedTimer(const char* func) :
    function_{func},
    start_{ClockType::now()} { }

  ScopedTimer(const ScopedTimer&) = delete;
  ScopedTimer(ScopedTimer&&) = delete;
  auto& operator=(const ScopedTimer&) -> ScopedTimer& = delete;
  auto& operator=(ScopedTimer&&) -> ScopedTimer& = delete;

  ~ScopedTimer() {
    using namespace std::chrono;
    auto stop = ClockType::now();
    auto duration = (stop - start_);
    auto ms = duration_cast<milliseconds>(duration).count();
    std::cout << ms << " ms " << function_ <<  '\n';
  }

private:
  const char* function_{};
  const ClockType::time_point start_{};
};
```

The ScopedTimer class will measure the time from when it was created to the time it went out of scope, that is, destructed. We are using the only std::chrono::steady_clock available since C++11, which was designed for measuring time intervals. The steady_clock is monotonic, which means that it will never decrease between two consecutive calls to clock_type::now(). This is not the case for the system clock, for example, which can be adjusted at any time.

We can now use our time class by measuring each function in a program by creating a ScopedTimer instance at the beginning of each function:

```
auto some_function() {
  ScopedTimer timer{"some_function"};
  ...
}
```

Even though we don't recommend the use of preprocessor macros in general, this might be a case for using one:

```
#if USE_TIMER
  #define MEASURE_FUNCTION() ScopedTimer timer{__func__}
#else
  #define MEASURE_FUNCTION()
#endif
```

We are using the only predefined function-local __func__ variable available since C++11 to get the name of the function. There are other nonstandard predefined macros that are supported by most compilers and can be really useful for debugging purposes, for example, __FUNCTION__, __FILE__, and __LINE__.

Now, our ScopedTimer class can be used like this:

```
auto some_function() {
  MEASURE_FUNCTION();
  ...
}
```

Assuming that we have defined USE_TIMER when compiling our timer, it will produce the following output each time some_function() returns:

```
2.3 ms some_function
```

Sampling profilers

Sampling profilers create a profile by looking at the running program's state at even intervals—typically, every 10 ms. Sampling profilers usually have a minimum impact on the program's actual performance, and it's also possible to build the program in release mode with all optimizations turned on. A drawback of sampling profilers is their inaccuracy and statistical approach, which is usually not a problem as long as you are aware of it. The following figure shows a sampling session of a running program with five functions: `main()`, `f1()`, `f2()`, `f3()`, and `f4()`. The $\mathbf{t_1}$-$\mathbf{t_{10}}$ labels indicate when each sample was taken. The boxes indicate the entry and exit point of each executing function:

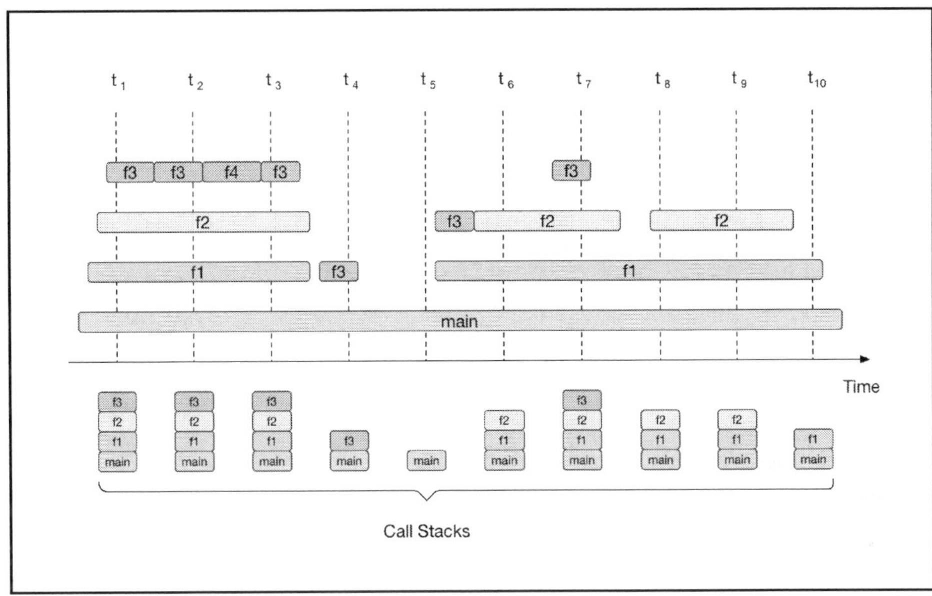

Example of a sampling profiler session

The profile is summarized in the following table:

Function	Total	Self
`main()`	100%	10%
`f1()`	80%	10%
`f2()`	70%	30%
`f3()`	50%	50%

The **Total** column in the preceding table shows the amount of call stacks that contained a certain function. In our example, the main function was present in all 10 out of 10 call stacks (100%), whereas the `f2()` function was only detected in 7 call stacks, which corresponds to 70% of all call stacks.

The **Self** column shows, for each function, how many times it occurred on top of the call stack. The `main()` function was detected once on top of the call stack at the fifth sample, $\mathbf{t_5}$, whereas the `f2()` function was on top of the call stack at samples $\mathbf{t_6}$, $\mathbf{t_8}$, and $\mathbf{t_9}$, which corresponds to 3/10 = **30%**. The `f3()` function had the highest self value (5/10) and was on top of the call stack whenever it was detected.

Conceptually, a sampling profiler stores samples of call stacks at even time intervals. It detects what is currently running on the CPU. Pure sampling profilers usually only detect functions that are currently being executed in a thread that is in a running state, since sleeping threads do not get scheduled on the CPU. This means that if a function is waiting for a lock that causes the thread to sleep, that time will not show up in the time profile. This is important, because your bottlenecks might be caused by thread synchronization that might be invisible for the sampling profiler.

What happened to the `f4()` function? According to the graph, it was called by the `f2()` function between samples two and three, but it never showed up in our statistical profile since it was never registered in any of the call stacks. This is also an important property of sampling profilers to be aware of: If the time between each sample is too big or the total sampling session is too short, short and infrequently-called functions will not show up in the profile. This is usually not a problem since these functions are rarely the functions you need to tune anyway. One can note that the `f3()` function was also missed between $\mathbf{t_5}$ and $\mathbf{t_6}$, but since `f3()` was called very frequently, it had a big impact on the profile anyway.

Make sure you understand what your time profiler actually registers. Be aware of its limitations and strengths in order to use it as effectively as possible.

Summary

In this chapter, you learned how to compare the efficiency of algorithms by using big O notation. We now know that the C++ STL has complexity guarantees. All STL algorithms specify their worst-case or average-case performance guarantees, whereas containers and iterators specify amortized complexity.

You also learned how to quantify software performance by measuring latency and throughput.

Lastly, you learned how to detect hotspots in your code by using CPU profilers.

4
Data Structures

In the last chapter, we discussed how to analyze time and memory complexity, and how to measure performance. In this chapter, we are going to talk about how to choose and use data structures from the Standard Template Library. To understand why certain data structures work very well on the computers of today, we first need to cover some basics about computer memory. In this chapter, you will learn about:

- The properties of computer memory
- The STL containers: sequence containers, associative containers, and container adapters
- Parallel arrays

Properties of computer memory

Before we start walking through the STL containers and some other useful data structures, we will briefly discuss some properties of computer memory.

C++ treats memory as a sequence of cells. The size of each cell is one byte, and each cell has an address. Accessing a byte in memory by its address is a constant time operation, *O(1)*, that is independent of the total number of memory cells. On a 32-bit machine, one can theoretically address 2^{32} bytes, that is, around 4 GB, which restricts the amount of memory a process is allowed to use at once. On a 64-bit machine, one can theoretically address 2^{64} bytes, which is so big that there is hardly any risk of running out of addresses.

The following image shows a sequence of memory cells laid out in memory. Each cell contains eight bits. The hexadecimal numbers are the addresses of the memory cells:

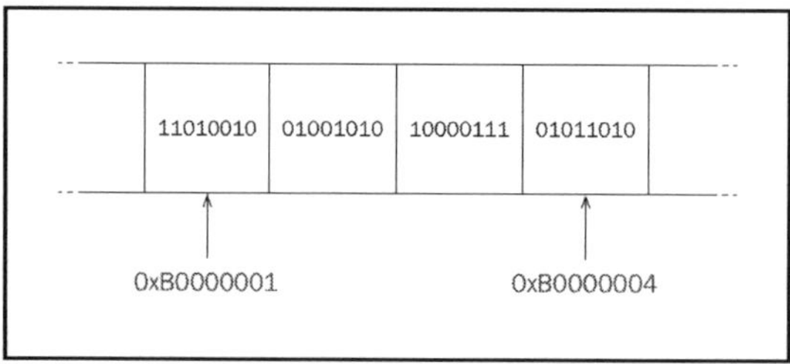

A sequence of memory cells laid out in memory.

Since accessing a byte by its address is an *O(1)* operation, from a programmer's perspective, it's tempting to believe that each memory cell is equally quick to access. This is a good and useful approach in many cases, but when choosing data structures for efficient use, one needs to take into account the memory hierarchy that exists in modern computers. The importance of the memory hierarchy has increased, since the time it takes to read and write from the main memory has become more expensive compared to the speed of today's processors. The following figure shows the architecture of a machine with one CPU with four cores:

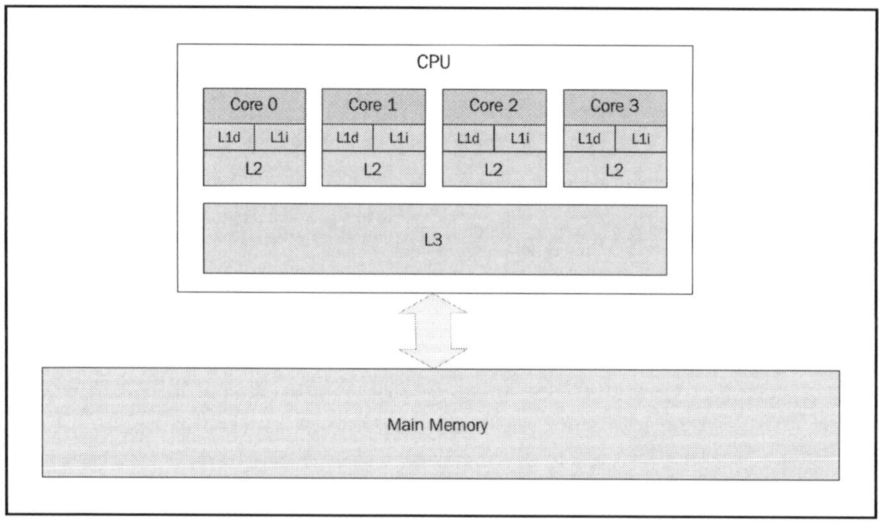

An example of a processor with 4 cores. The boxes labeled L1i, L1d, L2, and L3 are memory caches.

I'm currently writing this chapter on a MacBook Pro from 2013, which is equipped with an Intel Quad-Core i7 CPU. On this processor, each core has its own L1 and L2 caches, whereas the L3 cache is shared among all four cores. Running the `sysctl -a hw` command from a terminal gives me, among other things, the following information:

```
hw.memsize: 17179869184
hw.cachelinesize: 64
hw.l1icachesize: 32768
hw.l1dcachesize: 32768
hw.l2cachesize: 262144
hw.l3cachesize: 6291456
```

The reported `hw.memsize` is the total amount of main memory, which is 16 GB in this case.

The `hw.cachelinesize`, which is reported to be 64 bytes, is the size of the cache lines, also known as blocks. When accessing a byte in memory, the machine is not only fetching the byte we asked for; instead, the machine always fetches a cache line, which in this case is 64 bytes. The various caches between the CPU and main memory keep track of 64 byte blocks instead of individual bytes.

The `hw.l1icachesize` is the size of the L1 instruction cache. This is a 32 KB cache dedicated to store instructions that have been recently used by the CPU. The `hw.l1dcachesize` is also 32 KB and is dedicated for data as opposed to instructions.

Lastly, we can read the size of the L2 cache and the L3 cache, which is 2 MB and 6 MB respectively. An important observation is that the caches are tiny compared to the amount of main memory available.

Without presenting any detailed facts about the actual number of cycles required to access data from each layer in the cache hierarchy, a very rough guideline is that there are order of magnitude differences of latency between two adjacent layers (for example, L1 and L2). The following table shows an extract from the latency numbers presented in an article by *Peter Norvig, Teach yourself programming in ten years, 2001* (`http://norvig.com/21-days.html`). The full table is usually referred to as *Latency numbers every programmer should know* and is credited to Jeff Dean:

```
L1 cache reference          0.5 ns
L2 cache reference            7  ns
Main memory reference       100  ns
```

Structuring the data in such a way that the caches can be fully utilized can have a dramatic effect on the performance. Accessing data that has recently been used and, therefore, potentially already resides in the cache will make your program faster. This is known as **temporal locality**.

Also, accessing data that is located near some other data you are using will increase the likelihood that the data you need is already in a cache line fetched from main memory earlier. This is known as **spatial locality**.

Constantly wiping out the cache lines in inner loops might result in very bad performance. This is sometimes called cache thrashing. Let's look at an example:

```
constexpr auto kL1CacheCapacity = 32768; // The L1 Data cache size
constexpr auto kSize = kL1CacheCapacity / sizeof(int);
using MatrixType = std::array<std::array<int, kSize>, kSize>;

auto cache_thrashing(MatrixType& matrix) {
  auto counter = 0;
  for (auto i = 0; i < kSize; ++i) {
    for (auto j = 0; j < kSize; ++j) {
      matrix[i][j] = counter++;
    }
  }
}
```

This version takes about 40 ms to run on my computer. However, by only changing the line in the inner loop to the following, the time it takes to complete the function increases from 40 ms to over 800 ms:

```
matrix[j][i] = counter++;
```

In the first example when using `matrix[i][j]`, we will most of the time access memory that is already in the L1 cache, whereas in the modified version using `matrix[j][i]`, every access will generate an L1 cache miss. So, even if memory accesses are constant time operations, caching can have dramatic effects on the actual time it takes to access the memory.

STL containers

STL offers a set of extremely useful container types. A container is a data structure that contains a collection of elements. The container manages the memory of the elements it holds. This means that we don't have to explicitly create and delete our objects that we put in a container. We can pass objects created on the stack to a container and the container will copy and store them on the free store.

Iterators are used for accessing elements in containers, and are therefore a fundamental concept for understanding STL. The iterator concept is covered in `Chapter 5`, *A Deeper Look at Iterators*. For this chapter, it's enough to know that an iterator can be thought of as a pointer to an element and that the iterators have different operators defined depending on the container they belong to. For example, array-like data structures provide random access iterators to their elements. These iterators support arithmetic expressions using + and -, whereas an iterator to a linked list, for example, only supports ++ and -- operators.

The containers are divided into three categories: sequence containers, associative containers, and container adaptors. This section will contain a brief introduction to the containers in each of the three categories and also address the most important things to consider when performance is an issue.

Sequence containers

The sequence containers keep the elements in the order you specify when adding the elements to the container. The sequence containers are `std::array`, `std::vector`, `std::deque`, `std::basic_string`, `std::list`, and `std::forward_list`. Things you need to know before choosing a sequence container are as follows:

1. Number of elements (order of magnitude).
2. Usage patterns: How often are you going to add data? Read/traverse data? Delete data? Rearrange data?
3. Do you need to sort the elements?

When adding elements to a sequence container, you always specify where in the sequence the should be located. For example, when adding an element to a vector you can call `push_back`, which will add the new element last in the container.

Vector and array

`std::vector` is probably the most commonly used container type, and for good reason. A vector is an array that grows dynamically when needed. The elements added to a vector are guaranteed to be laid out contiguously in memory, which means that you can access any element in the array by its index in constant time. It also means that it provides excellent performance when traversing the elements in the order they are laid out, thanks to the spatial locality mentioned earlier.

The vector has a size and a capacity. The size is the number of elements that are currently held in the container, and the capacity is the number of elements that the vector can hold until it needs to allocate more space:

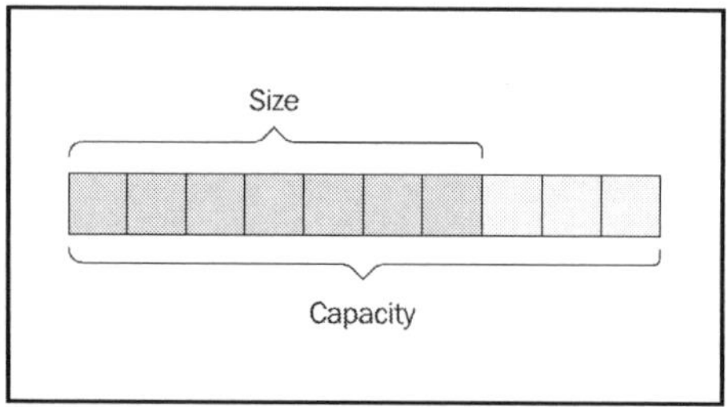

Adding elements to the end of the vector using the `push_back` function is fast, as long as the size is less than the capacity. When adding an element when there is no room for more, the vector will allocate a new internal buffer and then move all the elements to the new space. The capacity grows in a way that resizing the buffer happens seldom enough to make `push_back` an amortized constant time operation, as we discussed in `Chapter 3`, *Measuring Performance.*

A vector template instance of type `std::vector<Person>` will store `Person` objects by value. When the vector needs to rearrange the `Person` objects (for example, as a result of an insert), the values are copy constructed or moved. Objects are moved if they have a `nothrow` move constructor. Otherwise, the objects will be copy constructed in order to guarantee strong exception safety:

```
Person(Person&& other) { // Will be copied
    ...
}
Person(Person&& other) noexcept { // Will be moved
    ...
}
```

Internally, `std::vector` uses `std::move_if_noexcept` in order to determine whether the object should be copied or moved. The type support library can help you verify at compile time that your classes are guaranteed to not throw when being moved:

```
static_assert(std::is_nothrow_move_constructible<Person>::value, "")
```

If you are adding newly created objects to the vector, you can take advantage of the `emplace_back` function, which will create the object in place for you, instead of creating an object and then copy/moving it to the vector using the `push_back` function:

```
persons.emplace_back("John", 65);
```

The capacity of the vector can change in the following ways:

- By adding an element to the vector when the `capacity == size`
- By calling `reserve()`
- By calling `shrink_to_fit()`

Other than that, the vector will not change the capacity, and hence not allocate any new memory on the free store, which makes the vector usable even in real-time contexts.

As an alternative to the dynamically sized vector, STL also provides a fixed size version named `std::array` that manages its elements by using the stack as opposed to the free store. The size of the array is a template argument specified at compile time, which means that the size and type elements become a part of the concrete type:

```
auto a = std::array<int, 16>{};
auto b = std::array<int, 1024>{};
```

In this example, `a` and `b` are not the same type, which means that you have to specify the size when using the type as a function parameter:

```
auto f(const std::array<int, 1024>& input) {
  ...
}

f(a);  // Does not compile, f requires an int array of size 1024
```

This might seem a bit tedious at first, but this is in fact the big advantage over the built-in array type (`c` arrays) that lose the size information when passed to a function since it automatically converts to a pointer to the first element of the array:

```
// input looks like an array, but is in fact a pointer
auto f(const int input[]) {
  ...
}

int a[16];
int b[1024];
f(a); // Compiles, but unsafe
```

Deque

Sometimes you need to add elements to the end and the beginning of a sequence. If you are using a vector and need to speed up the inserts at the front, you can instead use `std::deque`, short for double-ended queue. `std::deque` is usually implemented as a collection of fixed-size arrays, which makes it possible to access elements by their index in constant time. However, as can be seen in the following image, all elements are not stored contiguously in memory, which is the case with vector and array:

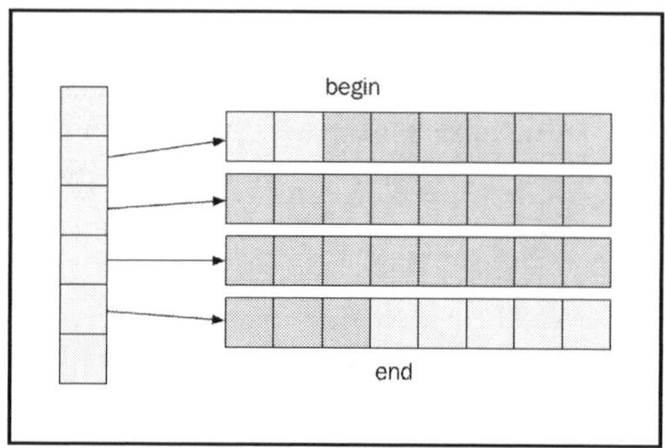

List and forward_list

The `std::list` is a doubly linked list, meaning that each element has one link to the next element and one link to its previous element. This makes it possible to iterate over the list both backwards and forwards. There is also a singly linked list named `std::forward_list`. The reason why you wouldn't always choose the doubly linked list over `std::forward_list` is because of the excessive memory occupied by the back pointers in the double linked list. So, if you don't need to traverse the list backwards, use `std::forward_list`. Another interesting feature of the forward list is that it's optimized for very short lists. When the list is empty, it only occupies one word, which makes it a good data structure for sparse data.

Note that even if the elements are ordered in a sequence, they are *not* laid out contiguously in memory as the vector and array are, which means that iterating a linked list will most likely generate a lot more cache misses compared to the vector.

The `std::list` is a doubly linked list with pointers to the next and previous elements:

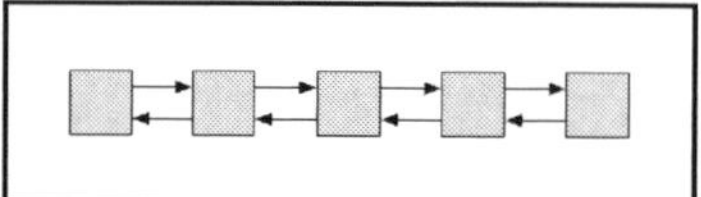

The `std::forward_list` is a single linked list with pointers to the next element:

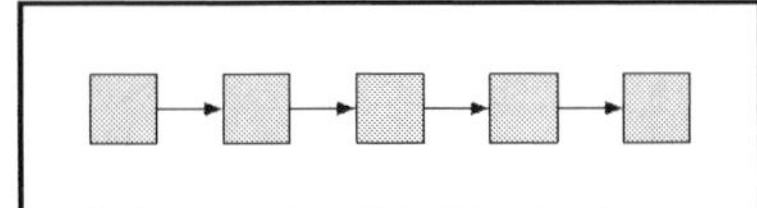

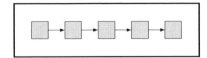

The `std::forward_list` is more memory efficient since it only has one pointer to the next element.

The basic_string

The last sequence container that we will cover is the `std::basic_string`. The `std::string` is a `typedef` for `std::basic_string<char>`. Historically, `std::basic_string` was not guaranteed to be laid out contiguously in memory. This has now changed since C++17, which makes it possible to pass the string to APIs that require an array of characters. For example, the following code reads an entire file into a string:

```
auto in = std::ifstream{"file.txt", std::ios::binary | std::ios::ate};
if (in.is_open()) {
  auto size = in.tellg();
  auto content = std::string(size, '\0');
  in.seekg(0);
  in.read(&content[0], size);
  // "content" now contains the entire file
}
```

Most implementations of `std::basic_string` utilize something called **small-size optimization**, which means that they do not allocate any dynamic memory if the size of the string is small. We will talk more about small-size optimization later in the book.

Associative containers

The associative containers place their elements based on the element itself. For example, it's not possible to add an element at the back or front in an associative container. Instead, the elements are added in a way that makes it possible to find the element without the need to scan the entire container. Therefore, the associative containers have some requirements for the objects we want to store in a container. We will look at these requirements later.

There are two main categories of associative containers:

- **Ordered associative containers**: These containers are based on trees. These containers use a tree for storing their elements. They require that the elements are ordered by the less than operator (<). The functions for adding, deleting, and finding elements are all *O(log n)* in the tree-based containers. The containers are named `std::set`, `std::map`, `std::multiset`, and `std::multimap`.
- **Unordered associative containers**: These containers are based on hash tables. These containers uses a hash table for storing their elements. They require that the elements are compared with the equality operator (==) and that there is a way to compute a hash value based on the element. More on that later. The functions for adding, deleting, and finding elements are all *O(1)* in the hash table-based containers. The containers are named `std::unordered_set`, `std::unordered_map`, `std::unordered_multiset`, and `std::unordered_multimap`.

Ordered sets and maps

The ordered associative containers guarantee that insert, delete, and search can be done in logarithmic time, *O(log n)*. How that is achieved is up to the implementation of the Standard Library. However, the implementations we know about use some kind of self-balancing binary search tree. The fact that the tree stays approximately balanced is necessary for controlling the height of the tree, and hence also the worst case running time of accessing the elements. There is no need for the tree to pre-allocate memory, so typically a tree will allocate memory on the free store each time an element is inserted and also free up memory whenever elements are erased. Check out the following diagram, which shows that the height of a balanced tree is *O(log n)*:

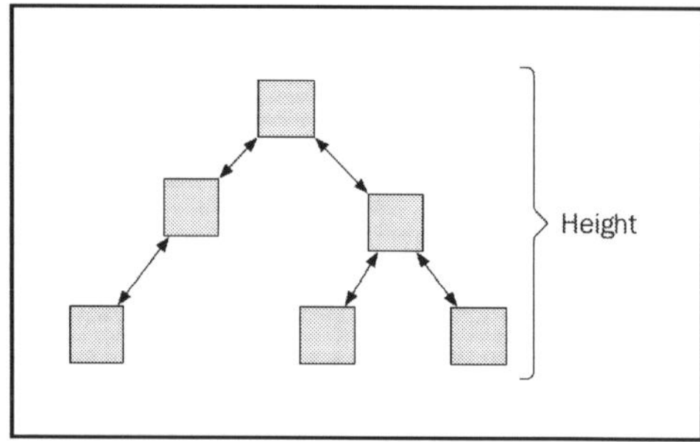

The height of the tree is O(log n) if it's balanced.

Unordered sets and maps

The unordered versions of sets and maps offer a hash-based alternative to the tree-based versions. This data structure is in general referred to as hash tables. In theory, hash tables offer constant-time insert, add, and delete operations, which are, of course, better than the tree-based versions that operate in *O(log n)*. However, in practice the difference might not be so obvious, especially if you are not storing a very large amount of elements in your container.

Let's see how a hash table can offer *O(1)* operations. A hash table keeps its elements in some sort of array. When adding an element to the hash table, an integer is computed for the element using a hash function. The integer is usually called the *hash* of the element. The hash value is then limited to the size of the array (by using the modulo operation, for example) so that the new limited value can be used as an index in the array. Once the index is computed, the hash table can store the element in the array at that index. The lookup of an element works in a similar manner by first computing a hash value for the element we are looking for and then accessing the array.

Apart from computing the hash value, this technique seems easy and straightforward. This is just half of the story, though. What if two different elements generate the same index, either because they produced the same hash value, or because two different hash values are being limited to the same index? When two non-equal elements end up at the same index, we call that a hash collision. This is not just an edge case, this will happen a lot even if we are using a good hash function, especially if the array is small compared to the number of elements we are adding. There are various ways of dealing with hash collisions. Here, we will focus on the one this is being used in the Standard Library, which is called separate chaining.

Separate chaining solves the problem of two unequal elements ending up at the same index. Instead of just storing the elements directly in the array, the array is a sequence of buckets. Each bucket can contain multiple elements, that is, all elements that are hashed to the same index. So, each bucket is also some sort of container. The exact data structure used for the buckets is not defined, but can vary for different implementations. However, we can think of it as a linked list and assume that finding an element in a specific bucket is slow since it needs to scan the elements in the buckets linearly.

The following image shows a hash table with eight buckets. The elements have landed in three separate buckets. The bucket with index **2** contains four elements, the bucket with index **4** contains two elements, and the bucket with index **5** contains only one element. The other buckets are empty:

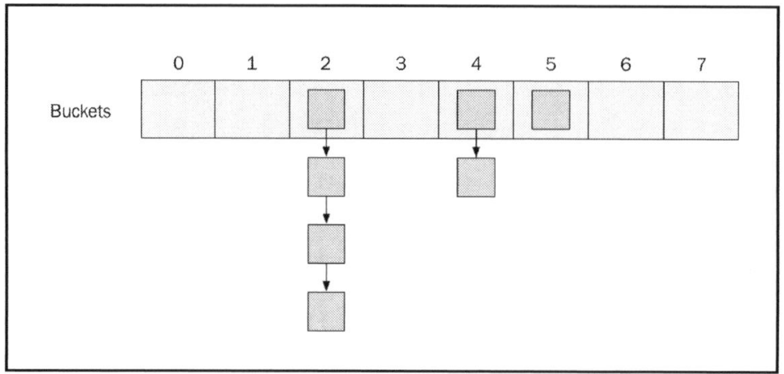

Each bucket contains 0 or more elements.

Hash and equals

The hash value, which can be computed in constant time with respect to the size of the container, determines in which bucket an element will be placed. Since it's possible that more than one object will generate the same hash value and therefore end up in the same bucket, each key also needs to provide an equals function, which is used to compare the key we are looking for with all the keys in the bucket.

If two keys are equal, they are required to generate the same hash value. However, it's perfectly legal for two objects to return the same hash value while not being equal to each other.

A good hash function is quick to compute and will also distribute the keys evenly among the buckets in order to minimize the number of elements in each bucket.

The following is an example of a *very bad* but perfectly valid hash function:

```
auto my_hash = [](const Person& person) {
  return 47; // Bad, don't do this!
};
```

It is valid because it will return the same hash value for two objects that are equal. The hash function is also very quick. However, since all elements will produce the same hash value, all keys will end up in the same bucket, which means finding an element is *O(n)* instead of *O(1)*, which we aimed at.

A good hash function, on the other hand, ensures that the elements are distributed evenly among the buckets to minimize hash collisions. STL already provides us with good hash functions for basic types. In many cases, we can reuse these functions when writing our own hash functions for user-defined types.

Suppose we want to use a `Person` class as a key in an `unorordered_set`. The `Person` class has two data members: `age`, which is an `int`, and `name`, which is a `std::string`. We start by writing the equal predicate:

```
auto person_eq = [](const Person& lhs, const Person& rhs) {
  return lhs.name() == rhs.name() && lhs.age() == rhs.age();
};
```

For two `Person` objects to be equal, they need to have the same name and the same age. We can now define the hash predicate by combining the hash values of all the data members that are included in the equals predicate. Unfortunately, there is no function in the C++ standard yet to combine hash values, but there is a good one available in Boost, which we use here:

```
auto person_hash = [](const Person& person) {
  auto seed = size_t{0};
  boost::hash_combine(seed, person.name());
  boost::hash_combine(seed, person.age());
  return seed;
};
```

If for some reason you cannot use Boost, the `boost::hash_combine` is really just a one-liner that can be copied from the documentation found at `http://www.boost.org/doc/libs/1_55_0/doc/html/hash/reference.html#boost.hash_combine`.

With the equality and hash predicates defined, we can finally create our `unordered_set`:

```
using Set = std::unordered_set<Person, decltype(person_hash),
decltype(person_eq)>;
auto persons = Set{100, person_hash, person_eq};
```

A good rule of thumb is to always use all data members that are being used in the equal function when producing the hash value. In that way, we adhere to the contract between equals and hash, and at the same time, this enables us to provide an effective hash value. For example, it would be correct but inefficient to only use the name when computing the hash value, since that would mean that all `Person` objects with the same name would end up in the same bucket. Even worse, though, would be to include data members in the hash function that are not being used in the equals function. This would most likely result in a disaster where you cannot find objects in your `unordered_set` that in fact compare equal.

Hash policy

Apart from creating hash values that distribute the keys evenly among the buckets, one can reduce the number of collisions by having many buckets. The average number of elements per bucket is called the `load_factor`. In the preceding example, we created an `unordered_set` with 100 buckets. If we add 50 persons to the set, the `load_factor` would be 0.5. The `max_load_factor` is an upper limit of the load factor, and when that value is reached, the set will need to increase the number of buckets, and as a consequence also rehash all the elements that are currently in the set. It's also possible to trigger a rehash manually with the `rehash` and `reserve` member functions.

Container adaptors

The last category of STL containers is *container adaptors*. There are three container adaptors in STL: `stack`, `queue`, and `priority_queue`. Container adaptors are quite different from the sequence containers and the associative containers since they represent *abstract data structures* that can be implemented by the underlying sequence container. For example, the stack, which is a **last in, first out** (**LIFO**) data structure supporting push and pop on the top of the stack, can be implemented by using a `vector`, `list`, `deque`, or any other custom sequence container that supports `back()`, `push_back()`, and `pop_back()`. The same goes for `queue`, which is a **first in, first out** (**FIFO**) data structure, and `priortiy_queue`.

In this section, we will focus on the `priority_queue`, which is a pretty useful data structure that is easy to forget.

Priority queues

A priority queue offers constant time lookup of the element with the highest priority. The priority is defined using the less than operator of the elements. Insert and delete both run in logarithmic time. A priority queue is a partially ordered data structure, and it might not be obvious when to use it instead of a completely sorted data structure, for example, a tree or a sorted vector. But in some cases, a priority queue can offer you the functionality you need, and for a lower cost than a completely sorted container.

The Standard Library already provides a partial sort algorithm, so we don't need to write our own. But let's see how we can implement a partial sort algorithm using a priority queue. Suppose we are writing a program for searching documents given a query. The matching document (search hits) should be ordered by a rank, and we are only interested in finding the first 10 search hits with the highest rank.

Each document is represented by a class:

```
class Document {
public:
  Document(const std::string& title)
  : title_{title}
  {}
private:
  std::string title_;
  ...
};
```

When searching, an algorithm is selecting the documents that match the query and computes a rank of the search hits. Each matching document is represented by a `Hit`:

```
struct Hit {
  float rank_{};
  std::shared_ptr<Document> document_;
};
```

Finally, we need to sort the hits and return the top *m* documents. What are the options for sorting the hits? If the hits are contained in a container that provides random access iterators, we could use `std::sort` and only return the *m* first elements. Or, if the total number of hits is much larger than the *m* documents we are to return, we could use `std::partial_sort`, which would be more efficient than `std::sort`. `std::partial_sort`, and also requires random access iterators.

But what if we don't have random access iterators? Maybe the matching algorithm only provides forward iterators to the hits. We could then use a priority queue and still come up with an efficient solution. Our sort interface would look like this:

```
template<typename It>
auto sort_hits(It begin, It end, size_t m) -> std::vector<Hit> {
```

We could call this function with any iterator that has the increment operator defined. Next, we create a `std::priority_queue` backed by a `std::vector` using a custom compare function for keeping the *lowest* ranking hits at the top of the queue:

```
  auto cmp = [](const Hit& a, const Hit& b) {
    return a.rank_ > b.rank_; // Note, we are using greater than
  };
  auto queue = std::priority_queue<
    Hit, std::vector<Hit>, decltype(cmp)>{cmp};
```

We will only insert at most *m* elements in the priority queue. The priority queue will contain the highest ranking hits seen so far. Among the elements that are currently in the priority queue, the hit with the lowest rank will be the topmost element:

```
  for (auto it = begin; it != end; ++it) {
    if (queue.size() < m) {
      queue.push(*it);
    }
    else if (it->rank_ > queue.top().rank_) {
      queue.pop();
      queue.push(*it);
    }
  }
```

Now, we have collected the highest ranking hits in the priority queue, so the only thing left is to put them in a vector in reverse order and return the *m* sorted hits:

```
  auto result = std::vector<Hit>{};
  while (!queue.empty()) {
    result.push_back(queue.top());
    queue.pop();
  }
  std::reverse(result.begin(), result.end());
  return result;
} // end of sort_hits
```

What is the complexity of this algorithm? If we denote the number of hits with *n* and the number of returned hits with *m*, we can see that the memory consumption is *O(m)*, whereas the time complexity is *O(n * log m)* since we are iterating over *n* elements, and in each iteration we might have to do a push and/or pop, which both run in *O(log m)* time.

Parallel arrays

We are finishing this chapter by talking about iterating over elements and looking at some ways to improve the performance when iterating over array-like data structures. We already mentioned two important factors for performance when accessing data: spatial locality and temporal locality. When iterating over elements stored in contiguous memory, we will see that by keeping our objects small, we will increase the probability that the data we need is already cached thanks to spatial locality. Obviously, this will have a great impact on the performance.

Recall the cache thrashing example shown in the beginning of this chapter where we iterated over a matrix. It demonstrated that we sometimes need to think about in what way we access data, even if we have a fairly compact representation of the data. Next, we will compare how long it takes to iterate over objects of different sizes. We start out by defining two structs, `SmallObject` and `BigObject`:

```
struct SmallObject {
  SmallObject() : score_{std::rand()} {}
  std::array<char, 4> data_{};
  int score_{};
};

struct BigObject {
 BigObject() : score_{std::rand()} {}
 std::array<char, 256> data_{};
 int score_{};
};
```

`SmallObject` and `BigObject` are identical except, for the size of the initial data array. Both structs contain an `int` named score, which we initialize to some random value just for testing purposes. We can let the compiler tell us the size of the objects by using the `sizeof` operator:

```
std::cout << sizeof(SmallObject); // Possible output is 8
std::cout << sizeof(BigObject);   // Possible output is 260
```

We need plenty of objects in order to evaluate the performance. Create one million objects of each kind:

```
auto small_objects = std::vector<SmallObject>(1'000'000);
auto big_objects = std::vector<BigObject>(1'000'000);
```

Now for the iteration. Let's say we want to sum the scores of all the objects. We could preferably use `std::accumulate()`, which we will cover later in the book, but for now a simple `for`-loop will do. We write this function as a template so that we don't have to manually write one version for each type of object. The function iterates over the objects and sums all the scores:

```
template <class T>
auto sum_scores(const std::vector<T>& objects) {
  ScopedTimer t{"sum_scores"};

  auto sum = 0;
  for (const auto& obj : objects) {
    sum += obj.score_;
  }
  return sum;
}
```

Now, we are ready to see how long it takes to sum the scores in the small objects compared to the big objects:

```
auto sum = 0;
sum += sum_scores(small_objects);
sum += sum_scores(big_objects);
```

To achieve reliable results, we need to repeat the test a couple of times. On my computer, it takes about 1 ms to compute the sum of the small objects and 10 ms to compute the sum of the big objects. This example is similar to the cache thrashing example we looked at the beginning of the chapter, and one reason for the big difference is again because of the way the computer uses the cache hierarchy to fetch data from the main memory.

How can we utilize the fact that it's faster to iterate over collections of smaller objects than bigger objects when working with more realistic scenarios than the preceding example?

Obviously, we can do our best to keep the size of our classes small, but it's often easier said than done. Also, if you are working with an old code base that has been growing for some time, the chances are high that you will stumble across some really large classes with too many data members and too many responsibilities. We will now look at a class that represents a user in an online game system and see how we can split it into smaller parts. The class has the following data members:

```
struct User {
  std::string name_;
  std::string username_;
  std::string password_;
  std::string security_question_;
  std::string security_answer_;
  short level_{};
  bool is_playing_{};
};
```

A user has a name that is frequently used, and a password and some username information for authentication that are rarely used. The class also keeps track of which level the player is currently playing at. Finally, the `User` struct also knows whether the user is currently playing by storing the `is_playing` boolean.

The `sizeof` operator reports that the user class is 128 bytes when compiling for a 64-bit architecture. An approximate layout of the data members can be seen in the following figure:

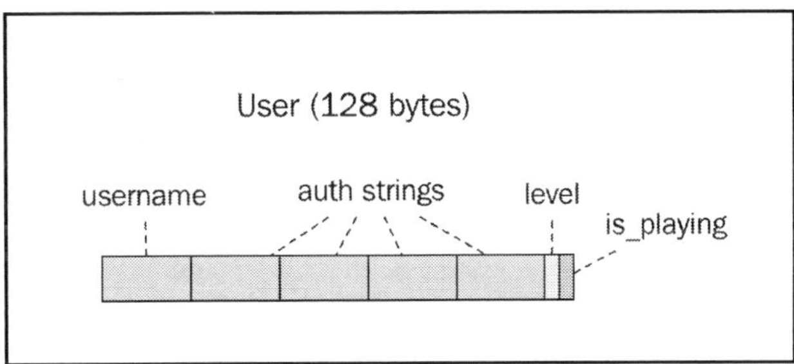

All users are kept in a `std::vector`, and there are two global functions that are being called very often and need to run fast: `num_users_at_level()` and `num_playing_users()`. Both functions iterate over all users, and therefore we need to make iterations over the user vector fast. The first function returns the number of users that have reached a certain level:

```
auto num_users_at_level(short level, const std::vector<User>& users) {
  ScopedTimer t{"num_users_at_level (using 128 bytes User)"};

  auto num_users = 0;
  for (const auto& user : users)
    if (user.level_ == level)
      ++num_users;

  return num_users;
}
```

The second function computes how many users are currently playing:

```
auto num_playing_users(const std::vector<User>& users) {
  ScopedTimer t{"num_playing_users (using 128 bytes User)"};
  return std::count_if(
    users.begin(),
    users.end(),
    [](const auto& user) {
      return user.is_playing_;
    });
}
```

Here, we use the STL algorithm `std::count_if()` instead of a handwritten loop, as we did in `num_users_at_level()`. `std::count_if()` will call the predicate we provide for each user in the users vector and return the number of times the predicate returns true. This is basically what we are doing in the first function as well, so we could also have used `std::count_if()` in the first case. Both functions run in linear time.

Calling the two functions with a vector of one million users results in the following output:

```
11 ms num_users_at_level (using 128 bytes User)
10 ms num_playing_users (using 128 bytes User)
```

Our hypothesis is that by making the user class smaller, it would be faster to iterate over the vector. As mentioned before, the password and security data fields are rarely used and could be grouped in a separate struct. That would give us the following classes:

```
struct AuthInfo {
  std::string username_;
```

```
  std::string password_;
  std::string security_question_;
  std::string security_answer_;
};

struct User {
  std::string name_;
  std::unique_ptr<AuthInfo> auth_info_;
  short level_{};
  bool is_playing_{};
};
```

This change decreases the size of the `User` class from 128 bytes to 40 bytes. Instead of storing four strings in the user class, we use a pointer to refer to the new `AuthInfo` object. The following figure shows how we have split up the `User` class into two smaller classes:

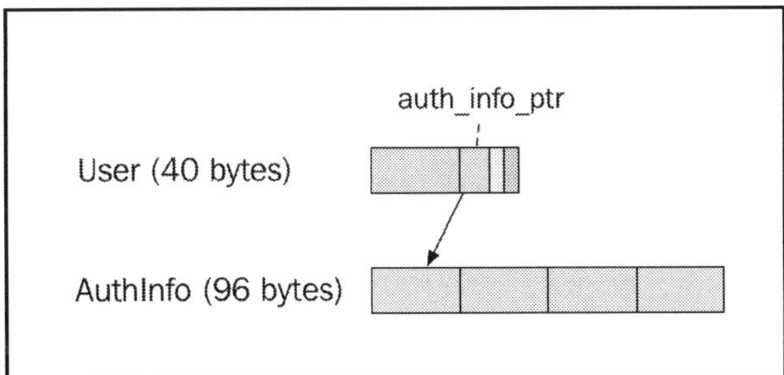

This change makes sense from a design perspective too. Keeping the authentication data in a separate class increases the cohesion of the user class. The `User` class contains a pointer to the authentication information. The total amount of memory that the user data occupies has not decreased, of course, but the important thing right now is to shrink the `User` class in order to speed up the functions that iterate over all users.

From an optimization point of view, we have to measure again to verify that our hypothesis regarding smaller data is valid. It turns out that both functions run more than twice as fast with the smaller `User` class. The output when running the modified version is:

```
4 ms num_users_at_level with User
3 ms num_playing_users with User
```

Next, we are going to try a more aggressive way of shrinking the amount of data we need to iterate through by using parallel arrays. First, a warning: This is an optimization that, in many cases, has too many drawbacks to be a viable alternative. So don't take this as a general technique and apply it without thinking twice. We will come back to the pros and cons of parallel arrays after we have seen a few examples.

By using parallel arrays, we simply split the large structures into smaller types, similar to what we did with the authentication information for our user class. But instead of using pointers to relate objects, we store the smaller structures in separate arrays of equal size. The smaller objects in the different arrays that share the same index form the complete original object.

An example will clarify the technique. The user class we have worked with consists of 40 bytes. It now only contains a username string, a pointer to the authentication information, an integer for the current level, and the `is_playing` boolean. By making the user objects smaller, we saw the performance was improved when iterating over the objects. The memory layout of an array of user objects would look something like the one shown in the following figure. We will ignore memory alignment and padding for now, but will get back to that later:

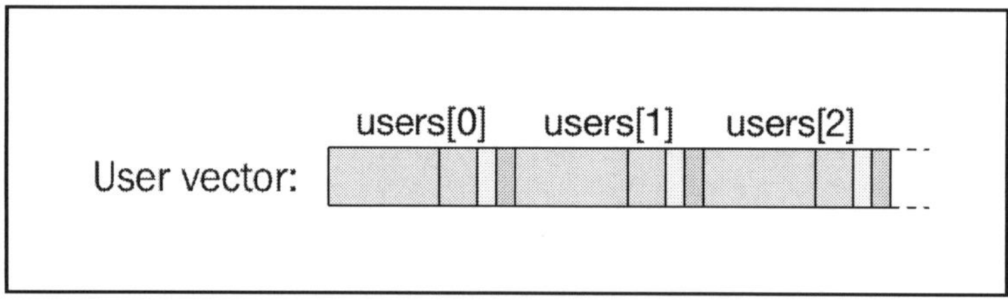

User objects stored contiguously in a vector

Instead of having one vector with user objects, we can store all the integer levels and `is_playing` flags in separate vectors. The current level for the user at index 0 in the user array is also stored at index 0 in the level array. In that way, we can avoid having pointers to the levels, and instead just use the index for connecting the data fields. We could do the same thing with the `boolean is_playing` field and end up with three parallel arrays instead of just one. The memory layout of the three vectors would look something like this:

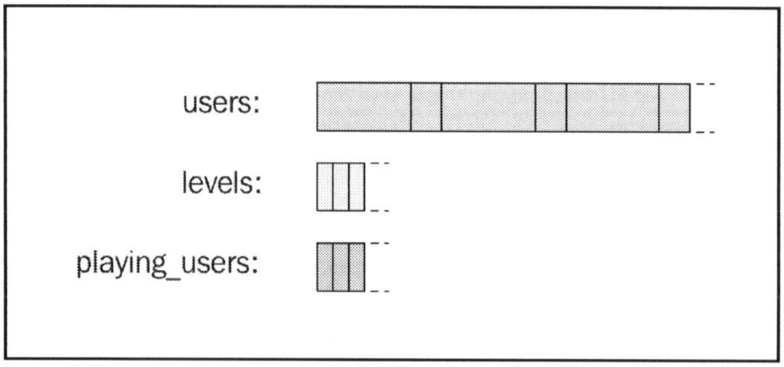

users:

levels:

playing_users:

We are using three parallel arrays to make iteration over one particular field fast.

The `num_users_at_level()` function can now compute the number of users at a specific level by only using the level array. The implementation is now simply a wrapper around `std::count()`:

```
auto num_users_at_level(int level, const std::vector<int>& users) {
  ScopedTimer t{"num_users_at_level using int vector"};
  return std::count(users.begin(), users.end(), level);
}
```

Likewise, the `num_playing_users()` function only needs to iterate over the vector of booleans to determine the number of playing users. Again, we use `std::count()`:

```
auto num_playing_users(const std::vector<bool>& users) {
  ScopedTimer t{"num_playing_users using vector<bool>"};
  return std::count(users.begin(), users.end(), true);
}
```

With the parallel arrays, we don't have to use the user array at all. The amount of memory that is occupied by the extracted arrays is substantially smaller than the user array, so let's see if we have gained any performance when running the functions on one million users again:

```
auto users = std::vector<User>{1000000};
auto levels = std::vector<int>{1000000};
auto playing_users = std::vector<bool>{1000000};

// Initialize data
...

auto num_users_at_level_5 = num_users_at_level(levels, 5);
auto num_playing_users = num_playing_users(playing_users);
```

Counting the number of users at a certain level only takes about 0.7 ms when using the array of integers. To recap, the initial version using the `User` class with a size of 128 bytes took around 11 ms. The smaller `User` class executed in 4 ms, and now, by only using the `user_level` array, we are down to 0.7 ms. Quite a dramatic change.

For the second function, `num_playing_users()`, the change is even bigger - it only takes around 0.03 ms to count how many users are currently playing. The reason why it can be so fast is thanks to a data structure called bit arrays. It turns out that `std::vector<bool>` is not at all a standard vector of C++ `bool` objects. Instead, internally, it's a bit array. Operations such as count and find can be optimized very efficiently in a bit array since it can process 64 bits at a time (on a 64-bit machine). The future of `std::vector<bool>` is unclear, and it might be deprecated soon in favor of the fixed size `std::bitset` and a new dynamically sized bitset. There is already a version in Boost named `boost::dynamic_bitset`.

This is all fantastic, but we warned you about some drawbacks. First of all, extracting the fields from the classes where they actually belong will have a big impact on the structure of the code. In some cases, it makes perfect sense to split large classes into smaller parts, but in other cases it totally breaks encapsulation and exposes data that could have been hidden behind interfaces with higher abstraction.

It's also cumbersome to ensure that the arrays are in sync, such that we always need to ensure that fields that comprise one object are stored at the same index in all arrays. Implicit relationships like this can be hard to maintain and are error prone.

The last drawback is actually related to performance. In the preceding example, we saw that for algorithms that iterate over one field at a time, there was a big performance gain. However, if we have an algorithm that would need to access multiple fields that have been extracted to different arrays, it would be substantially slower than iterating over one array with bigger objects.

So, as is always the case when working with performance, there is nothing that comes without a cost, and the cost for exposing data and split one simple array into multiple arrays may or may not be too high. It all depends on the scenario you are facing and what performance gain you encounter after measuring. Don't consider parallel arrays before you actually face a real performance issue. Always opt for sound design principles at first and prefer explicit ways of expressing relationships between objects rather than implicit ones.

Summary

In this chapter, we have introduced the container types from STL. We have seen that the way we structure data has a big impact on how efficiently we can perform certain operations on a collection of objects. The asymptotic complexity specifications of STL containers are key factors to consider when choosing among the different data structures.

In addition, we have seen how the cache hierarchy in modern processors impacts the way we need to organize data for efficient access to memory. The importance of utilizing the cache levels efficiently cannot be stressed enough. This is one of the reasons why the containers that keep their elements contiguously in memory have become the most used containers, such as `std::vector` and `std::string`.

5
A Deeper Look at Iterators

In this chapter, you will learn about the C++ iterator concept and how versatile it can be, even though its syntax mimics a plain old C-pointer. By looking at some examples, you will also learn how to create a custom iterator that iterates a linear range.

The iterator concept

Before going further into STL algorithms, we are going to take a deeper look at iterators in C++, as they form the basis of STL algorithms. Note that the iterator concept is not at all a C++ exclusive concept, rather it exists in most programming languages. What differentiates the C++ implementation of the iterator concept from other programming languages is that C++ mimics the syntax of raw memory pointers.

A simplified basic iterator is an object which represent a position in a sequence and therefore basically incorporate the following functionality:

- Are we out of the sequence? (denoted as `is_end() -> bool`)
- Retrieve the value at the current position (denoted `read() -> T`)
- Step to the next position (denoted `step_fwd() -> void`)

Note that the named functions `is_end()`, `read()` and so on, does not exist in C++, they are only here for readability. In practice they are implemented in terms of C-pointer semantics, which will be discussed further below.

The functions listed above are sufficient for reading all elements in any standard C++ container, but many algorithms requires iterators to be able to step backwards, as well as write a value to a specific position. In other words, the following three functions are also sometimes needed:

- Write to the current position (denoted `write(T val) -> void`)
- Step to the previous position(denoted `step_bwd() -> void`)
- Step an auxiliary number of elements (denoted `step(int n) -> void`)

In addition to algorithmic requirements, iterators might operate data sources where a write or read implies a step forward. Examples of such data sources could be user input, a network connection or a file. These data sources requires the following functions:

- Write and step forward (denoted `write_step_fwd(T val) -> void`)
- Read and step forward (denoted `read_step_fwd(T val) -> void`)

The function `step(int n)` might seems superfluous as it can be implemented as a number of `step_fwd()` or `step_bwd()`. However, algorithms such as binary search, requires iterators which can step several positions in constant time to perform effectively. Therefore STL differentiates between iterators which can be stepped several position in constant time. Binary search algorithms are explained in `Chapter 3`, *Measuring Performance*.

Iterator categories

If we think about a few basic algorithms, it becomes obvious that the requirements on the iterators vary between different algorithms:

- If an algorithm count the number of occurrences of a value, it requires `is_end()`, `read()` and `step_fwd()`
- If an algorithm fill a container with a value, it requires `is_end()`, `write()`, `step_fwd()`
- A binary search algorithm on a sorted range requires `step()` and `read()`
- An algorithm which rearrange the elements requires `read()`, `write()`, `step_fwd()` and `step_bwd()`

These requirements are categorized into four basic iterator categories in STL:

- `forward_iterator`: The iterator can step forward
- `bidirectional_iterator`: The iterator can step forward and backward
- `random_access_iterator`: The iterator can be stepped any number of steps in constant time
- `contiguous_iterator`: Special case where the underlying data is a contiguous block of memory, such as `std::string`, `std::vector`, `std::array`, and the (rarely used) `std::valarray`.

Additionally, iterators compliant with the functions we denoted `read_step_fwd()` and `write_step_fwd()` also have named categories:

- `input_iterator`: The iterator supports `read_step_fwd() -> T`
- `output_iterator`: The iterator supports `write_step_fwd(T) -> void`

Pointer-mimicking syntax

Now that we covered the basics of iterators, let's see how C++ implements it syntactically. As mentioned above, the syntax of C++ iterators are implemented in terms of standard C pointer notation. This means that any algorithm built upon iterators will also work with regular C pointers.

The step functions are implemented using pointer arithmetic. The following table shows which operator is overloaded for each step function, and how to invoke the function on an imagined iterator object called `it`:

Denoted function	**Overloaded operator**	**Usage example**
`step_fwd() -> void;`	`operator++()`	`++it;`
`step_bwd() -> void;`	`operator--()`	`--it;`
`step(int n) -> void;`	`operator+=(int n)`	`it += 5;`

The `read()` and `write()` functions are implemented by `operator*`, just like dereferencing a pointer. The following table shows how they are used:

Denoted function	**Usage example**
`read() -> T;`	`auto value = *it;`
`write(T val) -> void;`	`*it = T{};`

The `is_end() -> bool` function is implemented by comparing with a value which indicates the iterator is pointing out of the range bounds. The following table shows how we would implement `is_end()` in regular C-array pointer arithmetic iterating a standard C-array and a linked list:

<table>
<tr><th>C-style array</th><th>C-style linked list</th></tr>
<tr><td><pre>// Construct an array
int array[3] = {22, 44, 66};
// Iterate
int* begin = &array[0];
int* end = &array[3];
for(
  int* ptr = begin;
  ptr != end;
  ++ptr
) {
}</pre></td><td><pre>// Construct a simple Linked List
struct Element { Element* next_;};
Element a, b, c;
a.next_ = &b;
b.next_ = &c;
c.next_ = nullptr;
// Iterate
Element* begin = &a;
Element* end = nullptr;
for(
  auto ptr = begin;
  ptr != nullptr;
  ptr = ptr->next_
) {
}</pre></td></tr>
</table>

When implementing an iterator in C++, whatever the iterator iterates, the same methodology has to be used. The equivalent of implementing the function denoted `is_end()` is to compare the iterator to a value which indicates the end of the sequence.

The functions utilized by input/output iterators, `read_step_fwd()` and `write_step_fwd()` are only possible to express with two succeeding expressions. The first expression has the post-condition that the second expression must be valid.

Denoted function:	**Usage example:**
`read_step_fwd() -> T;`	`auto val = *it; ++it;`
`write_step_fwd(T val) -> void;`	`*it = val; ++it;`

When implementing an advanced iterator, it's advantageous to use the Boost library *iterator facade*, in which you can implement the functionality in named functions, similar to the example functions above. The iterator facade then handles the conversion to operators. More information is available at `http://www.boost.org`.

Iterators as generators

Looking deeper into the iterator concept, one can see that it does not actually need to point to actual data; we could simply generate values on the fly. Here is a simple implementation of a forward iterator that generates integers on the fly. It only fulfills two iterator categories; `forward_iterator` and `input_iterator`:

```
class IntIterator {
public:
  IntIterator(int v) : v_{v} {}
  auto operator==(const IntIterator& it)const{ return v_ == it.v_; }
  auto operator!=(const IntIterator& it)const{ return !(*this==it); }
  auto& operator*() const { return v_; }
  auto& operator++() { ++v_; return *this; }
private:
  int v_{};
};
```

The `IntIterator` can then be used to iterate an increasing range of integers just like if it was a container of values:

```
auto first = IntIterator{12}; // Start at 12
auto last = IntIterator{16};  // Stop when equal to 16
for(auto it = first; it != last; ++it) {
  std::cout << (*it) << " ";
}
// Prints 12 13 14 15
```

Iterator traits

As mentioned, STL differentiates iterators by which categories they fulfill. This is achieved by defining the following five specific types in the iterator class:

- `iterator_category`, the category the iterator fulfills
- `difference_type`, the type used to store the distance between two iterators
- `value_type`, the value the iterator returns when dereferenced
- `reference`, the type used for referencing the `value_type`
- `pointer`, the type of pointer used for pointing to the `value_type`

For the `IntIterator`, the following types would be defined:

```
class IntIterator {
public:
  ...
  using difference_type = int;
  using value_type = int;
  using reference = int&;
  using pointer = int*;
  using iterator_category = std::forward_iterator_tag;
  ...
}
```

It might seem superfluous to define both reference and pointer, but for many iterators these types are either not applicable (they are then defined as `void`), or they use other mechanism to point to, or reference, the `value_type`. Examples of such iterators will be discussed later in this chapter.

Now we can use `IntIterators` to create a vector of numbers from 5 to 12 by copying from `IntIterator` to `std::vector`. Note how we use the `copy` function even though the copied values are generated on the fly:

```
auto numbers = std::vector<int>{};
std::copy(IntIterator(5), IntIterator(12), std::back_inserter(numbers));
// numbers is {5, 6, 7, 8, 9, 10, 11}
```

Note that this example uses the C++17 way of defining iterator traits for a custom iterator. Prior to C++17, defining iterator traits was more complex, as it required overloading the `std::iterator_traits` class or inheriting `std::iterator` (which is now deprecated).

Implementing a function using iterator categories

In order to read properties of an iterator, the STL class `std::iterator_traits` shall be utilized, not the raw iterator type.
Correct: `using Category = std::iterator_traits<Iterator>::iterator_category`
Incorrect: `using Category = Iterator::iterator_category;`

Let's say we want to implement a template function called `iterator_distance()`, equivalent of `std::distance()`, which returns the number of steps between two iterators:

- If the iterator category is random access we simply subtract the difference between the iterator `a` and `b`.
- Otherwise, we have to calculate the number of steps from iterator `a` to iterator `b`.

Using `iterator_category` tag and `difference_type`, the distance function is implemented as follows:

```
template <typename Iterator>
auto iterator_distance(Iterator a, Iterator b) {
  using Traits = typename std::iterator_traits<Iterator>;
  using Category = typename Traits::iterator_category;
  using Difference = typename Traits::difference_type;
  constexpr auto is_random_access =
    std::is_same_v<Category, std::random_access_iterator_tag>;
  if constexpr(is_random_access) {
    return b - a;
  }
  else {
    auto steps = Difference{};
    while(a != b) { ++steps; ++a; }
    return steps;
  }
}
```

The `iterator_distance()` function can now be used with any compliant iterator, as well as regular C-pointers and chooses a correct implementation depending on the iterator category.

Extending the IntIterator to bidirectional

In order to make it possible to iterate a range of numbers in reverse, we add the `operator--()` method to `IntIterator` and upgrade `iterator_category` to `std::bidirectional_iterator_tag`:

```
class IntIterator {
  ...
  using iterator_category = std::bidirectional_iterator_tag;
  ...
  auto& operator--() { --value_; return *this; }
  ...
};
```

This is an example of iterating in reverse order:

```
for(auto it = IntIterator{12}; it != IntIterator{-1}; --it) {
  std::cout << *it << " ";
}
// Prints: 12 11 10 9 8 7 6 5 4 3 2 1 0
```

Practical example – iterating floating point values within a range

Let's address a fundamental problem with floating point values; they are very often not exact representations of the values assigned to them, rather they often represent something very near the assigned value.

For example, often when I would like to iterate from `0.0` to `1.0` with a step length of `0.1`, I conveniently start with something like this:

```
for(float t = 0.0f; t <= 1.0f; t += 0.1f) {
  std::cout << t << ", ";
}
// Prints 0.0, 0.1, 0.2, 0.3, 0.4, 0.5, 0.6, 0.7, 0.8, 0.9,
```

The subtle problem here is that `0.1` cannot be represented by a floating point value; instead, it is represented by something slightly larger than `0.1`, and therefore the loop will not reach `1.0f`.

To solve this, we can represent this range of floating points as a start value, a stop value, and a number of steps instead. Basically, we are required to do something like this:

```
for(size_t i = 0; i <= 10; ++i) {
  float t = float(i) / 10.0f;
  std::cout << t << ", ";
}
// Prints 0.0, 0.1, 0.2, 0.3, 0.4, 0.5, 0.6, 0.7, 0.8, 0.9, 1.0,
```

As this code is quite obscure for such a simple case, we'd like to wrap it in a range so that we can simply type this:

```
for(auto t: make_linear_range(0.0f, 1.0f, 11)) {
  std::cout << t << ", ";
}
// Prints 0.0, 0.1, 0.2, 0.3, 0.4, 0.5, 0.6, 0.7, 0.8, 0.9, 1.0,
```

We use the number of values when iterating, not the number of steps, so the last parameter is `11`.

Illustrated usage examples

Iterating from `0.0` to `1.0` at a step length of `0.1` will result in ten steps, and eleven values evaluated:

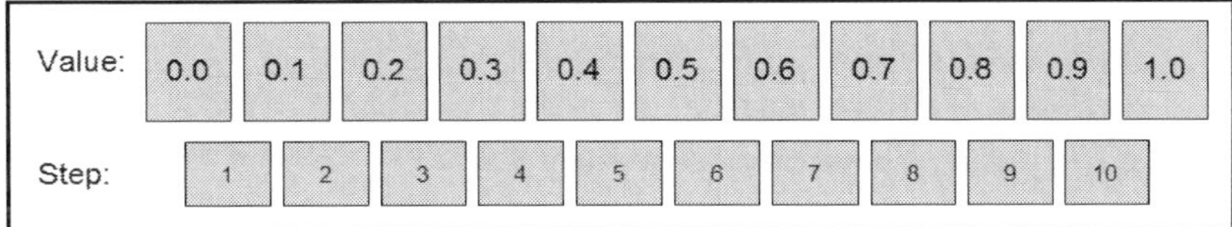

Values when iterating from 0.0 to 1.0 with eleven values

Iterating from `0.0` to `1.0` at a step length of 0.33 will result in three steps and four values:

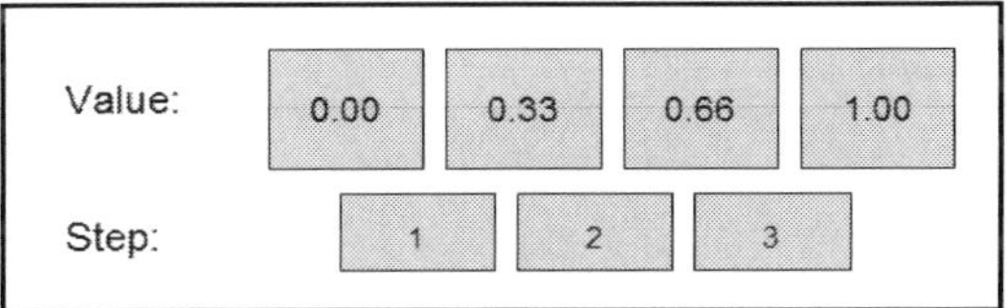

Values when iterating from 0.0 to 1.0 with four values

Utility functions

The iterators we are about to create will be built upon two utility functions: one for calculating the step size, and one for retrieving the value of a specific step index using the start value and the step index. For simplicity, we prevented a range from having fewer than two values.

To calculate the step size, we will need the start, stop value, and the number of values parameters:

```
template <typename T>
auto get_step_size(T start, T stop, size_t n) {
  assert(n >= 2);
  return (stop-start) / (n-1);
}
```

To calculate a linear value at a specific index, we will need the start, step size, and value index parameters:

```
template <typename T>
auto get_linear_value(T start, T step_size, size_t idx) {
  return start + step_size * idx;
}
```

Using these utility functions, we can iterate a range of floating point numbers by referring to their index in a range, rather than the actual number, as shown below:

```
auto start = 0.0f;
auto stop = 1.0f;
auto num_values = size_t{11};
auto step_size = get_step_size(start, stop, num_values);
for(size_t i = 0; i < num_values; ++i) {
  auto t = get_linear_value(start, step_size, i);
  std::cout << t << ", ";
}
// Prints 0.0, 0.1, 0.2, 0.3, 0.4, 0.5, 0.6, 0.7, 0.8, 0.9, 1.0,
```

Using the index is advantageous as it relieves us from making mistakes related to floating point inaccuracy.

How to construct a linear range iterator

Now, let's generalize this functionality into something usable with `for`-loops by wrapping it into iterators and a range. This way, we can utilize it as a first class citizen of C++ in both STL algorithms and range-based `for`-loop. The following table demonstrate this property:

<table>
<tr><th>Linear Range and an STL algorithm</th><th>Linear Range and a range based for-loop</th></tr>
<tr><td><pre>auto r =LinearRange<float>{0,1,4};
auto vec =std::vector<float>{};
std::copy(
  r.begin(),
  r.end(),
  std::back_inserter(vec)
);
// vec is {0.0, 0.33, 0.66, 1.0}</pre></td><td><pre>auto r =LinearRange<float>{0,1,4};
auto vec =std::vector<float>{};
for(auto t: r) {
  vec.push_back(t);
}
// vec is {0.0, 0.33, 0.66, 1.0}</pre></td></tr>
</table>

First, we need an iterator that is aware of the start value, the step length, and the current step it is currently at. As the iterator merely represents a position in the linear range, we do not need to store the stop value. Note how similar the `LinearRangeIterator` is to the `IntIterator`. The main difference is that it returns a calculated value instead of just a value when `operator*` is invoked:

```
template <typename T>
class LinearRangeIterator {
public:
  using difference_type = size_t;
  using value_type = T;
  using reference = T;
  using pointer = void;
  using iterator_category = std::bidirectional_iterator_tag;

  LinearRangeIterator(T start, T step_size, size_t idx)
  : start_{start}
  , step_size_{step_size}
  , idx_{idx}
  {}
  auto operator==(const LinearRangeIterator& lri) const{
    return idx_==lri.idx_;
  }
  auto operator!=(const LinearRangeIterator& lri) const{
    return !(*this==lri);
  }
```

```
    auto& operator++() { ++idx_; return *this; }
    auto& operator--() { --idx_; return *this; }
    auto operator*() const { return start_ + (idx_*step_size_); }
  private:
    size_t idx_{};
    T start_{};
    T step_size_{};
  };
```

Note that, in contrast to the simple `IntIterator`, `value_type` is generated on the fly, and therefore neither pointer nor reference can be defined like a regular reference or pointer. As we are required to define all five types, we define the reference as being a regular `value_type` and `pointer` is simply set to `void`.

Iterator usage example

Now this linear range iterator can be used without having it wrapped into a range. In the following code two standalone iterators representing a range are created:

```
auto start = 0.0f;
auto stop = 1.0f;
auto num_values = size_t{6};
auto step_size = get_step_size(start, stop, num_values);
auto first = LinearRangeIterator<float>{start, step_size, 0};
auto last = LinearRangeIterator<float>{start, step_size, num_values};
```

These two iterators can now be utilized in a regular `for`-loop, or an STL algorithm as shown in the following table:

Copy into std::set using a for-loop	**Copy into std::set using std::copy**

`auto s = std::set<float>{};`
`for(auto it=first; it!=last; ++it){`
`  s.insert(*it);`
`}`
	`auto s = std::set<float>{};`
	`auto dst = std::inserter(s, s.end());`
	`std::copy(first, last, dst);`

As you see, in practice our linear range iterator looks- and behaves just like any iterator which would iterate a container of numbers.

Generalizing the iterator pair to a range

Even though the previous example works, it is quite bloated as we need to duplicate the start and step length values. A more generalized solution is to let the range mimic a container, where `begin()` and `end()` correspond to the start and stop iterators:

```
template <typename T>
class LinearRange {
  using iterator = LinearRangeIterator<T>;
public:
  LinearRange(T start, T stop, size_t num_values)
  : start_{start}
  , step_size_{get_step_size(start, stop, num_values)}
  , num_values_{num_values}
  {}
  auto begin()const{ return iterator{start_, step_size_, 0}; }
  auto end()const{ return iterator{start_, step_size_, num_values_}; }
private:
  T start_{};
  T step_size_{};
  size_t num_values_{};
};
```

The make_linear_range convenience function

In order to avoid explicitly specifying the floating point type when using the `LinearRange` template, we do as the STL does with `make_pair()`: we create a convenience function called `make_linear_range()` which returns a `LinearRange` object where its type has been deduced from the arguments.

Here is how we implement the `make_linear_range()` function:

```
template <typename T>
auto make_linear_range(T start, T stop, size_t n) {
  return LinearRange<T>{ start, stop, n };
}
```

Without the `make_linear_range()` function, we need to explicitly specify the contained value type to create a range:

```
auto r = LinearRange<double>{0.0, 1.0, 4};
// r evaluates to {0.0, 0.33, 0.66, 1.0}
```

Using the `make_range_function` we the `<double>` is deduced automatically:

```
auto r = make_linear_range(0.0, 1.0, 4);
// r evaluates to {0.0, 0.33, 0.66, 1.0}
```

As you see, the `double` does not have to be specified as types are automatically deduced in template functions.

In C++17, even template class types get deduced from constructor parameters, and therefore the `make_linear_range` function is superfluous. In other words, the following code is also valid in C++17: `auto r = LinearRange{0.0f, 1.0f, 4};`

Linear range usage examples

Now that we have the foundation functions, the iterator and its corresponding `type_traits`, the `range` class, and the `make_linear_range` convenience function, we can use them to iterate a range of numbers as simple as this:

```
for(auto t: make_linear_range(0.0, 1.0, 4)) { std::cout << t << ", "; }
// Output: 0, 0.33, 0.66, 1.0,
```

What happens here is that the `make_linear_range` function returns a `LinearRange` class. When a range-based `for`-loop is invoked, the compiler internally generates code that looks similar to this:

```
auto r = make_linear_range(0.0, 1.0, 4); // r is a LinearRange<double>
auto first = r.begin(); // first is a LinearRangeIterator<double>
auto last = r.end(); // last is a LinearRangeIterator<double>
for(auto it = first; it != last; ++it) {
  std::cout << (*it) << ", ";
}
```

Therefore, the values of `LinearRange` get iterated just as if it was a container explicitly holding the values, like this:

```
for(auto t: {0.0, 0.33, 0.66, 1.0}) { std::cout << t << ", "; }
```

The linear range can also be used for iterating numbers in reverse order:

```
for(auto t: make_linear_range(1.0, 0.0, 4)) { std::cout << t << ", "; }
// Output: 1.0, 0.66, 0.33, 0.0,
```

Summary

In this chapter, you learned how to create a custom iterator and how to use `iterator_traits` to inform the STL library of how your custom iterator can be used.

In the next chapter, we will look into the algorithm library of STL, and also learn how to use the new ranges library for a more expressive C++ syntax.

6
STL Algorithms and Beyond

In this chapter, we will take a look at how we can write efficient algorithms in C++. You will learn the benefits of using the STL algorithms as building blocks in your application, both performance-wise and readability-wise. In the end, we will take a look at the limitations of the STL algorithms and take a look at how the *ranges library* can compose algorithms for a more expressive code base.

Using STL algorithms as building blocks

The **Standard Template Library** (**STL**) is a set of data types, containers, and algorithms included in the C++ standard. Even though we use containers on a daily basis, we tend to underuse the STL algorithms.

It's easy to forget that complex algorithms can be implemented by combining algorithms from the STL, so consider STL as the first choice before writing algorithms manually.

STL algorithm concepts

To get a better understanding of the STL algorithms, it's good to know a bit about the concepts and common patterns used by all STL algorithms.

Algorithms operate on iterators

The algorithms in the STL library operate only on iterators, not containers (that is, `std::vector`, `std::map`, and so on). Basically, an iterator could be considered an object with the same properties as a regular C-pointer; it can be stepped to the next element and dereferenced (if pointing to a valid address). The algorithms only use a few of the operations that a pointer allows, although the iterator may internally be a heavy object traversing a tree-like `std::map`.

Implementing a generic algorithm that can be used with any container

Implementing a generic algorithm allows programmers to easily implement their own algorithms, compatible with any container. In the following example, the `contains()` function can be used with any container:

```
template <typename Iterator, typename T>
auto contains(Iterator begin, Iterator end, const T& v) {
  for (auto it = begin; it != end; ++it) {
    if (*it == v) {
      return true;
    }
  }
  return false;
}
```

Vice versa, a new container can also use all the algorithms if it exposes the iterators. As a simple example, if we implement a two-dimensional `Grid` structure as shown below, where rows are exposed as pair of iterators:

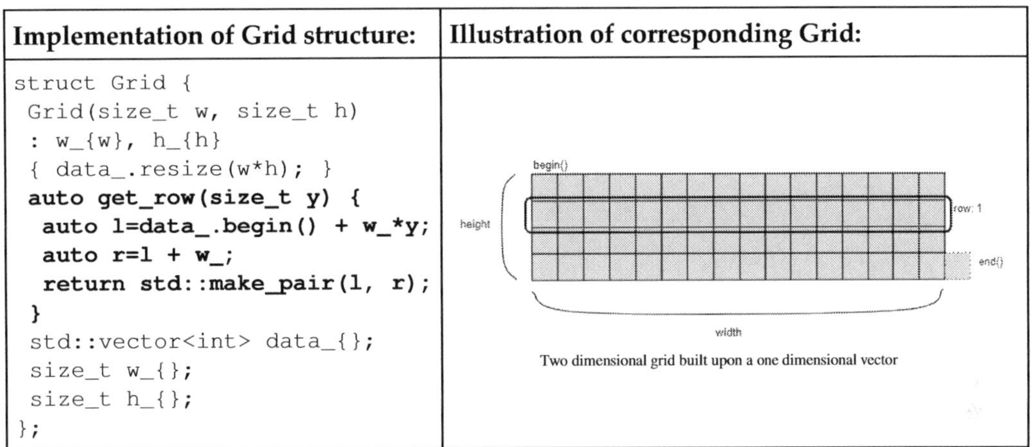

Implementation of Grid structure:

```
struct Grid {
 Grid(size_t w, size_t h)
 : w_{w}, h_{h}
 { data_.resize(w*h); }
 auto get_row(size_t y) {
  auto l=data_.begin() + w_*y;
  auto r=l + w_;
  return std::make_pair(l, r);
 }
 std::vector<int> data_{};
 size_t w_{};
 size_t h_{};
};
```

Illustration of corresponding Grid:

Two dimensional grid built upon a one dimensional vector

The iterator-pair representing a row can then be utilized by any STL algorithm:

```
auto grid = Grid{10, 10};
auto y = 3;
auto r = grid.get_row(y);
std::generate(r.first, r.second, std::rand);
auto num_fives = std::count(r.first, r.second, 5);
```

Iterators for a range point to the first element and the element after the last

All algorithms take a pair of iterators, where the first one points to the first element in the range and the second one points to one element beyond the last element in the range. Take a look at the following code snippet:

`auto vec=std::vector<std::string>{`
`  "a","b","c","d","e","f"};`
`auto first = vec.begin();`
`auto last = vec.end();`
	"a" "b" "c" "d" "e" "f"
	first last

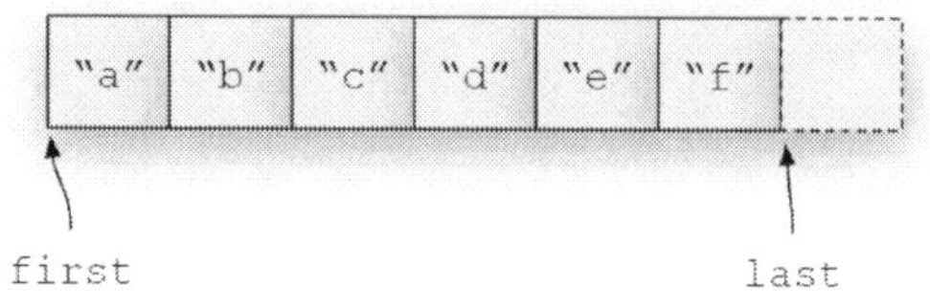

As seen in the image, the `last` iterator now points to an imagined element after "f":

Algorithms do not change the size of the container

The STL algorithms can only modify the elements in a specified range; the elements are never added or removed from the container.

For example, `std::remove()` or `std::unique()` does not actually remove elements from a container. Rather, it rearranges the elements so that the removed elements are placed at the back. It then returns an iterator to the first element of the removed elements.

Code example	**Resulting vector**

`// Example with std::remove`
`auto vec = std::vector<int>{1,1,2,2,3,3};`
`auto new_end = std::remove(`
`  vec.begin(), vec.end(), 2`
`);`
`vec.erase(new_end, vec.end());`
	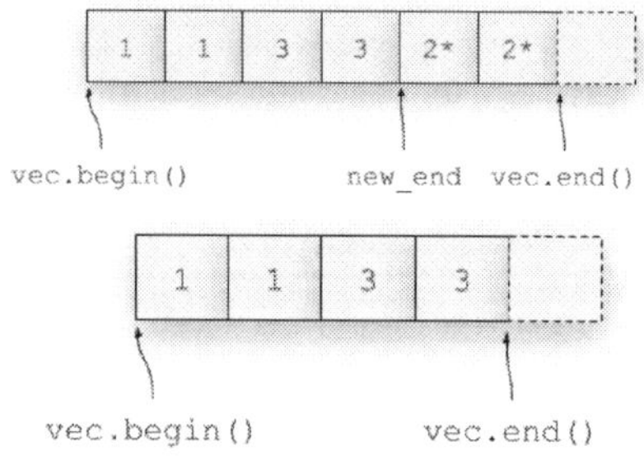 1 1 3 3 2* 2*
	vec.begin() new_end vec.end()
	1 1 3 3
	vec.begin() vec.end()

```
// Example with std::unique
auto vec = std::vector<int>{1,1,2,2,3,3};
auto new_end = std::unique(
  vec.begin(), vec.end());
vec.erase(new_end, vec.end();
```

Algorithms with output require allocated data

Algorithms that write data to an output iterator, such as `std::copy()` or `std::transform()`, requires already allocated data reserved for the output. As the algorithms only use iterators as arguments, they cannot allocate data by themselves. To enlarge the container the algorithms operate on, they rely on the iterator to be capable of enlarging the container it iterates.

If an iterator to an empty container is passed to the algorithms for output, the program will crash. The following example, where `squared` is empty, illustrates the problem:

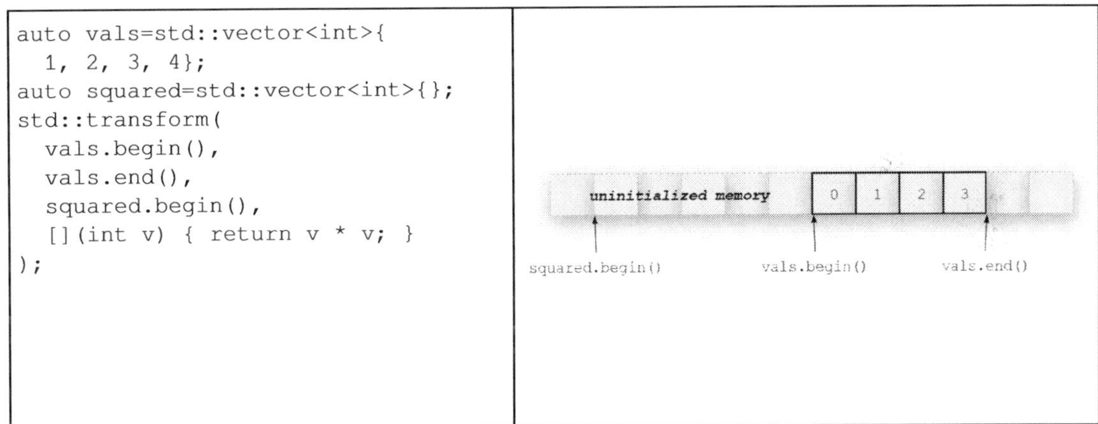

```
auto vals=std::vector<int>{
  1, 2, 3, 4};
auto squared=std::vector<int>{};
std::transform(
  vals.begin(),
  vals.end(),
  squared.begin(),
  [](int v) { return v * v; }
);
```


Instead, you have to do either of the following:

- Preallocate the required size for the resulting container
- Use an `insert`-iterator, which inserts elements into a container while iterating

The following snippet shows how to use preallocated space:

```
auto square_func = [](int v) { return v * v; };
auto vals = std::vector<int>{1,2,3};
auto squared = std::vector<int>{};
squared.resize(vals.size());
auto dst = squared.begin();
std::transform(vals.begin(), vals.end(), dst, square_func);
```

The following snippet shows how to use `std::back_inserter` and `std::inserter` to insert values into a container which is not preallocated:

```
auto square_func = [](int v) { return v * v; };
auto c = std::vector<int>{1,2,3};
// Insert into back of vector using std::back_inserter
auto squared_vec = std::vector<int>{};
auto dst_vec = std::back_inserter(squared_vec);
std::transform(c.begin(), c.end(), dst_vec, square_func);
// Insert into a std::set using std::inserter
auto squared_set = std::set<int>{};
auto dst_set = std::inserter(squared_set, squared_set.end());
std::transform(c.begin(), c.end(), dst_set, square_func);
```

If you are operating on `std::vector` and know the expected size of the resulting container, you can use the `reserve()` member function before executing the algorithm in order to avoid unnecessary allocations. Otherwise, the vector will reallocate a new chunk of memory several times during the algorithm.

Algorithms use operator== and operator< by default

For comparison, an algorithm relies on the fundamental == and < operators, as in the case of an integer. To be able to use your own classes with algorithms, `operator==` and `operator<` must either be provided by the class or as an argument to the algorithm.

The following example shows these operators implemented in a simple `Flower` class, where `operator==` is utilized by `std::find`, and `operator<` is utilized by `std::max_element`.

```
struct Flower {
  // Is equal operation, used when finding
  auto operator==(const Flower& f) const {
    return height_ == f.height_; }
  // Is less than operation, used when sorting
```

```
  auto operator<(const Flower& f) const {
    return height_ < f.height_; }
  int height_{};
};
auto garden = std::vector<Flower>{Flower{12}, Flower{13}, Flower{4}};
// std::max_element uses operator<
auto tallest_flower = std::max_element(garden.begin(), garden.end());
// std::find uses operator==
auto magic_flower = *std::find(garden.begin(), garden.end(), Flower{13});
```

Custom comparator function

If, however, you would like to use another comparison function, for example, sorting or finding a string by length, a custom function can be provided as an additional argument. While the original algorithm uses a value (for example, `std::find()`), the version with a specific operator has the same name with `_if` attached at the end (`std::find_if(...)`, `std::count_if(...)`, and so on):

```
auto names = std::vector<std::string> {
  "Ralph", "Lisa", "Homer", "Maggie", "Apu", "Bart"
};
std::sort(names.begin(), names.end(),
  [](const std::string& a,const std::string& b){
    return a.size() < b.size();
  });
// names is now "Apu", "Lisa", "Bart", "Ralph", "Homer", "Maggie"

auto target_sz = size_t{3};
auto x = std::find_if(names.begin(), names.end(),
  [target_sz](const auto& v){ return v.size() == target_sz;}
);
// x points to "Apu"
```

General-purpose predicates

When you are building a code base, we'd suggest building a namespace (named `preds` or something similar) of general-purpose predicates to make the code more readable. For example, in the previous example, the predicates could be generalized to this:

```
auto less_by_size = [](const auto& a, const auto& b){
  return a.size() < b.size();
};
auto equal_by_size = [](auto size){
  return [size](const auto& v){ return size == v.size(); };
};
```

With these named predicates, the user code becomes more readable:

```
std::sort(names.begin(), names.end(), preds::less_by_size);
auto x = std::find_if(names.begin(), names.end(), equal_by_size(3));
// x points to "Apu"
```

Candidates for this namespace could be `equal_case_insensitive`, which compares `std::string` case insensitively:

```
auto equal_case_insensitive=[](const std::string& needle){
  // Note that a lambda is returned
  return [&needle](const std::string& s){
    if(needle.size() != s.size())
      return false;
    auto eq_lower = [](char a, char b){
      return std::tolower(a)==std::to_lower(b);
    };
    return std::equal(s.begin(), s.end(), needle.begin(), eq_lower);
  };
};
```

Now, we can find a string using a case insensitive target:

```
auto num_maggies = std::count_if(names.begin(), names.end(),
  equal_case_insensitive(std::string{"maggie"}));
assert(num_maggies == 1);
```

Algorithms require move operators not to throw

All algorithms use `std::swap` and `std::move` when moving elements around, but only if the move-constructor and move-assignment are marked `noexcept`. Therefore, it is important to have these implemented for heavy objects when using algorithms. If they are not available and exception free, the elements will be copied instead.

Note that if you implement the `move` construction and `move` assignment in your class, `std::swap` will utilize them and, therefore, a specified `std::swap` overload is not needed.

Algorithms have complexity guarantees

The complexity of each STL algorithm is specified using big O notation. STL algorithms are created with performance in mind. Therefore, they do not allocate memory nor have a time complexity higher than $O(n \log n)$. Algorithms that do not fit these criteria are not included even if they are fairly common operations.

Note the exception of `std::stable_sort()`, `std::inplace_merge()`, and `std::stable_partition()`. Many STL implementations tend to temporarily allocate memory during these operation.

For example, an algorithm which tests whether a non-sorted range contains duplicates. One option is to implement it by iterating through the range and search the rest of the range for a duplicate. This will result in an algorithm with $O(n^2)$ complexity:

```
template <typename Iterator>
auto contains_duplicates(Iterator first, Iterator last) {
  for(auto it = first; it != last; ++it)
    if(std::find(std::next(it), last, *it) != last)
      return true;
  return false;
}
```

Another option is to make a copy of the full range, sort it, and look for adjacent equal elements. This will result in a time complexity of $O(n \log n)$, the average complexity of `std::sort()`, which satisfies the performance requirement. However, since it needs to make a copy of the full range, it still doesn't qualify as a building block algorithm. Allocating means that we cannot trust it not to throw:

```
template <typename Iterator>
auto contains_duplicates(Iterator first, Iterator last) {
  // As (*first) returns a reference, we have to get
  // the base type using std::decay_t
  using ValueType = std::decay_t<decltype(*first)>;
  auto c = std::vector<ValueType>(first, last);
  std::sort(c.begin(), c.end());
  return std::adjacent_find(c.begin(),c.end()) != c.end();
}
```

Algorithms perform just as well as C library function equivalents

The standard C library comes with a couple of low-level algorithms such as `memcpy()`, `memmove()`, `memcmp()`, and `memset()`. In our experience, sometimes people tend to use these functions instead of their equivalents in the STL algorithm library. The reason is that people tend to believe that the C library functions are faster and, therefore, accept the trade off in type safety.

This is not true for modern STL implementation; the equivalent STL algorithms, `std::copy()`, `std::equal()`, and `std::fill()`, resort to these low-level C functions where plausible; hence, they provide both performance and type safety.

Note that there might be exceptions where the C++ compiler is not able to detect that it is safe to resort to the low-level C-functions. These cases should be rare though.

STL algorithms versus handcrafted for-loops

We promote the use of algorithms over hand-written `for`-loops for a number of reasons. First, they are more readable, less error-prone, and future-proof in the sense that it is easier to revisit the code and modify or optimize it. We will try to illustrate this with a few examples.

Let's look at the advantages of STL algorithms over handcrafted `for`-loops:

- STL algorithms deliver performance. Even though some of the algorithms in STL may sometimes seem trivial, they are often optimally designed in ways that are not obvious at first glance.
- STL algorithms provide safety; even simpler algorithms may have corner cases which is easy to overlook.
- STL algorithms are future-proof; algorithms can be replaced by a more suitable algorithm if one wants to take advantage of SIMD extensions, parallelism, or even the GPU at a later stage (`Chapter 11`, *Parallel STL*, will cover the basics of parallel algorithms).
- STL algorithms are very well documented.

Readability and future-proofing

By using algorithms instead of `for`-loops, the intention of each operation is clearly indicated by the name and, more importantly, algorithms are very well-documented. The reader of a function does not need to inspect every `for`-loop in order to determine exactly what it does. It might not be obvious looking at a single algorithm, but when several algorithms are followed upon, as in the next example, the advantages are obvious. Note that when reading `for`-loops, you have to inspect every detail, whereas STL algorithms immediately show how the data is being used.

Also, from an optimization point of view, the algorithms in the example can be easily replaced by parallelized equivalents (this will be further explained in `Chapter 11`, *Parallel STL*).

Once you get into the habit of thinking in terms of algorithms rather than `for`-loops, you'll realize that most `for`-loops are most often a variation of a few simple algorithms such as `std::transform()`, `std::remove_if()`, `std::copy_if()`, and `std::find()`.

Due to the importance of utilizing the STL algorithms instead of `for`-loops in high-performance C++, we'd like to show a few examples. Resorting to handwritten `for`-loops might be convenient, as one might have developed a habit of thinking in terms of `for`-loops; however, using algorithms has many advantages, which we will try to demonstrate with examples.

Part of the syntax verbosity was solved in C++11, when lambda functions were introduced in the language. As explained in `Chapter 2`, *Modern C++ Concepts*, prior to the introduction of lambda functions in C++11, programmers had to use complicated functor objects when incorporating algorithms.

Real-world code base example

This example is from a real-world code base, although variable names has been disguised. As it is only a cut-out, you don't have to understand the logic of the code. The example is here just to show you how the complexity is lowered when using algorithms compared with nested `for`-loops.

Using algorithms will also make the code cleaner. You can often write functions without nesting. In the `for`-loop version, it's hard to grasp when conflicting textures are set to `true`, whereas in the algorithm version, you can instinctively see that it happens if `info` fulfills a predicate.

Note that **kvp** is short for **key-value-pair**.

<table>
<tr><th>The for-loop version</th><th>The STL algorithm version</th></tr>
<tr><td>

```
auto varies() -> bool {...}
auto conflicting = false;
for (auto&& kvp : infos) {
 auto usage = kvp.second;
 auto par = usage.params();
 if (par==output.params()){
  if(varies(usage.flags())){
   conflicting = true;
   break;
  }
 }
 else {
  conflicting = true;
  break;
 }
}
```

</td><td>

```
auto varies() -> bool {...}
auto conflicting=std::any_of(
 infos.begin(),
 infos.end(),
 [&](const auto& kvp) {
  auto usage = kvp.second;
  auto par = usage.params();
  return
   par!=output.params() ||
   varies(usage.flags());
 }
);
```

</td></tr>
</table>

Although it may overstate the point, imagine if one were to track a bug or parallelizing it, the right version would be far easier to understand and reason about.

Usage examples of STL algorithms versus handcrafted for-loops

To state the importance of using algorithms rather than `for`-loops, we'd like to show a few examples of not-so-obvious problems that one may bump into when using handcrafted `for`-loops rather than STL algorithms.

Example 1 – Unfortunate exceptions and performance problems

Let's say we need a function that moves the first *n* elements from the front of a container to the back, like this:

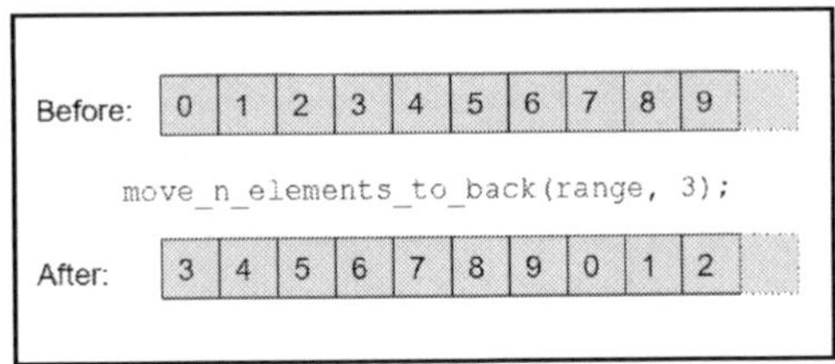

Moving the first three elements to back of a range

Approach 1 – Use a traditional for-loop:

A very naive approach would be to copy the first *n* elements to the back while iterating over them and then erasing the first *n* elements:

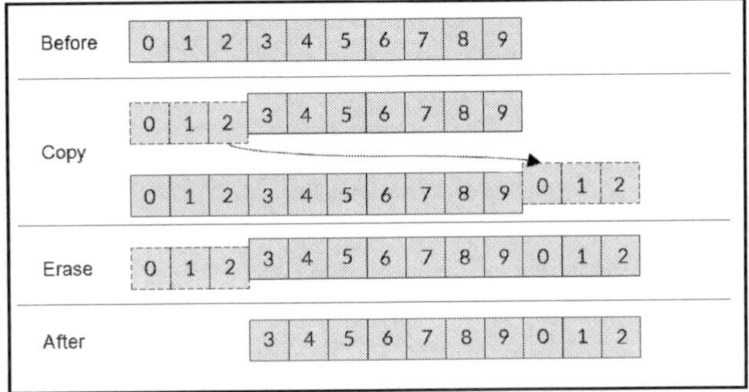

Allocating and deallocating in order to move elements to back of range

Here's the corresponding implementation:

```
template <typename Container>
auto move_n_elements_to_back(Container& c, size_t n) {
  // Copy the first n elements to the end of the container
  for(auto it = c.begin(); it != std::next(c.begin(), n); ++it) {
    c.emplace_back(std::move(*it));
  }
  // Erase the copied elements from front of container
  c.erase(c.begin(), std::next(c.begin(), n));
}
```

At first glance, it might look plausible, but inspecting it reveals a severe problem—if the container reallocates during the iteration due to `push_back()`, the iterator `it` will no longer be valid. As the algorithm tries to access an invalid iterator, the algorithm will throw an exception.

Approach 2 – Safe for-loop safe at the expense of performance:

As a thrown exception is quite an obvious problem, we'll have to rewrite the algorithm. We are still using a handcrafted `for`-loop, but we'll utilize the index instead of the iterator:

```
template <typename Container>
auto move_n_elements_to_back(Container& c, size_t n) {
  for(size_t i = 0; i < n; ++i) {
    auto value = *std::next(c.begin(), i);
    c.emplace_back(std::move(value));
  }
  c.erase(c.begin(), std::next(c.begin(), n));
}
```

The solution works; it doesn't crash anymore. But now, it has a subtle performance problem. The algorithm is significantly slower on `std::list` than on `std::vector`. The reason is that `std::next(it, n)` used with `std::list::iterator` is *O(n)*, and *O(1)* on a `std::vector::iterator`. As `std::next(it, n)` is invoked in every step of the `for`-loop, this algorithm will have a time complexity of $O(n^2)$ on containers such as `std::list`. Apart from this performance limitation, the preceding code also has the following limitations:

- It doesn't work with containers of a static size, such as `std::array`, due to `emplate_back()`
- It might throw an exception, since `emplace_back()` may allocate memory and fail (okay, probably rare)

Approach 3 – Find, and use, a suitable STL algorithm:

When we have reached this stage, we should browse through STL and see if they contain a suitable algorithm to be used as a building block. Conveniently, STL provides an algorithm called `std::rotate()`, which does exactly what we are looking for while avoiding all the disadvantages mentioned before. Let's use the `std::rotate()` algorithm:

```
template <typename Container>
auto move_n_elements_to_back(Container& c, size_t n) {
  auto new_begin = std::next(c.begin(), n);
  std::rotate(c.begin(), new_begin, c.end());
}
```

Let's have a look at the advantages of using `std::rotate()`:

- The algorithm does not throw exceptions, as it does not allocate memory (the contained object might throw exceptions though)
- It works with containers whose size cannot be changed, such as `std::array`
- Performance is *O(n)* regardless of the container it operates on
- STL implementations are often optimized with specific hardware in mind

Maybe you find this comparison between `for`-loops and STL algorithms unfair because there are other solutions to this problem that are both elegant and efficient without using STL. Still, in the real world, it's not uncommon to see implementations like the ones we just saw, when there are algorithms in STL just waiting to solve your problems.

Example 2 – STL has subtle optimizations even in simple algorithms

Even algorithms that may seem very simple might contain optimizations you wouldn't consider. Let's have a look at `std::find()`, for example. At a glance, it seems that the obvious implementation couldn't be optimized further. Here is a possible implementation of the `std::find()` algorithm:

```
template <typename It, typename Value>
auto find_slow(It first, It last, const Value& value) {
  for(auto it = first; it != last; ++it)
    if(*it == value)
      return it;
  return last;
}
```

However, looking through the `libstdc++` implementation, when being used with `RandomAccessIterator` (in other words, `std::vector`, `std::string`, `std::deque`, and `std::array`), the libc++ implementers have unrolled the `for`-loop in parts of four, resulting in the comparison (`it != last`) being executed one-fourth as many times.

Here is the optimized version of `std::find()` taken from the `libstdc++` library:

```
template <typename It, typename Value>
auto find_fast(It first, It last, const Value& value) {
  // Main loop unrolled into chunks of four
  auto num_trips = (last - first) / 4;
  for (auto trip_count = num_trips; trip_count > 0; --trip_count) {
    if (*first == value) {return first;} ++first;
    if (*first == value) {return first;} ++first;
```

```
    if (*first == value) {return first;} ++first;
    if (*first == value) {return first;} ++first;
  }
  // Handle the remaining elements
  switch (last - first) {
    case 3: if (*first == value) {return first;} ++first;
    case 2: if (*first == value) {return first;} ++first;
    case 1: if (*first == value) {return first;} ++first;
    case 0:
    default: return last;
  }
}
```

Note that it is actually the `std::find_if()`, not `std::find()` which utilizes this loop unrolling optimization. But the `std::find()` is implemented using `std::find_if()`. In addition to `std::find()`, a multitude of algorithms in *libstdc++* is implemented using `std::find_if()`, for example `std::any_of()`, `std::all_of()`, `std::none_of()`, `std::find_if_not()`, `std::search()`, `std::is_partitioned()`, `std::remove_if()`, `std::is_permutation()`, which means that all of these are slightly faster than a handcrafted `for`-loop.

And by slightly, I really mean slightly; the performance benefit is roughly half a percent, as shown in the following table:

Find an integer in a std::vector of 10'000'000 elements		
Algorithm	**Microseconds**	**Speed up**
`find_slow`	3420	1.000 x
`find_fast`	3402	**1.005 x**

However, even though the benefit is almost negligible, using STL algorithms, you get it for free.

"Compare with zero" optimization

In addition to the loop unrolling, a very subtle optimization is that `trip_count` is iterated backwards in order to compare with zero instead of a value. On some CPUs comparing with zero is slightly faster than any other value, as it uses another assembler instruction (on the x86 platform it uses `test` instead of `cmp`). However, do not rearrange your handmade loops in order to benefit from this optimization, unless it's a (very) hot spot. Doing so will heavily reduce the readability of your code; let the algorithms handle these kinds of optimizations instead.

The following table show the difference in assembly output

Action	C++	Assembler x86

Compare with zero	`auto is_above_zero(size_t v) {`
	`  return v > 0;`
	`}`
		`test edi, edi`
		`setne al`
		`ret`

Compare with other value	`auto is_above_123(size_t v) {`
	`  return v > 123;`
	`}`
		`cmp edi, 123`
		`seta al`
		`ret`

Sorting only for the data you need to retrieve

STL contains three basic sorting algorithms: `std::sort()`, `std::partial_sort()`, and `std::nth_element()`. In addition, it also contains a few abbreviations of those, but we will focus on these three as, in our experience, it is easy to forget that, in many cases, a complete sort can be avoided by using `nth_element()` or `partial_sort()` instead.

While `std::sort()` sorts the whole range, `std::partial_sort()` and `std::nth_element()` could be thought of as algorithms for inspecting parts of that sorted range. In many cases, you are only interested in a certain part of the sorted range.

For example;

- If you want to calculate the median of a range, you require the value in the middle of the sorted range.
- If you want to create a body scanner which can be used by the mean 80% by length of a population, you require two values in the sorted range; the value located 10% from the tallest person, and 10% from the shortest person.

The following image illustrates how `std::nth_element` and `std::partial_sort` processes a range, compared to a fully sorted range:

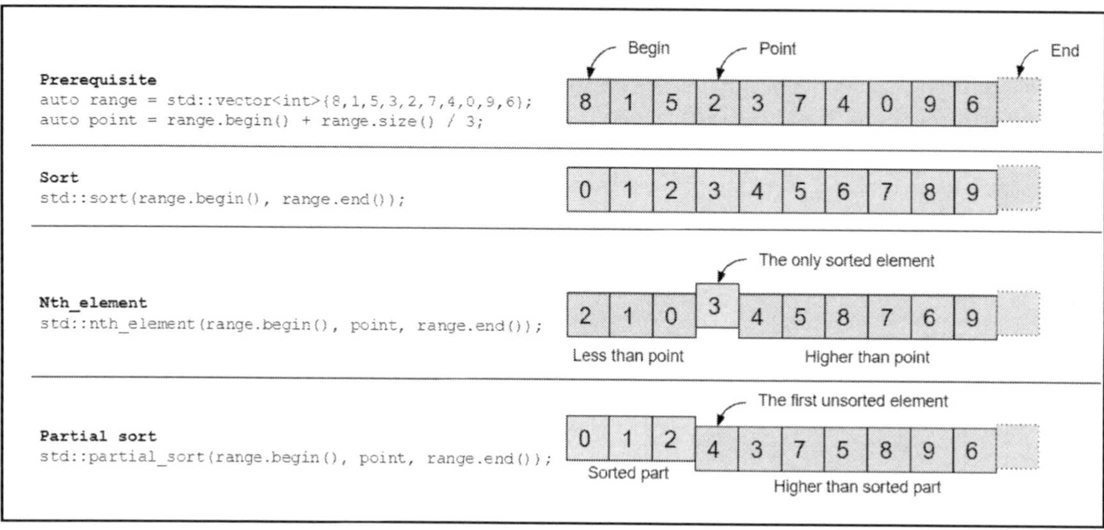

Sorted and non-sorted elements of a range using different algorithms

The following table shows their algorithmic complexity; note that *m* denotes the sub range, which is being fully sorted:

Algorithm	Complexity	Example at n = 10000, m = 3333
`std::sort()`	$O(n \log n)$	40'000
`std::partial_sort()`	$O(n \log m)$	35'229
`std::nth_element()`	$O(n)$	10'000

Use cases

Now that we have insights into `std:nth_element()` and `std::partial_sort()`, let's see how we can combine them to inspect parts of a range as if the entire range were sorted:

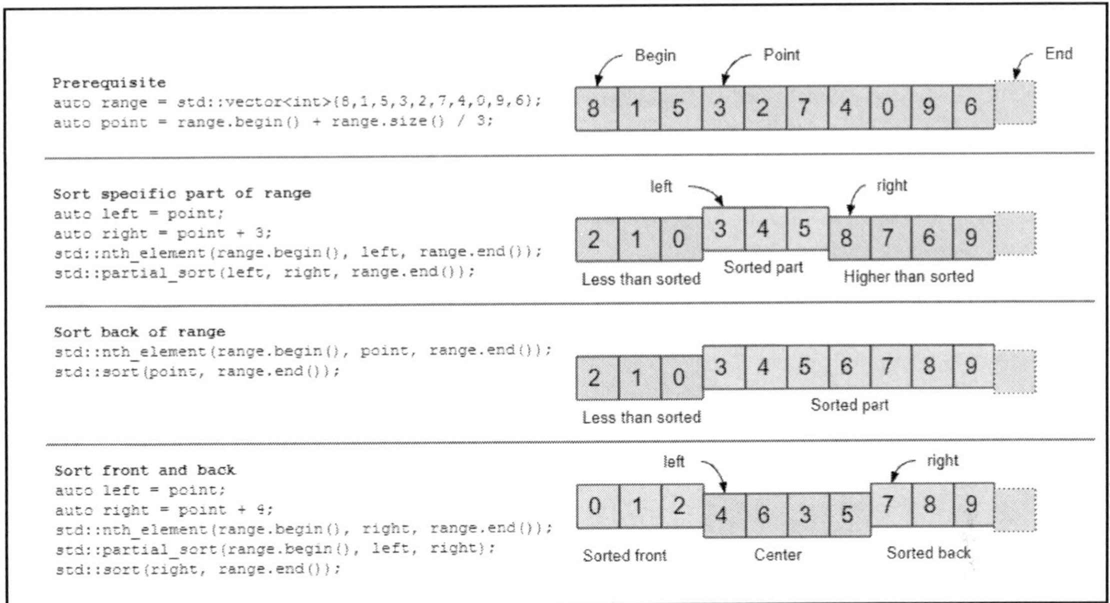

Combining algorithms and corresponding partially ordered result

Performance evaluation

Let's see how `std::nth_element()` and `std::partial_sort()` measure up against `std::sort()`. We've measured with 10,000,000 elements in total and a partial range of 1,000,000 elements:

Operation	Code, where r is the range operated on	Speed up:
Sort	`sort(r.begin(), r.end());`	1.00x
Find median	`auto middle = r.begin() + r.size() / 2;` `nth_element(r.begin(), middle, r.end());`	12.41x

Find the values as if fully ordered
From `left_idx` to `right_idx`
List unordered
	`auto left_it = r.begin() + left_idx;`
	`auto right_it = r.begin() + right_idx;`
	`nth_element(r.begin(), left_it,r.end());`
	`nth_element(left_it, right_it, r.end());`
		8.70x

Find the values as if fully ordered
From `left_idx` to `right_idx`
List ordered
	`auto left_it = r.begin() + left_idx;`
	`auto right_it = r.begin() + right_idx;`
	`nth_element(r.begin(), left_it, r.end());`
	`partial_sort(left_it, right_it, r.end());`
		4.58x

The future of STL and the ranges library

This section deals with a library that is proposed for the upcoming C++ standard, C++20. As of now, it is available at `https://github.com/ericniebler/range-v3`. Compiling these examples will require an updated compiler.

Limitations of the iterators in STL

Although the iterator and algorithm concepts in STL have quite a few good properties, they lack composability.

Let's say, we have some sort of a `Warrior` class with an ability and a level of ability, as implemented below:

```
enum class EAbility { Fencing, Archery };
class Warrior {
public:
  EAbility ability_{};
  int level_{};
  std::string name_{};
};
```

Now, let's say we want to find the `Warrior` with the highest level of `Archery` in the list of `warriors`.

If we were to use STL, the algorithm we'd use is `std::max_element()`, operating on `level_`, but as we only want to take the `warriors` with the ability of `Archery` into account, it gets tricky. Essentially, we want to compose a new algorithm out of a combination of `std::copy_if()` and `std::max_element()`, but composing algorithms is not possible with STL.

Instead, we would have to make a copy of all the `warriors` with `Archery` to a new container and then iterate the new container to the maximum level, leaving us with code that is both verbose and quite ineffective due to the copy.

The code would look something like this; as you can see, it is quite verbose for a simple task:

```
auto is_archer = [](Warrior w){return w.ability_==EAbility::Archery;};
auto compare_level = [](Warrior a,Warrior b){return a.level_<b.level_;};

auto get_max_archor_level(const std::vector<Warrior>& warriors) {
  auto archery = std::vector<Warrior>{};
  // The warrior list needs to be copied in order
  // to filter to archery only
  std::copy_if(
    warriors.begin(),
    warriors.end(),
    std::back_inserter(archery),
    is_archer
  );
  auto max_level_it = std::max_element(
    archery.begin(),
    archery.end(),
    compare_level
  );
  return *max_level_it;
}
```

Here's a usage example:

```
auto warriors = std::vector<Warrior> {
  Warrior{EAbility::Fencing, 12, "Zorro"},
  Warrior{EAbility::Archery, 10, "Legolas"},
  Warrior{EAbility::Archery, 7, "Link"}
};
auto max_archor_level = get_max_archor_level(warriors);
// max_archor_level equals 10
```

Of course, you may now be thinking that `get_max_archor_level()` could be written as a simple `for`-loop, which relieves us of the extra allocation due to `copy_if()`:

```
auto get_max_archor_level(const std::vector<Warrior>& warriors){
  auto max_level = int{0};
  for(const auto& w: warriors) {
    if(w.ability_ == EAbility::Archer) {
      max_level = std::max(max_level, w.level_);
    }
  }
  return max_level;
}
```

Although easily achievable, we would then miss the readability of an algorithm; as mentioned earlier, a code base full of `for`-loops simply isn't readable, as every algorithm looks the same, more or less.

What we would like is a syntax as readable as using algorithms, but with the ability to avoid constructing new containers for every step in the algorithm. This is where the future ranges library takes off . Although the ranges library is huge, the essential difference from the STL library is its ability to compose what is essentially a different kind of iterators into a lazily evaluated range.

This is what the previous example would look like if it were written using the ranges library:

```
namespace rv = ranges::view;
auto get_max_archor_level(const std::vector<Warrior>&warriors){
  auto archer_levels = warriors
    | rv::filter(is_archer)
    | rv::transform([](const auto& w) { return w.level_; });
  auto max_level_it = ranges::max_element(archer_levels);
  return *max_level_it;
}
```

All we do is simply compose a range view which, when iterated by `ranges::max_element()`, simply exposes the level of all archers. The range, `archer_levels`, is simply all `warriors`, filtered by `is_archer` and transformed into exposing the level.

Although not part of the standard yet, the ranges library is available at `https://github.com/ericniebler/range-v3`. We think it's a far too important enhancement of C++ to ignore in this book, so let's give you a brief introduction to the ranges library.

Introduction to the ranges library

As mentioned earlier, the STL algorithm library has quite a verbose syntax, where every algorithm requires a pair of iterators as parameters. The ranges library has overloaded these functions but by taking a range as a parameter instead of a pair of iterators:

STL algorithms operates on iterators	Ranges library operates on containers
`std::sort(a.begin(), a.end());` `std::count(a.begin(), a.end(), 12);`	`ranges::sort(a);` `ranges::count(a, 12);`

This makes the syntax of algorithms neater, but the main feature with the ranges library is the introduction of views.

Views in the range library are lazily evaluated iterations over a range. Technically they are only iterators with built in logic, but syntactically, they provide a very pleasant syntax for many common operations. Following is an example of how a view is used to iterate a vector of numbers like if it contained the squares of the original numbers:

```
namespace rv = ranges::view;
auto numbers = std::vector<int>{1,2,3,4,5,6,7};
auto squared_view = rv::transform(numbers, [](auto v){
  return v * v;
});
for(auto s: squared_view) {
  std::cout << s << " ";
}
// Output: 1 4 9 16 25 36 49
```

The variable, `squared_view`, is not a copy of the `numbers` vector with the values squared; it is a proxy object for `numbers` with one slight difference—every time you access an element, the `transform` function is invoked.

From the outside, you can still iterate over `squared_view` as any regular container and, therefore, perform regular algorithms such as `find` or `count`, but internally, you haven't created another container.

If you want to store the range, the view can be simply assigned to the container of your choice. Once copied back to a container, there is no longer any dependency between the original, and the transformed container.

```
std::vector<int> v = squared_view;
std::list<int> l = squared_view;
```

With ranges, it is also possible to create a filtered view where only a part of the range is visible. In this case, only the elements that satisfy the condition are visible when iterating the view:

View odd values	View fives

`namespace rv = ranges::view;`
`auto vals = std::vector<int>{`
`  4,5,6,7,6,5,4`
`};`
`auto odd_view = rv::filter(`
`  vals,`
`  [](auto v){return(v%2)==1;}`
`);`
`for(auto v: odd_view) {`
`  std::cout << v << " ";`
`}`
`// Output: 5 7 5`
	`namespace rv =ranges::view;`
	`auto vals=std::vector<int>{`
	`  4,5,6,7,6,5,4`
	`};`
	`auto five_view=rv::filter(`
	`  vals,`
	`  [](auto v){return v==5;}`
	`);`
	`for(auto v: five_view) {`
	`  std::cout << v << " ";`
	`}`
	`// Output: 5 5`

Another example of the versatility of the ranges library is the possibility it offers of creating a view that can iterate over several containers as if they were a single list:

```
auto list_of_lists = std::vector<std::vector<int>> {
  {1, 2},
  {3, 4, 5},
  {5},
  {4, 3, 2, 1}
};
auto flattened_view = rv::join(list_of_lists);
for(auto v: flattened_view)
  std::cout << v << ", ";
// Output: 1, 2, 3, 4, 5, 5, 4, 3, 2, 1,

auto max_value = *ranges::max_element(flattened_view);
// max_value is 5
```

Composability and pipeability

The full power of views comes from the ability to combine them. As they don't copy the actual data, you can express multiple operations on a dataset while, internally, only iterating over it once.

```
namespace rv = ranges::view;
auto numbers = std::vector<int>{1,2,3,4,5,6,7};

// Create a squared view
auto squared_view = rv::transform(numbers, [](auto v){
  return v * v;
});
// squared_view evaluates to "1, 4, 9, 16, 25, 36, 49"

// Add a filter onto the squared view
auto odd_squared_view = rv::filter(squared_view, [](auto v){
  return (v % 2) == 1;
});
// odd_squared_view evaluates to "1, 9, 25, 49"
```

Now this might not look syntactically elegant, but the ranges library also allows us to compose the views using a the pipe operator for a much more elegant syntax (you will learn more about using the pipe operator in your own code in `Chapter 9`, *Proxy Objects and Lazy Evaluation*):

```
namespace rv = ranges::view;
auto numbers = std::vector<int>{1,2,3,4,5,6,7};
auto odd_squares_view = numbers
  | rv::transform([](auto v){ return v * v; })
  | rv::filter([](auto v){ return (v % 2) == 1; });

// odd_squared_view evaluates to "1, 9, 25, 49"
```

The ability to read a statement from left to the right, rather than inside-out as is the case with a regular syntax using parenthesis, makes the code much easier to read.

Actions, views, and algorithms

The ranges library consists of three types of operations: algorithms, actions, and views. It's important to know the difference between views and actions, the following code snippet shows what a simple procedure corresponds to when using actions versus using views. Note how the actions mutate the vector, whereas the view simply iterates it:

```
// Prerequisite
auto is_odd = [](int v){ return (v % 2) == 1; }
auto square = [](int v){ return v*v; }
auto get() { return std::vector<int>{1,2,3,4}; }
using ra = ranges::action;
using rv = ranges::view;

// Print odd squares using actions...
for(auto v: get() | ra::remove_if(is_odd) | ra::transform(square)) {
 std::cout << v << " ";
}
// ... corresponds to the following code where c is mutated:
auto c = get();
auto new_end = std::remove_if(c.begin(), c.end(), is_odd);
c.erase(new_end, c.end());
std::transform(c.begin(), c.end(), c.begin(), square);
for(auto v: c) { std::cout << v << " "; }

// Print odd squares using a view...
for(auto v: get() | rv::remove_if(is_odd) | rv::transform(square)) {
  std::cout << v << " ";
}
// ... corresponds to the following code where get() is only iterated
for(auto v: get()) {
  if(is_odd(v)) {
    auto s = square(v)
    std::cout << s << " ";
  }
}
```

Actions

Actions work like standard STL algorithms, but instead of using iterators as input/output, they take containers and return new modified containers.

Unlike STL algorithms, the actions of **ranges modify the size of the container**, that is, `ranges::action::remove_if()` returns a container where the elements have been erased from the container, whereas `std::remove_if(...)` simply returns an iterator to the last unique element and leaves it to the programmer to actually erase the elements. Same goes with `std::unique`; a new range containing only the unique values are returned:

<table>
<tr><th>Erasing duplicates using STL algorithms</th><th>Erasing duplicates using the ranges library</th></tr>
<tr><td><pre>auto a = std::vector<int>{
  1, 2, 1, 3, 2, 4
};
std::sort(a.begin(),a.end());
// ints is "1, 1, 2, 2, 3, 4"
auto it = std::unique(
  a.begin(),
  a.end()
);
// a is "1, 2, 3, 4, 3, 4"
// it points to the fifth element
a.erase(it, a.end());
// a is "1, 2, 3, 4"</pre></td><td><pre>namespace ra = ranges::action;
auto a =
  std::vector<int>{1,2,1,3,2,4}
  | ra::sort
  | ra::unique;
// a is 1, 2, 3, 4</pre></td></tr>
</table>

As **actions mutate data**, they cannot operate on views. Hence, the following example does not compile:

```
auto numbers = std::vector<int>{ 1, 2, 1, 3, 2, 4 };
numbers = std::move(numbers)
  | ranges::view::unique
  | ranges::action::sort; // Does not compile, cannot sort a view
```

In order to mutate a container using actions you must choose one of the following:

- Provide the container as an *r-value*, that is, the range is returned from a function or via `std::move()`
- Initiate the action with `|=` instead of `|`, which mutates the container in place.

The following are examples of how the approaches look syntactically:

Initialization code	`namespace ra = ranges::action;`
	`auto get(){return std::vector<int>{1,3,5,7};}`
	`auto above_5 = [](auto v){ return v >= 5; };`

Use`get()` straight away	`auto vals = get() | ra::remove_if(above_5);` `// vals is "1, 3"`

Constructed r-value, using`std::move()`	`auto vals = get();`
	`vals = std::move(vals) | ra::remove_if(above_5);`
	`// vals is "1, 3"`

Mutate container, using `|= operator`	`auto vals = get();`
	`vals |= ra::remove_if(above_5);`
	`// vals is "1, 3"`

Views

Views might seem similar to actions, but on the inside, they are completely different. While an action operates on the input container and returns a mutated version, views simply return a proxy view, which, when iterated, looks like a mutated container.

However, the container is not mutated at all; all the processing is performed in the iterators.

Comparing `ranges::view::transform()` with `ranges::action::transform()` clarifies the difference. As actions transforms the container, they cannot transform the type, whereas views can transform to a view of any type.

The following transformation, where an `int` is transformed to a `std::string`, can only be performed using `ranges::view`. Note that `str_view` is just a proxy; the actual returned string is not constructed until the view is accessed.

```
namespace ra = ranges::action;
namespace rv = ranges::view;
auto get_numbers() { return std::vector<int>{1,3,5,7}; }
// An action cannot transform the type
auto strings = get_numbers() | ra::transform([](auto v){
  return std::to_string(v); // Does not compile
});
// A view can transform the type
auto ints = get_numbers();
auto str_view = ints | rv::transform([](auto v){
  return std::to_string(v);
});
```

To mimic the behavior of `std::transform()` which can transform data to a container with a different value type, the view can be converted to a container. This can be performed either by using the functions `ranges::to_vector`, `ranges::to_list` etc, or by simply assigning the view to the range of choice.

<table>
<tr><th>Assign using explicit container type</th><th>Assign using <code>auto</code> and <code>to_list</code></th></tr>
<tr><td><pre>namespace rv = ranges::view;
auto a = std::list<int>{2,4};
std::list<std::string> b = a
 | rv::transform([](auto v){
   return std::to_string(v);
 });</pre></td><td><pre>namespace rv = ranges::view;
auto a = std::list<int>{2,4};
auto b = a
  | rv::transform([](auto v){
    return std::to_string(v);
  })
  | ranges::to_list;</pre></td></tr>
</table>

Algorithms

The algorithms in the ranges library that do not return a view or a mutated container are simply referred to as algorithms. Examples of such algorithms are `ranges::count`, `ranges::any_of`, and so on. They work exactly as non-mutating algorithms in STL, with the exception that they use a range as input instead of a pair of iterators.

Unlike actions and views, algorithms cannot be chained with the `|` operator:

```
auto cars = std::vector<std::string>{"volvo","saab","trabant"};
// Using the STL library
auto num_volvos_a = std::count(cars.begin(), cars.end(), "volvo");
// Using the ranges library
auto num_volvos_b = ranges::count(cars, "volvo");
```

Summary

In this chapter, you learned how to use the basic concepts in the STL algorithm library, the advantages of using them as building blocks instead of handwritten `for`-loops, and why using the STL algorithm library is beneficial for optimizing your code at a later stage. We also discussed the guarantees and trade-offs of the STL algorithms, meaning that you can, from now on, use them with confidence.

In the end, we had a brief look at the upcoming ranges library, which simplifies range handling a lot more.

By using the advantages of the algorithms instead of manual `for`-loops, your code base is well prepared for the parallelization techniques that will be discussed in the coming chapters of this book.

7
Memory Management

After reading the previous chapters, it should no longer come as a surprise that the way we handle memory can have a huge impact on the performance. The CPU spends a lot of time shuffling data between the CPU registers and the main memory (loading and storing data to and from the main memory). As shown in `Chapter 4`, *Data Structures*, the CPU uses memory caches to speed up the access of memory, and the programs need to be cache-friendly in order to run quickly. This chapter will reveal more aspects of how computers work with memory so that we know which things must be considered when tuning memory usage. We will discuss automatic memory allocation and dynamic memory management, and look at the life cycle of a C++ object. Sometimes there are hard memory limits that force us to keep our data representation compact, and sometimes we have plenty of memory available but need the program to go faster by making the memory management more efficient. Allocating and deallocating dynamic memory is relatively expensive and, at times, we need to avoid unnecessary allocations to make the program run faster.

We will start this chapter by explaining some concepts that we need to understand before we dig deeper into C++ memory management. This introduction will explain virtual memory and virtual address space, stack memory versus heap memory, paging, and swap space.

Computer memory

The physical memory of a computer is shared among all the processes running on a system. If one process uses a lot of memory, the other processes will most likely be affected. But from a programmer's perspective, we usually don't have to bother about the memory that is being used by other processes. This isolation of memory is due to the fact that most operating systems today are *virtual memory* operating systems, which provide the illusion that a process has all the memory for itself. Each process has its own *virtual address space*.

The virtual address space

Addresses in the virtual address space that programmers see are mapped to physical addresses by the operating system and the **memory management unit** (**MMU**), which is a part of the processor. This mapping or translation happens each time we access a memory address.

This extra layer of indirection makes it possible for the operating system to use physical memory for the parts of a process that are currently being used and back up the rest of the virtual memory on-disk. In this sense, we can see the physical main memory as a cache for the virtual memory space, which resides on secondary storage. The areas of the secondary storage that are used for backing up memory pages are usually called swap space, swap file, or, simply, pagefile depending on the operating system.

Virtual memory makes it possible for processes to have a virtual address space bigger than the physical address space, since virtual memory that is not in use does not have to occupy physical memory.

Memory pages

The most common way to implement virtual memory today is to divide the address space in fixed sized blocks called *memory pages*. When a process accesses memory at a virtual address, the operating system checks whether the memory page is backed by physical memory (a page frame). If the memory page is not mapped in the main memory, a hardware exception occurs and the page is loaded from disk into memory. This type of hardware exception is called a *page fault*. This is not an error but a necessary interrupt in order to load data from disk to memory. As you may have guessed though, this is very slow compared to reading data that is already resident in memory.

When there are no more available page frames in the main memory, a page frame has to be evicted. If the page to be evicted is dirty, that is, it has been modified since it was last loaded from disk, it needs to be written to disk before it can be replaced. This mechanism is called *paging*. If the memory page has not been modified, the memory page is simply evicted.

Not all operating systems that support virtual memory support paging. iOS, for example, does have virtual memory but dirty pages are never stored to disk; only clean pages can be evicted from memory. If the main memory is full, iOS will start terminating processes until there is enough free memory again.

The following diagram shows two running processes. They both have their own virtual memory space. Some of the pages are mapped to the physical memory and some are not. If process 1 needs to use memory in the memory page that starts at address 0x1000, a page fault will occur. The memory page will then be mapped to a vacant memory frame. Also, note that the virtual memory addresses are not the same as the physical addresses. The first memory page of process 1, which starts at the virtual address 0x0000, is mapped to a memory frame that starts at the physical address 0x4000:

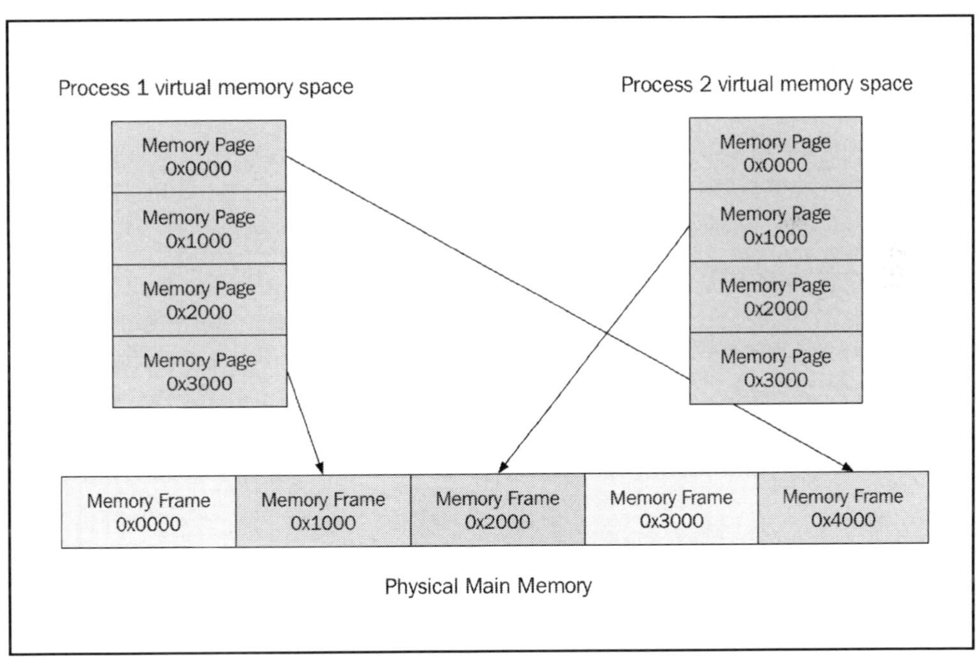

Virtual memory pages mapped to memory frames in physical memory. Virtual memory pages that are not in use do not have to occupy physical memory.

Thrashing

Thrashing can happen when a system runs low on physical memory and is, therefore, constantly paging. Whenever a process gets time scheduled on the CPU, it tries to access memory that has been paged out. Loading new memory pages means that the other pages first have to be stored on-disk. Moving data back and forth between disk and memory is usually very slow, so in some cases, this more or less stalls the computer, since the system spends all its time paging. Looking at the system's page fault frequency is a good way to determine whether the program has started thrashing.

Process memory

The stack and the heap are the two most important memory segments in a C++ program. There is also static storage and thread local storage, but more on that later. Actually, to be formally correct, C++ doesn't talk about stack and heap; instead, it talks about storage classes and the storage duration of objects. However, since the concepts of stack and heap are widely used in the C++ community, and all the implementations of C++ that we are aware of use a stack to implement function calls and manage automatic storage of local variables, we think it is important to understand what stack and heap are. In this book, we are also using the terms stack and heap rather than the storage duration of objects.

Both the stack and the heap reside in the process' virtual memory space. The stack is a place where all the local variables reside; this also includes arguments to functions. The stack grows each time a function is being called and contracts when a function returns. Each thread has its own stack and, hence, stack memory can be considered thread-safe. The heap on the other side is a global memory area that is being shared among all the threads in a running process. The heap grows when we allocate memory with `new` (or the C-library function, `malloc()`) and contracts when we free the memory with `delete` (or `free()`). Usually, the heap starts at a low address and grows in an upward direction, whereas the stack starts at a high address and grows in the downward direction. The following image shows how the stack and heap grow in opposite directions in a virtual address space:

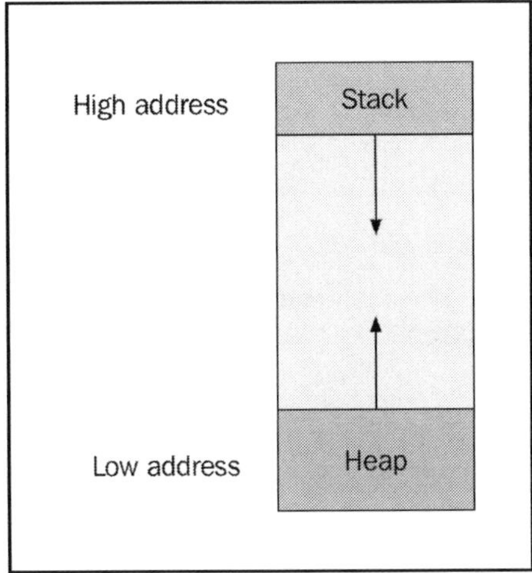

An address space of a process. The stack and the heap grows in opposite directions.

Stack memory

The stack differs in many ways compared to the heap. Here are some of the unique properties of the stack:

- The stack is a contiguous memory block.
- It has a fixed maximum size. If a program exceeds the maximum stack size, the program will crash.
- The stack memory never becomes fragmented.
- Allocating memory from the stack is always fast.
- Each thread in a program has its own stack.

The code examples that follow in this section will examine some of these properties. Let's start with allocations and deallocations to get a feel for how the stack is used in a program.

We can easily find out in which direction the stack grows by inspecting the address of stack-allocated data. The following example code demonstrates how the stack grows and contracts when entering and leaving functions:

```
auto func2() {
  auto i = 0;
  std::cout << "func2(): " << std::addressof(i) << '\n';
}
```

```
auto func1() {
  auto i = 0;
  std::cout << "func1(): " << std::addressof(i) << '\n';
  func2();
}

auto main() -> int {
  auto i = 0;
  std::cout << "main(): " << std::addressof(i) << '\n';
  fun1();
  fun2();
}
```

A possible output when running the program could look like this:

```
main(): 0x7ea075ac
func1(): 0x7ea07594
func2(): 0x7ea0757c
func2(): 0x7ea07594
```

By printing the address of the stack allocated integer, we can determine how much and in which direction the stack grows on my platform. The stack grows by 24 bytes each time we enter either `func1()` or `func2()`. The integer `i`, which will be allocated on the stack, is 4 bytes long. The remaining 20 bytes contain data needed when the function ends, such as the return address. The following diagram illustrates how the stack grows and contracts during the execution of the program. The first box illustrates how the memory looks when the program has just entered the `main()` function. The second box shows how the stack has increased when we execute `func1()` and so on:

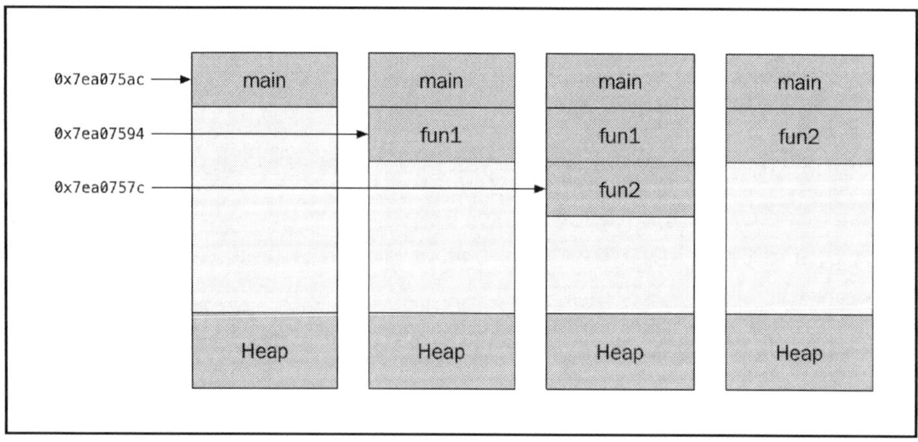

The stack grows and contracts when functions are entered and returns.

The total memory allocated for the stack is a fixed size contiguous memory block created at thread startup. So, how big is the stack and what happens when we reach the limit of the stack? As mentioned earlier, the stack grows each time the program enters a function and contracts when the function returns. The most common reason for the stack to overflow is by deep recursive calls and/or by using large automatic variables on the stack. The maximum size of the stack differs among platforms and can also be configured for individual processes.

Let's see if we can write a program to see how big the stack is by default on my system. We begin by writing a function `func()`, which will recurse infinitely. At the beginning of each function, we'll allocate a one-kilobyte variable, which will be placed onto the stack every time we enter `func()`. Every time `func()` is executed, we print the current size of the stack:

```
auto func(char* stack_bottom_addr) -> void {
  char data[1024];
  std::cout << stack_bottom_addr - data << '\n';
  func(stack_bottom_addr);
}

auto main() -> int {
  char c;
  func(&c);
}
```

The size of the stack is only an estimate. We compute it by subtracting the address of the first local variable in `main()` with the first local variable defined in `func()`.

When I compiled the code with Clang, I got a warning that `func()` will never return. Normally, this is a warning that we should not ignore, but this time, this is just what we want, so we ignore the warning and run the program anyway. The program crashes after a short while when the stack has reached its limit. Before the program crashes, it manages to print out thousands of lines with the current size of the stack. The last lines of the output look like this:

```
...
8378667
8379755
8380843
```

Since we are subtracting `char` pointers, the size is in bytes, so it looks like the maximum size of the stack is around 8 MB on my system. On Unix-like systems, it is possible to set and get the stack size for processes by using the `ulimit` command with the option, `-s`:

```
$ ulimit -s
$ 8192
```

Ulimit (short for user limit) returns the current setting for the maximum stack size in kilobytes. The output of `ulimit` confirms the results from our experiment: the stack is about 8 MB on my Mac if I don't configure it explicitly.

With this example, we can also conclude that we don't want to run out of stack memory since the program will crash when that happens. Later in this chapter, we will see how to implement a rudimentary memory allocator to handle fixed-size allocations. We will then understand that the stack is just another type of memory allocator that can be implemented very efficiently because the usage pattern is always sequential. We always request and release memory at the top of the stack (the end of the contiguous memory). This ensures that the stack memory will never become fragmented and that we can allocate and deallocate memory by only moving a stack pointer.

Heap memory

The heap or the free store, which is a more correct term in C++, is where data with dynamic storage lives. As mentioned earlier, the heap is shared among multiple threads, which means that memory management for the heap needs to take concurrency into account.

This makes memory allocations in the heap more complicated than stack allocations, which are local per thread.

The allocation and deallocation pattern for stack memory is sequential in the sense that memory is always deallocated in the reverse order to that in which it was allocated. On the other hand, for dynamic memory, the allocations and deallocations can happen arbitrarily. The dynamic lifetime of objects and the variable sizes of memory allocations increase the risk for fragmented memory.

An easy way to understand the issue with memory fragmentation is to go through an example of how fragmented memory can occur. Suppose that we have a small contiguous memory block of 16 KB that we are allocating memory from. We are allocating objects of two types: type **A**, which is 1 KB, and type **B**, which is 2 KB. We first allocate an object of type **A** followed by an object of type **B**. This repeats until the memory looks like the following image:

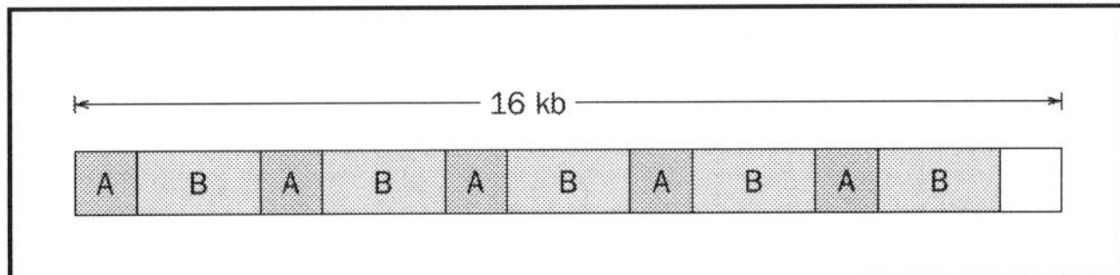

Next, all objects of type **A** are no longer needed, so they can be deallocated. The memory now looks like this:

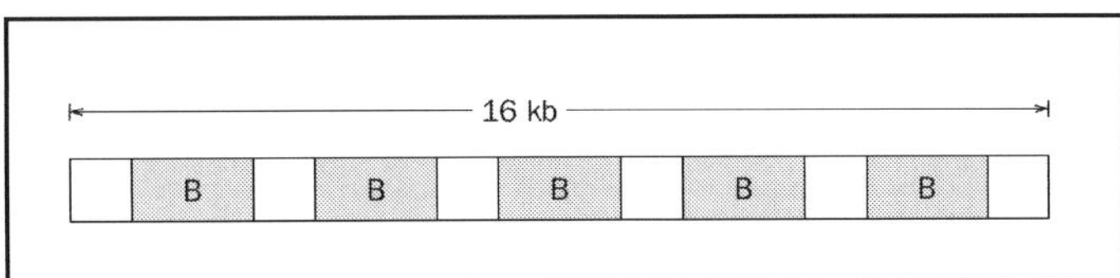

There is now 10 KB of memory in use and 6 KB is available. Now, suppose we want to allocate a new object of type **B**, which is 2 KB. Although there is 6 KB of free memory, there is nowhere we can find a 2 KB memory block because the memory has become fragmented.

Objects in memory

All the objects we use in a C++ program reside in memory. Here, we will explore how objects are created and deleted from memory and also describe how objects are laid out in memory.

Creating and deleting objects

In this section, we will dig into the details of using `new` and `delete`. We are all familiar with the standard way of using new for creating an object on the free store and then deleting it using `delete`:

```
auto user = new User{"John"};  // allocate and construct
user->print_name();            // use object
delete user;                   // destruct and deallocate
```

As the comments suggest, `new` actually does two things:

1. Allocates memory to hold a new object of the `User` type
2. Constructs a new `User` object in the allocated memory space by calling the constructor of the `User` class

The same thing goes with `delete`:

1. Destructs the `User` object by calling its destructor
2. Deallocates/frees the memory that the `User` object was placed in

Placement new

C++ allows us to separate memory allocation from object construction. We could, for example, allocate a byte array with `malloc()` and construct a new `User` object in that region of memory. Have a look at the following code snippet:

```
auto memory = std::malloc(sizeof(User));
auto user = new (memory) User("john");
```

The perhaps unfamiliar syntax using `new (memory)` is called *placement new*. It is a non-allocating form of new, which only constructs an object. In the preceding example, placement new constructs the `User` object and places it at the specified memory location. Since we are allocating the memory with `std::malloc()` for a single object, it is guaranteed to be correctly aligned. Later on, we will explore cases where we have to take alignment into account when using placement new.

There is no placement delete, so in order to destruct the object and free the memory, we need to call the destructor explicitly and then free the memory:

```
user->~User();
std::free(memory);
```

Note: this is the only time you should call a destructor explicitly. Never ever call a destructor like this unless you have created an object with placement new.

C++17 introduces a set of utility functions in `<memory>` for constructing and destroying objects without allocating or deallocating memory. So, instead of calling placement new, it is now possible to use some of the functions from `<memory>` whose names begin with `std::uninitialized_` for constructing, copying, and moving objects to an uninitialized memory area. And instead of calling the destructor explicitly, we can now use `std::destroy_at()` to destruct an object at a specific memory address without deallocating the memory.

The previous example could be rewritten using these new functions. Here is how it would look:

```
auto memory = std::malloc(sizeof(User));
auto user_ptr = reinterpret_cast<User*>(memory);
std::uninitialized_fill_n(user_ptr, 1, User{"john"});
std::destroy_at(user_ptr);
std::free(memory);
```

The new and delete operators

The function `operator new` is responsible for allocating memory when a new expression is invoked. The `new` operator can either be a globally defined function or a static member function of a class. It is possible to overload the global operators, `new` and `delete`. Later on in this chapter, we will see that this can be useful when analyzing memory usage. Here is how to do it:

```
auto operator new(size_t size) -> void* {
  void* p = std::malloc(size);
  std::cout << "allocated " << size << " byte(s)" << '\n';
  return p;
}

auto operator delete(void* p) noexcept -> void {
  std::cout << "deleted memory\n";
  return std::free(p);
}
```

We can verify that our overloaded operators are actually being used when creating and deleting a `char` object:

```
auto* p = new char{'a'}; // Outputs "allocated 1 byte(s)"
delete p;                // Outputs "deleted memory"
```

When creating and deleting an array of objects using the `new[]` and `delete[]` expressions, there is another pair of operators that are being used, namely `operator new[]` and `operator delete[]`. We can overload these operators in the same way:

```
auto operator new[](size_t size) -> void* {
  void* p = std::malloc(size);
  std::cout << "allocated " << size << " byte(s) with new[]" << '\n';
  return p;
}

auto operator delete[](void* p) noexcept -> void {
  std::cout << "deleted memory with delete[]\n";
  return std::free(p);
}
```

Keep in mind that if you overload `operator new`, you should also overload `operator delete`. Functions for allocating and deallocating memory come in pairs. Memory should be deallocated by the allocator that the memory was allocated by. For example, memory allocated with `std::malloc()` should always be freed using `std::free()`. Memory allocated with `operator new[]` should be deallocated using `operator delete[]`.

It is also possible to override a class-specific `operator new` and `operator delete`. This is probably more useful than overloading the global operators, since it is more likely that we need a custom dynamic memory allocator for a specific class. Here, we are overloading `operator new` and `operator delete` for the `Document` class:

```
class Document {
// ...
public:
  auto operator new(size_t size) -> void* {
    return ::operator new(size);
  }
  auto operator delete(void* p) -> void {
    ::operator delete(p);
  }
};
```

The class-specific version of `new` will be used when we create new dynamically allocated `Document` objects:

```
auto* p = new Document{}; // Uses class-specific operator new
delete p;
```

If we instead want to use global `new` and `delete`, it is still possible by using the global scope (`::`):

```
auto* p = ::new Document{}; // Uses global operator new
::delete p;
```

We will discuss memory allocators later in this chapter and we will then see the overloaded `new` and `delete` operators in use. To summarize what we have seen so far, a `new` expression involves two things: allocation and construction. `operator new` allocates memory and you can overload it globally or per class to customize dynamic memory management. Placement new can be used to construct an object in an already allocated memory area.

Memory alignment

The CPU reads memory into its registers one word at a time. The word size is 64 bits on a 64-bit architecture, 32 bits on a 32-bit architecture, and so forth. For the CPU to work efficiently when working with different data types, it has restrictions on the addresses where objects of different types are located. Every type in C++ has an alignment requirement that defines the addresses at which an object of a certain type should be located in memory. If the alignment of a type is 1, it means that the objects of that type can be located at any byte address. If the alignment of a type is 2, it means that the object of that type can only be located at addresses that are multiples of 2 and so on. We can use `alignof` to find out the alignment of a type:

```
// Possible output is 4
std::cout << alignof(int) << '\n';
```

When I run this code it outputs 4, which means that the alignment requirement of type `int` is 4 bytes on my platform, that is, objects of type `int` need to be located at an address that is a multiple of 4.

The following diagram shows two examples of memory from a system with 64-bit words. The upper row contains three 4-byte integers, which are located on addresses that are 4 bytes aligned. The CPU can load these integers into registers in an efficient way and never need to read multiple words when accessing one of the `int` members. Compare this with the second row, which contains two `int` members, which are located at unaligned addresses. The second `int` even spans over two-word boundaries. In the best case this is just inefficient, but on some platforms the program will crash:

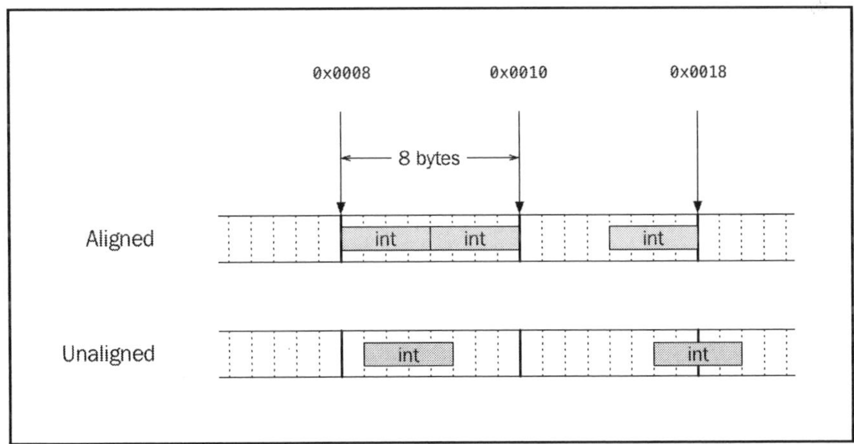

Two examples of memory which contains ints at aligned and unaligned memory addresses.

When allocating memory with new or std::malloc(), the memory we get back should be correctly aligned for the type we specify. The following code shows that the memory allocated for int is at least 4-bytes aligned:

```
auto p = new int();
auto address = reinterpret_cast<std::uintptr_t>(p);
std::cout << (address % 4ul) << '\n'; // Outputs 0
```

In fact, new and malloc() are guaranteed to always return memory suitably aligned for any scalar type (if it manages to return memory at all). The <cstddef> header provides us with a type called std::max_align_t, whose alignment requirement is at least as strict as all the scalar types. Later on, we will see that this type is useful when writing custom memory allocators. So, even if we only request memory for char on the free store, it will be aligned suitable for std::max_align_t. The following code shows that the memory returned from new is correctly aligned for std::max_align_t and also for any scalar type:

```
auto* p = new char{};
auto address = reinterpret_cast<std::uintptr_t>(p);
auto max_alignment = alignof(std::max_align_t);
std::cout << (address % max_alignment) << '\n'; // Outputs 0
```

Let's allocate char two times in a row with new:

```
auto* p1 = new char{'a'};
auto* p2 = new char{'b'};
```

Then, the memory may look something like this:

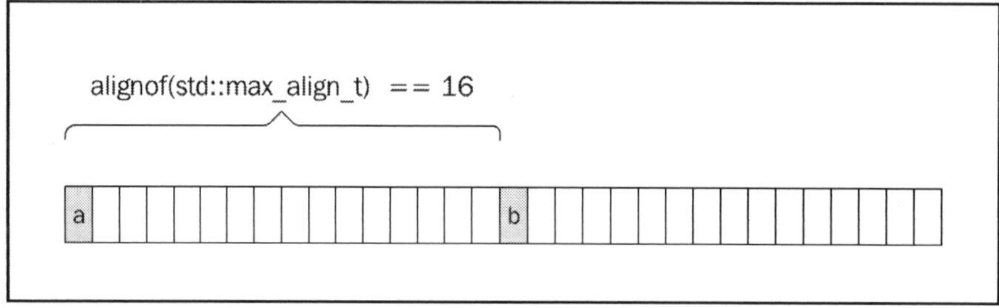

The space between p1 and p2 depends on the alignment requirements of std::max_align_t. On my system, it was 16 bytes and, therefore, there are 15 bytes between each char instance, even though the alignment of a char is only 1.

Padding

The compiler sometimes needs to add extra bytes, *padding*, in our user-defined types. When we define data members in a class or struct, the compiler is forced to place the members in the same order as we define them. However, the compiler also has to ensure that data members inside the class have the correct alignment; hence, it needs to add padding between data members if necessary. For example, assume we have a class defined as follows:

```
class Document {
  bool is_cached_{};
  double rank_{};
  int id_{};
};
std::cout << sizeof(Document) << '\n'; // Possible output is 24
```

The reason for the possible output being 24 is that the compiler inserts padding after `bool` and `int` to fulfill the alignment requirements of the individual data members and the entire class. The compiler converts the `Document` class to something like this:

```
class Document {
  bool is_cached_{};
  char padding1[7]; // Invisible padding inserted by compiler
  double rank_{};
  int id_{};
  char padding2[4]; // Invisible padding inserted by compiler
};
```

The first padding between `bool` and `double` is 7 bytes, since the `rank_` data member of the `double` type has an alignment of 8 bytes. The second padding that is added after `int` is 4 bytes. This is needed in order to fulfill the alignment requirements of the `Document` class itself. The member with the largest alignment requirement also determines the alignment requirement for the entire data structure. In our example, this means that the total size of the `Document` class must be a multiple of 8, since it contains a `double` value that is 8-byte aligned.

We now realize that we can rearrange the order of the data members in the `Document` class in a way that minimizes the padding inserted by the compiler, by starting with types with the biggest alignment requirements. Let's create a new version of the `Document` class:

```
// Version 2 of Document class
class Document {
  double rank_{};
  int id_{};
  bool is_cached_{};
};
```

With the rearrangement of the members, the compiler now only needs to pad after the `is_cached_` data member to adjust for the alignment of `Document`. This is how the class will look after padding:

```
// Version 2 of Document class after padding
class Document {
  double rank_{};
  int id_{};
  bool is_cached_{};
  char padding[3]; // Invisible padding inserted by compiler
};
```

The size of the new `Document` class is now only 16 bytes, compared to the first version, which was 24 bytes. We can verify this by using the `sizeof` operator again on our updated version of `Document`:

```
std::cout << sizeof(Document) << '\n'; // Possible output is 16
```

As a general rule, you can place the biggest data members in the beginning and the smallest members at the end. In this way, you can minimize the memory overhead caused by padding. Later on, we will see that we need to think about alignment when placing objects in memory regions that we have allocated, before we know the alignment of the objects that we are creating.

From a performance perspective, there can also be cases where you want to align objects to cache lines to minimize the number of cache lines an object spans over. While we are on the subject of cache friendliness, it should also be mentioned that it can be beneficial to place multiple data members that are frequently used together next to each other.

Memory ownership

Ownership of resources is a fundamental aspect to consider when programming. An owner of a resource is responsible for freeing the resource when it is no longer needed. A resource is typically a block of memory but could also be a database connection, a file handle, and so on. Ownership is important regardless of which programming language you are using. However, it is more apparent in languages such as C and C++, since dynamic memory is not garbage collected by default. Whenever we allocate dynamic memory in C++, we have to think about the ownership of that memory. Fortunately, there is now very good support in the language for expressing various types of ownership by using smart pointers, which we will cover later in this section.

The smart pointers from the standard library help us specify the ownership of dynamic variables. Other types of variables already have a defined ownership. For example, local variables are owned by the current scope. When the scope ends, the objects that have been created inside the scope will be automatically destroyed:

```
{
  auto user = User{};
} // user will automatically be destroyed when it goes out of scope
```

Static and global variables are owned by the program and will be destroyed when the program terminates:

```
static auto user = User{};
```

Data members are owned by the instances of the class that they belong to:

```
class Game {
  User user; // A Game object owns the User object
  // ...
};
```

It is only dynamic variables that do not have a default owner, and it is up to the programmer to make sure that all the dynamically allocated variables have an owner to control the lifetime of the variables:

```
auto user = new User{}; // Who owns user now?
```

With modern C++, we can write most of our code without explicit calls to `new` and `delete`, which is a great thing. Manually keeping track of calls to `new` and `delete` spread out over a large code base can easily become an issue. Raw pointers do not express any ownership, which makes ownership hard to track if we are only using raw pointers to refer to dynamic memory.

We recommend that you make ownership clear and explicit, but do strive to minimize explicit memory management. By following a few fairly simple rules for dealing with the ownership of memory, you will increase the likelihood of getting your code clean and correct without leaking resources. The coming sections will guide you through some best practices for that purpose.

Handling resources implicitly

First, make your objects implicitly handle the allocation/deallocation of dynamic memory:

```
auto func() {
  auto v = std::vector<int>{1, 2, 3, 4, 5};
}
```

In the preceding example, we are using both stack and dynamic memory, but we don't have to explicitly call `new` and `delete`. The `std::vector` object (of the `std::vector` class) we create is an automatic object that will live on the stack. Since it is owned by the scope, it will be automatically destroyed when the function returns. The `std::vector` object itself uses dynamic memory to store the integer elements. When the `std::vector` object goes out of scope, its destructor can safely free the dynamic memory. This pattern of letting destructors free dynamic memory makes it fairly easy to avoid memory leaks.

While we are on the subject of freeing resources, I think it makes sense to mention RAII. **RAII** is a well-known C++ technique, short for **Resource Acquisition Is Initialization**, where the lifetime of a resource is controlled by the lifetime of an object. The pattern is simple but extremely useful for handling resources (memory included). But let's say, for a change, that the resource we need is some sort of connection for sending requests. Whenever we are done using the connection, we (the owners) must remember to close it. Here is an example of how it looks when we open and close the connection explicitly to send a request:

```
auto send_request(const std::string& request) {
  auto connection = open_connection("http://www.example.com/");
  send_request(connection, request);
  close(connection);
}
```

As you can see, we have to remember to close the connection after we have used it or the connection will stay open (leak). In this example, it seems hard to forget, but once the code gets more complicated after inserting proper error handling and multiple exit paths, it will be hard to guarantee that the connection will always be closed. RAII solves this by relying on the fact that the lifetime of automatic variables is handled for us in a predictable way. What we need is an object that will have the same lifetime as the connection we get from the `open_connection()` call. We create a class for this, called `RAIIConnection`:

```
class RAIIConnection {
public:
  RAIIConnection(const std::string& url)
  : connection_{open_connection(url)} {}
  ~RAIIConnection() {
    try {
      close(connection_);
    }
    catch (const std::exception&) {
      // Handle error, but never throw from a destructor
    }
  }
  auto& get() { return connection_; }

private:
  Connection connection_;
};
```

The `Connection` object is now wrapped in a class that controls the lifetime of the connection (the resource). Instead of explicitly closing the connection, we can now let `RAIIConnection` handle this for us:

```
auto send_request(const std::string& request) {
  auto connection = RAIIConnection("http://www.example.com/");
  send_request(connection.get(), request);
  // No need to close the connection, it is implicitly handled
  // by the RAIIConnection destructor
}
```

Containers

Use standard containers to handle a collection of objects. The container you use will own the dynamic memory it needs to store the objects you add to it. This is a very effective way of minimizing explicit `new` and `delete` expressions in your code. We won't talk more about the containers here since they have already been covered in `Chapter 4`, *Data Structures*.

Smart pointers

The smart pointers from the standard library wrap a raw pointer and make the ownership of the object it points to explicit. When used correctly, there is no doubt about who is responsible for deleting a dynamic object. The three smart pointer types are `std::unique_ptr`, `std::shared_ptr`, and `std::weak_ptr`. As their names suggest, they represent three types of ownership of an object:

- Unique ownership expresses that I, and only I, own the object. When I'm done using it, I will delete it.
- Shared ownership expresses that I own the object along with others. When no one needs the object anymore, it will be deleted.
- Weak ownership expresses that I'll use the object if it exists, but don't keep it alive just for me.

Unique pointer

The safest and least complicated ownership is unique ownership and should be the first thing that pops into your mind when thinking about smart pointers. Unique pointers represent unique ownership, that is, a resource is owned by exactly one entity. A unique ownership can be transferred to someone else, but it cannot be copied, since that would break the uniqueness. Unique pointers are also very efficient since they do not add any performance overhead compared to ordinary raw pointers. Here is how to use a `sed::unique_ptr`:

```
auto owner = std::make_unique<User>("John");
auto new_owner = std::move(owner); // Transfer ownership
```

Shared pointer

Shared ownership means that an object can have multiple owners. When the last owner ceases to exist, the object will be deleted. This is a very useful pointer type, but is also more complicated than unique pointer.

The `std::shared_ptr` object uses reference counting to keep track of the number of owners an object has. When the counter reaches 0, the object will be deleted. The counter needs to be stored somewhere, so it does have some memory overhead compared with the unique pointer. Also, `std::shared_ptr` is thread-safe, so the counter needs to be updated atomically to prevent race conditions.

The recommended way of creating objects owned by shared pointers is to use `std::make_shared()`. It is both safer (from an exception-safety point of view) and more efficient than creating the object manually with `new` and then passing it to a `std::shared_ptr` constructor. By overloading `operator new` and `operator delete` again to track allocations, we can conduct an experiment to find out why using `std::make_shared()` is more efficient:

```
auto operator new(size_t size) -> void* {
  void* p = std::malloc(size);
  std::cout << "allocated " << size << " byte(s)" << '\n';
  return p;
}

auto operator delete(void* p) noexcept -> void {
  std::cout << "deleted memory\n";
  return std::free(p);
}
```

Now let's try the recommended way first, using `std::make_shared()`:

```
auto main() -> int {
 auto i = std::make_shared<double>(42.0);
 return 0;
}
```

The output when running the program is as follows:

```
allocated 32 bytes
deleted memory
```

Now, let's allocate the `int` value explicitly by using `new` and then pass it to the `std::shared_ptr` constructor:

```
auto main() -> int {
  auto i = std::shared_ptr<double>(new double{42.0});
  return 0;
}
```

The program will generate the following output:

```
allocated 4 bytes
allocated 32 bytes
deleted memory
deleted memory
```

We can conclude that the second version needs two allocations, one for the `double` and one for the `std::shared_ptr`, whereas the first version only needed one allocation. This also means that, by using `std::make_shared()`, our code will be more cache-friendly, thanks to spatial locality.

Weak pointer

Weak ownership doesn't keep any objects alive; it only allows us to use an object if someone else owns it. Why would you want such a fuzzy ownership as weak ownership? One common reason for using a weak pointer is to break a reference cycle. A reference cycle occurs when two or more objects refer to each other using shared pointers. Even if all external `std::shared_ptr` constructors are gone, the objects are kept alive by referring to themselves.

Why not just use a raw pointer? Isn't the weak pointer exactly what a raw pointer already is? Not at all. A weak pointer is safe to use since we cannot reference the object unless it actually exists, which is not the case with a dangling raw pointer. An example will clarify this:

```
auto i = std::make_shared<int>(10);
auto weak_i = std::weak_ptr<int>{i};
// Maybe i.reset() happens here so that the int is deleted...
if (auto shared_i = weak_i.lock()) {
  // We managed to convert our weak pointer to a shared pointer
  std::cout << *shared_i << '\n';
}
else {
  std::cout << "weak_i has expired, shared_ptr was nullptr\n";
}
```

Whenever we try to use the weak pointer, we need to convert it to a shared pointer first using the member function `lock()`. If the object hasn't expired, the shared pointer will be a valid pointer to that object; otherwise, we will get an empty `std::shared_ptr` back. This way, we can avoid dangling pointers when using `std::weak_ptr` instead of raw pointers.

Small size optimization

One of the great things about containers such as `std::vector` is that they automatically allocate dynamic memory when needed. Sometimes, though, the use of dynamic memory for container objects that only contain a few small elements can hurt the performance. It would be more efficient to keep the elements in the container itself and only use stack memory instead of allocating small regions of memory on the heap. Most modern implementations of `std::string` will take advantage of the fact that a lot of strings in a normal program are short and that short strings are more efficient to handle without the use of heap memory.

One alternative is to keep a small separate buffer in the string class itself, which can be used when the string content is short. This would increase the size of the string class even when the short buffer is not used. So, a more memory-efficient solution is to use a union, which can hold a short buffer when the string is in short mode and, otherwise, hold the data members it needs to handle a dynamically allocated buffer. The technique for optimizing a container for handling small data is usually referred to as small string optimization for strings, or small size optimization and small buffer optimization for other types. We have many names for the things we love.

A short code example will demonstrate how `std::string` from libc++ from LLVM behaves on my 64-bit system:

```
auto allocated = size_t{0};
// Overload operator new and delete to track allocations
auto operator new(size_t size) -> void* {
  void* p = std::malloc(size);
  allocated += size;
  return p;
}

auto operator delete(void* p) noexcept -> void {
  return std::free(p);
}

auto main() -> int {
  allocated = 0;
```

```
    auto s = std::string{""}; // Elaborate with different string sizes
    std::cout << "stack space = " << sizeof(s)
      << ", heap space = " << allocated
      << ", capacity = " << s.capacity() << '\n';
}
```

The code starts by overloading global `operator new` and `operator delete` for the purpose of tracking dynamic memory allocations. We can now start testing different sizes of the string `s` to see how `std::string` behaves. When building and running the preceding example in the release mode on my system, it generates the following output:

```
stack space = 24, heap space = 0, capacity = 22
```

This output tells us that `std::string` occupies 24 bytes on the stack and that it has a capacity of 22 chars without using any heap memory. Let's verify that this is actually true by replacing the empty string with a string of 22 chars:

```
auto s = std::string{"1234567890123456789012"};
```

The program still produces the same output and verifies that no dynamic memory has been allocated. But what happens when we increase the string to hold 23 characters instead?

```
auto s = std::string{"12345678901234567890123"};
```

Running the program now produces the following output:

```
stack space = 24, heap space = 32, capacity = 31
```

The `std::string` class has now been forced to use the heap for storing the string. It allocates 32 bytes and reports that the capacity is 31. This is because libc++ always stores a null-terminated string internally and, therefore, needs an extra byte at the end for the null character. It is still quite remarkable that the string class can be only 24 bytes and can hold strings of 22 characters in length without allocating any memory. How does it do it? As mentioned earlier, it is common to save memory by using a union with two different layouts: one for the short mode and one for the long mode. There is a lot of cleverness in the real libc++ implementation to make the maximum use of the 24 bytes that are available. The code here is simplified for the purpose of demonstrating the concept. The layout for the long mode looks like this:

```
struct Long {
  size_t capacity_{};
  size_t size_{};
  char* data_{};
};
```

Each member in the long layout is 8 bytes so the total size is 24 bytes. The `char` pointer `data_` is a pointer to the dynamically allocated memory that will hold long strings. The layout of the short mode looks something like this:

```
struct Short {
  unsigned char size_{};
  char data_[23]{};
};
```

In the short mode, there is no need to use a variable for the capacity, since it is a compile-time constant. It is also possible to use a smaller type for the `size_` data member in this layout, since we know that the length of the string can only range from 0 to 22 if it is a short string.

Both the layouts are combined using a union:

```
union u_ {
  Short short_layout_;
  Long long_layout_;
};
```

There is one piece missing, though: how can the string class know whether it is currently storing a short string or a long string? A flag is needed to indicate this, but where is it stored? It turns out that *libc++* uses the least significant bit on the `capactiy_` data member in the long mode and the least significant bit on the `size_` data member in the short mode. For the long mode, this bit is redundant anyway since the string always allocates memory sizes that are multiples of 2. In the short mode, it is possible to use only 7 bits for storing the size so that one bit can be used for the flag. It becomes even more complicated when writing this code to handle big endian byte order, since the bit needs to be placed in memory at the same location regardless of whether we are using the short struct or the long struct of the union. You can look up the details in the *libc++* implementation at `https://github.com/llvm-mirror/libcxx`.

Clever tricks like this are the reason that you should strive to use the efficient and well-tested classes provided by the standard library before you try to roll out your own. Nevertheless, knowing about those optimizations and how they work is important and useful, even if you never need to write one yourself.

The following diagram summarizes our simplified (but still, rather, complicated) memory layout of the union used by an efficient implementation of the small string optimization:

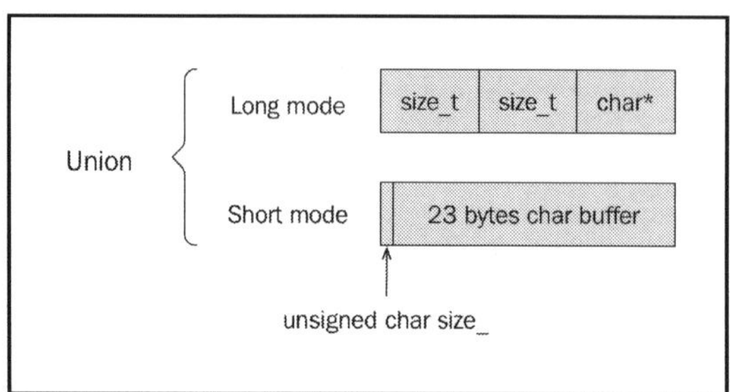

The union of the two different layouts used for handling short strings and long strings, respectively.

Custom memory management

We have come a long way in this chapter now. We have covered the basics of virtual memory, the stack and the heap, the `new` and `delete` expressions, memory ownership, and alignment and padding. But before we close this chapter, we are going to show how to customize the memory management in C++. We will see how the parts that we went through earlier in this chapter will come in handy when writing a custom memory allocator.

But first, what is a custom memory manager and why do we need one?

When using `new` or `malloc()` to allocate memory, we use the built-in memory management system in C++. Most implementations of `operator new` use `malloc()`, which is a general-purpose memory allocator. In other words, designing and building a general-purpose memory manager is a complicated task and there are many people who have already spent a lot of time researching this topic. Still, there are several reasons why you might want to write a custom memory manager. Here are some examples:

- **Debugging and diagnostics**: We have already done this a couple of times in this chapter by overloading `operator new` and `operator delete` just to print out some debugging information.
- **Sandboxing**: A custom memory manager can provide a sandbox for code that isn't allowed to allocate unrestricted memory. The sandbox can also track memory allocations and release memory when the sandboxed code finishes executing.

- **Performance**: If we need dynamic memory and can't avoid allocations, we may have to write a custom memory manager that performs better for our specific needs. Later on, we will cover some of the circumstances that we could utilize to outperform `malloc()`.

With that said, many experienced C++ programmers have never faced a problem that actually required them to customize the standard memory manager that comes with the system. This is a good indication of how well the general-purpose memory managers actually are today, despite all the requirements they have to fulfill without any knowledge about our specific use cases. The more we know about the memory usage patterns in our application, the better the chances are that we can actually write something more efficient than `malloc()`. Remember the stack, for example? Allocating and deallocating memory from the stack is very fast compared to the heap, thanks to the fact that it doesn't need to handle multiple threads and that allocations and deallocations are guaranteed to always happen in the reverse order.

Building a custom memory manager usually starts with analyzing the exact memory usage patterns and then implementing an arena.

Building an arena

Two frequently used terms when working with memory allocators are *arena* and *memory pool*. We will not distinguish between these terms in this book. By arena, we mean a block of contiguous memory including a strategy for handing out parts of that memory and reclaiming it later on. This could technically also be called an allocator, but we will use that term to refer to allocators used by the standard library. The custom allocator we will develop later will be implemented using the arena we create here.

There are some general strategies that can be used when designing an arena that will make allocations and deallocations likely to perform better than `malloc()` and `free()`:

- **Single-threaded**: If we know that an arena will only be used from one thread, there is no need to protect data with synchronization primitives, such as locks or atomics. There is no risk that the client using the arena may be blocked by some other thread, which is important in real-time contexts.
- **Fixed-size allocations**: If the arena only hands out memory blocks of fixed size, it is relatively easy to reclaim memory efficiently without memory fragmentation by using a free list.

- **Limited lifetime**: If you know that objects allocated from an arena only need to live during a limited and well-defined lifetime, the arena can postpone the reclamation and free the memory all at once. An example could be objects created while handling a request in a server application. When the request has finished, all the memory that was handed out during the request can be reclaimed in one step. Of course, the arena needs to be big enough to handle all the allocations during the request without reclaiming memory continually; otherwise, this strategy will not work.

We will not go into further details about these strategies, but it is good to be aware of the possibilities when looking for ways to improve memory management in your program. As is often the case with optimizing software, the key is to understand the circumstances under which your program will run and to analyze the specific memory usage patterns in order to find ways to improve a custom memory manager compared to a general-purpose one.

Next, we will have a look at a simple arena class template, which can be used for small or few objects that need dynamic storage duration, but where the memory it needs usually is so small that it can be placed on the stack. This code is based on Howard Hinnant's `short_alloc` published in the page, `https://howardhinnant.github.io/stack_alloc.html`. This is a great place to start if you want to dig deeper into custom memory management. We think it is a good example for demonstration purposes because it can handle multiple sized objects, which require proper handling of alignment. But again, keep in mind that this is a simplified version for demonstrating the concept rather than providing you with production-ready code:

```
template <size_t N>
class Arena {
  static constexpr size_t alignment = alignof(std::max_align_t);
public:
  Arena() noexcept : ptr_(buffer_) {}
  Arena(const Arena&) = delete;
  Arena& operator=(const Arena&) = delete;

  auto reset() noexcept { ptr_ = buffer_; }
  static constexpr auto size() noexcept { return N; }
  auto used() const noexcept {
    return static_cast<size_t>(ptr_ - buffer_);
  }
  auto allocate(size_t n) -> char*;
  auto deallocate(char* p, size_t n) noexcept -> void;
private:
  static auto align_up(size_t n) noexcept -> size_t {
    return (n + (alignment-1)) & ~(alignment-1);
  }
```

```
    auto pointer_in_buffer(const char* p) const noexcept -> bool {
      return buffer_ <= p && p <= buffer_ + N;
    }
    alignas(alignment) char buffer_[N];
    char* ptr_{};
};
```

The arena contains a `char` buffer, whose size is determined at compile time. This makes it possible to create an arena object on the stack or as a variable with static or thread local storage duration. The alignment of the memory that this version will hand out will be the same as when using `malloc()`—it's suitable for any type. This is a bit wasteful if we use the arena for small types with smaller alignment requirements, but we ignore this here. The buffer is a `char` array that might be allocated on the stack; hence, there is no guarantee that it will be aligned for types other than char unless we apply the `alignas` specifier to the array. The helper `align_up()` function may look complicated if you are not used to bitwise operations. However, it basically just rounds up to the alignment requirement that we use.

When reclaiming memory, we need to know whether the pointer we are asked to reclaim actually belongs to our arena. The `pointer_in_buffer()` function checks this by comparing a pointer address with the arena's address range.

Next, we need the implementation of allocate and deallocate:

```
template<size_t N>
auto Arena<N>::allocate(size_t n) -> char* {
  const auto aligned_n = align_up(n);
  const auto available_bytes =
  static_cast<decltype(aligned_n)>(buffer_ + N - ptr_);
  if (available_bytes >= aligned_n) {
    char* r = ptr_;
    ptr_ += aligned_n;
    return r;
  }
  return static_cast<char*>(::operator new(n));
}
```

Allocate returns a pointer to a correctly aligned memory with the specified size, n. If there is no available space in the buffer for the requested size, it will fall back to using `operator new` instead.

The following `deallocate()` function first checks whether the pointer to the memory to be deallocated is from the buffer or whether it has been allocated with `operator new`. If it is not from the buffer, we simply delete it with `operator delete`. Otherwise, we check whether the memory to be deallocated is the last memory we handed out from the buffer and, then, reclaim it by moving the current `ptr_`, just as a stack would do. We simply ignore other attempts to reclaim the memory:

```
template<size_t N>
auto Arena<N>::deallocate(char* p, size_t n) noexcept -> void {
  if (pointer_in_buffer(p)) {
    n = align_up(n);
    if (p + n == ptr_) {
      ptr_ = p;
    }
  }
  else {
    ::operator delete(p);
  }
}
```

That's about it; our arena is now ready to be used. Let's use it when allocating `User` objects:

```
auto user_arena = Arena<1024>{};

class User {
public:
  auto operator new(size_t size) -> void* {
    return user_arena.allocate(size);
  }
  auto operator delete(void* p) -> void {
    user_arena.deallocate(static_cast<char*>(p), sizeof(User));
  }
  auto operator new[](size_t size) -> void* {
    return user_arena.allocate(size);
  }
  auto operator delete[](void* p, size_t size) -> void {
    user_arena.deallocate(static_cast<char*>(p), size);
  }
private:
  int id_{};
};

auto main() -> int {
  // No dynamic memory is allocated when we create the users
  auto user1 = new User{};
  delete user1;
```

```
  auto users = new User[10];
  delete [] users;

  auto user2 = std::make_unique<User>();
  return 0;
}
```

A custom memory allocator

When trying our custom memory manager with a specific type, it worked great! There is a problem, though. It turns out that the class-specific `operator new` is not called on all the occasions that we first might have expected. Consider the following code:

```
auto user = std::make_shared<User>("John");
```

What happens when we want to have `std::vector` of 10 users?

```
auto users = std::vector<User>{};
users.reserve(10);
```

In neither of the two cases is our custom memory manager being used. Why? Starting with the shared pointer, we have to go back to the example earlier where we saw that `std::make_shared()` actually allocates memory for both reference counting data and the object it should point to. There is no way that `std::make_shared()` can use an expression such as `new User()` to create the user object and the counter with only one allocation. Instead, it allocates memory and constructs the user object using placement new.

The `std::vector` object is similar. It doesn't construct 10 objects by default in an array when we call `reserve()`. This would have required a default constructor for all the classes to be used with the vector. Instead, it allocates memory that can be used for holding 10 user objects when they are being added. Again, placement new is the tool for making this possible.

Fortunately, we can provide a *custom memory allocator* to both `std::vector` and `std::shared_ptr` in order to have them use our custom memory manager. This is true for the rest of the containers in the standard library as well. If we don't supply a custom allocator, the containers will use the default `std::allocator<T>` class. So, what we need in order to use our arena is to write an allocator that can be used by the containers.

Custom allocators have been a hot and well-debated topic for a long time in the C++ community. Many custom containers have been implemented to control how memory is managed instead of using the standard containers with custom allocators, probably for good reasons. However, the support and requirements for writing a custom allocator has been improved in C++11, and it is now a lot better than it used to be. Here, we will only focus on allocators from C++11 and beyond.

A minimal allocator in C++11 now looks like this:

```
template<typename T>
struct Alloc {
  using value_type = T;
  Alloc();
  template<typename U> Alloc(const Alloc<U>&);
  T* allocate(size_t n);
  auto deallocate(T*, size_t) const noexcept -> void;
};
template<typename T>
auto operator==(const Alloc<T>&, const Alloc<T>&) -> bool;
template<typename T>
auto operator!=(const Alloc<T>&, const Alloc<T>&) -> bool;
```

It's really not that much code anymore, thanks to the improvements in C++11. The container that uses the allocator actually uses `std::allocator_traits`, which provides reasonable defaults if the allocator omits them. I recommend you have a look at the `std::allocator_traits` to see what traits can be configured and what the defaults are.

By using `malloc()` and `free()`, we could quite easily implement a minimal custom allocator. Here, we will show the old and famous `Mallocator`, first published in a blog post by *Stephan T. Lavavej*, to demonstrate how to write a minimal custom allocator using `malloc()` and `free()`. Since then, it has been updated for C++11 to make it even slimmer. Here is how it looks:

```
template <class T>
struct Mallocator {

  using value_type = T;
  Mallocator() noexcept {} // default ctor not required

  template <class U>
  Mallocator(const Mallocator<U>&) noexcept {}

  template <class U>
  auto operator==(const Mallocator<U>&) const noexcept {
    return true;
```

```
  }

  template <class U>
  auto operator!=(const Mallocator<U>&) const noexcept {
    return false;
  }
  auto allocate(const size_t n) const -> T* {
    if (n == 0) {
      return nullptr;
    }
    if (n > std::numeric_limits<size_t>::max() / sizeof(T)) {
      throw std::bad_array_new_length{};
    }
    void* const pv = malloc(n * sizeof(T));
    if (pv == nullptr) {
      throw std::bad_alloc{};
    }
    return static_cast<T*>(pv);
  }
  auto deallocate(T* const p, size_t) const noexcept -> void {
    free(p);
  }
};
```

`Mallocator` is a stateless allocator, which means that the allocator instance itself doesn't have any mutable state; instead, it uses global functions for allocation and deallocation, namely `malloc()` and `free()`. A stateless allocator should always compare equal to the allocators of the same type. It indicates that memory allocated with `Mallocator` should also be deallocated with `Mallocator`, regardless of the `Mallocator` instance. A stateless allocator is the least complicated allocator to write but it is also limited, since it depends on the global state.

To use our arena as a stack-allocated object, we will need a stateful allocator that can reference the arena instance. Here, the arena class that we implemented really starts to make sense. Say, for example, that we want to use one of the standard containers in a function to do some processing. We know that, most of the time, we are dealing with very small amounts of data that will fit on the stack. But once we use the containers from the standard library, they will allocate memory from the heap, which, in this case, will hurt the performance.

What are the alternatives for using the stack to manage the data and avoid unnecessary heap allocations? One alternative is to build a custom container that uses a variation of the small size optimization we looked at for `std::string`. It is also possible to use a container from *Boost*, for example, `boost::container::small_vector`, which is based on LLVM's small vector. We advise you to check it out if you haven't already: `http://www.boost.org/doc/libs/1_64_0/doc/html/container/non_standard_containers.html`.

Yet another alternative, though, is to use a custom allocator, which we will explore next. Since we already have an arena template class ready, we could simply create the instance of an arena on the stack and have a custom allocator use it for the allocations. What we then need to do is to implement a stateful allocator, which could hold a reference to the stack-allocated arena object.

Again, this custom allocator that we will implement is a simplified version of Howard Hinnant's `short_alloc`:

```
template <class T, size_t N>
struct ShortAlloc {

  using value_type = T;
  using arena_type = Arena<N>;

  ShortAlloc(const ShortAlloc&) = default;
  ShortAlloc& operator=(const ShortAlloc&) = delete;

  ShortAlloc(arena_type& arena) noexcept : arena_{arena} { }

  template <class U>
  ShortAlloc(const ShortAlloc<U, N>& other) noexcept
  : arena_{other.arena_} {}

  template <class U> struct rebind {
    using other = ShortAlloc<U, N>;
  };

  auto allocate(size_t n) -> T* {
    return reinterpret_cast<T*>(arena_.allocate(n*sizeof(T)));
  }
  auto deallocate(T* p, size_t n) noexcept -> void {
    arena_.deallocate(reinterpret_cast<char*>(p), n*sizeof(T));
  }

  template <class U, size_t M>
  auto operator==(const ShortAlloc<U, M>& other) const noexcept {
    return
```

```
      N == M &&
      std::addressof(arena_) == std::addressof(other.arena_);
  }
  template <class U, size_t M>
  auto operator!=(const ShortAlloc<U, M>& other) const noexcept {
    return !(*this == other);
  }
  template <class U, size_t M> friend struct ShortAlloc;

private:
  arena_type& arena_;
};
```

The allocator holds a reference to the arena. This is the only state the allocator has. Allocate and deallocate simply forward their requests to the arena. The compare operators ensure that two instances of the `ShortAlloc` type are using the same arena.

Now, the allocator and arena we implemented can be used with a standard container to avoid dynamic memory allocations. When we are using small data, we can handle all allocations using the stack instead. Let's see an example using `std::set`:

```
auto main() -> int {

  using SmallSet =
    std::set<int, std::less<int>, ShortAlloc<int, 512>>;

  auto stack_arena = SmallSet::allocator_type::arena_type{};
  auto unique_numbers = SmallSet{stack_arena};
  // Read numbers from stdin
  auto n = int{};
  while (std::cin >> n)
    unique_numbers.insert(n);
  // Print unique numbers
  for (const auto& number : unique_numbers)
    std::cout << number << '\n';
}
```

The program reads integers from standard input until the end-of-file is reached (*Ctrl* + *D* on Unix-like systems and *Ctrl* + *Z* on Windows). It then prints the unique numbers in an ascending order. Depending on how many numbers are read from `stdin`, the program will use stack memory or dynamic memory by using our `ShortAlloc` allocator.

Summary

This chapter has covered a lot of ground, starting with the basics of virtual memory and finally implementing a custom allocator that can be used by containers from the standard library. A good understanding of how your program uses memory is important. Overuse of dynamic memory can be a performance bottleneck that you might need to optimize away. Before you start implementing your own containers or custom memory allocators, bear in mind that many people before you have probably had very similar memory issues to the ones you may face. So, there is a good chance that the right tool for you is already out there in a library. Building custom memory managers that are fast, safe, and robust is a challenge.

8

Metaprogramming and Compile-Time Evaluation

C++ has the ability to evaluate expressions at compile time, meaning that values are already calculated when the program executes. Even though metaprogramming has been possible since C++98; however, it was very complicated due to its complex template-based syntax. With the introduction of `constexpr` and, recently, `if constexpr`, metaprogramming has become much more similar to writing regular code.

This chapter will give you a brief introduction of compile-time expression evaluations in C++ and how they can be used for optimization.

Introduction to template metaprogramming

When writing regular C++ code, it is eventually transformed to machine code. Metaprogramming, on the other hand, is code that transforms itself into regular C++ code. When using metaprogramming, it is important to remember that its main use case is to make great libraries and, thereby, hide complex constructs/optimizations from the user code. So, remember that howsoever complex the interior of the metacode may be, it's important to hide it behind a good interface so that the user code base is easy to read and use.

In its simplest and most common form, template metaprogramming in C++ is used to generate functions, values, and classes that accept different types.

Let's take a look at a simple `pow()` function and a `Rectangle` class. By using a template parameter, the rectangle can be used with any integer or floating point type. Without templates, the programmer would have to create a separate function/class for every base type.

The compiler then compiles/generates the metacode to regular C++ code, which is further compiled to machine code. We will hereforth refer to C++ code generated from metaprogramming as regular C++ code.

Writing metaprogramming code can be very complex; something that can make it easier, is to imagine how the expected regular C++ code is intended to be.

Here is an example of a simple templated function:

```
// pow_n accepts any number type
template <typename T>
auto pow_n(const T& v, int n) {
  auto product = T{1};
  for(int i = 0; i < n; ++i) {
    product *= v;
  }
  return product;
}
```

Using this function will generate a function whose return type is dependent on the template parameter type:

```
auto x = pow_n<float>(2.0f, 3); // x is a float
auto y = pow_n<int>(3, 3);      // y is an int
```

Correspondingly, a simple template-based class is constructed like this:

```
// Rectangle can be of any type
template <typename T>
class Rectangle {
public:
  Rectangle(T x, T y, T w, T h) : x_{x}, y_{y}, w_{w}, h_{h} {}
  auto area() const { return w_ * h_; }
  auto width() const { return w_; }
  auto height() const { return h_; }
private:
  T x_{}, y_{}, w_{}, h_{};
};
```

When a template class is utilized, the programmer specifies the types for which the template should generate the code:

```
// rectf is a rectangle of floats
auto rectf = Rectangle<float>{2.0f, 2.0f, 4.0f, 4.0f};
// recti is a rectangle of integers
auto recti = Rectangle<int>{-2, -2, 4, 4};
```

A standalone function can then use a template to accept a rectangle with dimensions of any data type but no other class type than `Rectangle`, as follows:

```
template <typename T>
auto is_square(const Rectangle<T>& r) -> bool {
  return r.width() == r.height();
}
```

Using integers as template parameters

Beyond general types, a template can also be of any integral type, which means that the compiler generates a new function for every integer passed as the template argument:

```
template <int N, typename T>
auto const_pow_n(const T& v) {
  auto product = T{1};
  for(int i = 0; i < N; ++i) {
    product *= v;
  }
  return product;
}

// The compiler generates a function which squares the value
auto x2 = const_pow_n<float, 2>(4.0f);
// The compiler generates a function which cubes the value
auto x3 = const_pow_n<float, 3>(4.0f);
```

Note the difference between the template parameter `N` and the function parameter `v`. For every value of `N`, **the compiler generates a new function**. However, `v` is passed as a regular parameter and, as such, does not result in a new function.

How the compiler handles a template function

When the compiler deals with a template function, it constructs a regular function/class with the template parameters expanded. The following code will make the compiler generate regular functions, as it utilizes templates:

```
auto valuei = int{42};
auto valuei_cubed = pow_n(valuei, 3);
auto valuef = float{42.42f};
auto valuef_squared = pow_n(valuef, 2);
auto valuef_const_squared = const_pow_n<2, float>(valuef);
auto valuef_const_cubed = const_pow_n<3, float>(valuef);
```

Thus, when compiled, as distinguished from regular functions, the compiler will generate new functions for every template parameter. This means that it is the equivalent of manually creating four different functions looking something like this:

```
auto pow_n__float(float v, int n) {...}
auto pow_n__int(int v, int n) {...}
auto const_pow_n__float_2(float v) {...}
auto const_pow_n__float_3(float v) {...}
```

This is important for understanding how metaprogramming works. The template code generates non-templated C++ code, which is then executed as regular code. If the generated C++ code does not compile, the error will be caught at compile time.

Review the templated version of `pow_n()`, and let's say, we want to prevent it from being called with negative exponents (the `n` value).

To prevent this in the runtime version, where `n` is a regular argument, we add a regular runtime assertion. Now, if the function is called with a negative value for `n`, the program will break:

```
template <typename T>
auto pow_n(const T& v, int n) {
  assert(n >= 0); // Only works for positive numbers
  auto product = T{1};
  for(int i = 0; i < n; ++i) {
    product *= v;
  }
  return product;
}
```

Using static_assert to trigger errors at compile time

If we do the same to the template version, we can utilize `static_assert()`. The `static_assert()` declaration, unlike a regular assert, will refuse to compile if the condition isn't fulfilled. So, it's better to break the build than to break at runtime. In the following example, if the template parameter `N` is a negative number, `static_assert()` will prevent the function from compiling:

```
template <typename T, int N>
auto const_pow_n(const T& v) {
  static_assert(N >= 0, "N must be positive");
  auto product = T{1};
  for(int i = 0; i < N; ++i) {
    product *= v;
  }
  return product;
}

auto x = const_pow_n<5>(2); // Compiles, N is positive
auto y = const_pow_n<-1>(2); // Does not compile, N is negative
```

In other words, with regular variables, the compiler is only aware of the type and has no idea what it contains. With compile-time values, the compiler knows both the type and the value. This allows the compiler to calculate other compile-time values.

Type traits

When doing template metaprogramming, you may often find yourself in situations where you need information about the types you are dealing with at compile time. Since the result of metaprogramming is the generated C++ code, the generated C++ code needs to be correct. This is, of course, never the case for traditional functions, as they only deal with specified types.

Type trait categories

There are two categories of type traits:

- Type traits that return information about a type as a boolean or an integer value
- Type traits that return a new type

The first category returns `true` or `false` depending on the input and ends with `_v` (short for value).

The `_v` postfix has been added in C++17. If your STL implementation does not provide `_v` postfixes for type traits, then you can use the older version, `std::is_floating_point<float>::value`. In other words, remove the `_v` extension and add `::value` at the end.

Here are some examples of compile-time type checking using type traits:

```
auto same_type = std::is_same_v<uint8_t, unsigned char>;
auto flt = 0.3f;
auto is_float_or_double = std::is_floating_point_v<decltype(flt)>;
class Parent {};
class Child : public Parent {};
class Infant {};
static_assert(std::is_base_of_v<Child, Parent>, "");
static_assert(!std::is_base_of_v<Infant, Parent>, "");
```

The second category returns a new type and ends with `_t` (short for type):

```
// Examples of type traits which transforms types
using value_type = std::remove_pointer_t<int*>; // value_type is an "int"
using ptr_type = std::add_pointer_t<float>; // ptr_type is a"float*"
```

Using type traits

In order to extract information about template types, the STL provides a type traits library, available in the `<type_traits>` header. All type traits are evaluated at compile time. For example, this function, which returns `1` if the value is zero or above and `-1`, otherwise, can immediately return `1` for unsigned integers as follows:

```
template <typename T>
auto sign_func(const T& v) -> int {
  if (std::is_unsigned_v<T>) {
    return 1;
  }
  return v < 0 ? -1 : 1;
}
```

As they are evaluated at compile time, the compiler will generate codes as shown in the following table when invoked with an unsigned and signed integer, respectively:

Used with an unsigned integer...	**...generated function:**

auto unsigned_v = uint32_t{32};
auto sign=sign_func(unsigned_v);
	int sign_func(const uint32_t& v){
	  if (true) {
	    return 1;
	  }
	  return v < 0 ? -1 : 1;
	}

Used with a signed integer...	**...generated function:**

auto unsigned_v=int32_t{32};
auto sign=sign_func(unsigned_v);
	int sign_func(const int32_t& v){
	  if (false) {
	    return 1;
	  }
	  return v < 0 ? -1 : 1;
	}

Receiving the type of a variable with decltype

The `decltype` keyword is used to retrieve the type of a variable and is used when an explicit type name is not available.

Sometimes, an explicit type name is not available, only the variable name is available. For example, *polymorphic lambda functions* (lambdas with `auto` as a parameter) do not name the type (as opposed to templated functions, where the type name has its own parameter):

Regular template function	**Lambda function**

Here, the type of `v` is visible as `T`:
template <typename T>
auto square_func(const T& v){
  return v * v;
}
	Here, the type of `v` is not visible, as it is only denoted as `auto`:
	auto square_func_lbd=[](auto v){
	  return v * v;
	};

Take the previous sign function; if we would like to rewrite it as a lambda function, we would have to extract the type of the variable via `decltype`.

Be aware, though, that there is a glitch here. The variable `v` is actually a reference and, therefore, we have to get the referenced-to type. This is achieved by using the type trait, `std::remove_reference_t`, which returns a type with the reference attribute removed, as follows:

```
auto sign_func = [](const auto& v) -> int {
  using ReferenceType = decltype(v);
  using ValueType = std::remove_reference_t<ReferenceType>;
  if (std::is_unsigned_v<ValueType>) {
    return 1;
  }
  return v < 0 ? -1 : 1;
};
```

The `decltype` keyword not only retrieves the type of a variable but can also be used on an expression in order to retrieve the type the expression returns.

This example takes any range or container and converts it to a vector. To determine the type of the values in the vector, the type returned by the `begin()` function of the container is utilized:

```
template <typename Range>
auto to_vector(const Range& r) {
  using IteratorType = decltype(r.begin());
  using ReferenceType = decltype(*IteratorType());
  using ValueType = std::decay_t<ReferenceType>;
  return std::vector<ValueType>(r.begin(), r.end());
}
```

Conditionally enable functions based on types with std::enable_if_t

The `std::enable_if_t` type trait is used for function overloading when dealing with a template function. While regular function overloading requires you to overload a function for every type you intend to use it with, `std::enable_if_t` uses a compile-time predicate for overloading.

Let's say we'd like to create an interpolate function, which mixes two values weighted by a power parameter from zero to one:

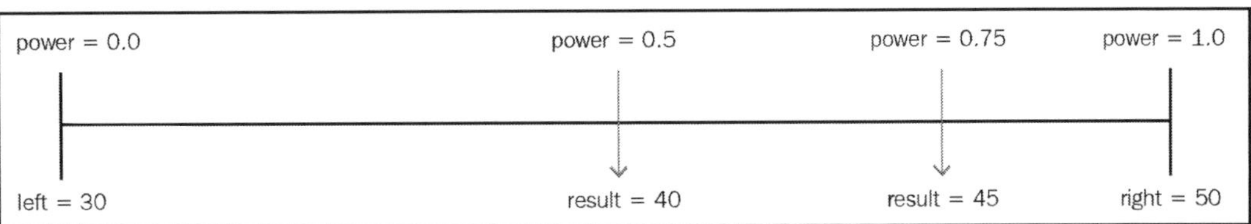

Illustration of interpolation function

As the power must be a decimal number, the function only works with floats and doubles. Using regular function overloading, we have to create two functions, one for floats and one for doubles:

```
auto interpolate(float left, float right, float power) {
  return left * (1 - power) + right * power;
}
auto interpolate(double left, double right, double power) {
  return left * (1 - power) + right * power;
}
```

If we template this function, we need to disallow its use for integers, as integers cannot hold decimal numbers. In order to prevent the user from accidentally calling the function with an integer type, `std::enable_if_t` is used to make the function visible only when a certain condition is fulfilled. In this case, the condition is that it is used with a floating point type.

The syntax for `std::enable_if_t` may seem a bit odd, but its syntax is as follows:

- It is used as a return type
- The first templated parameter is the condition
- The second parameter is the returned value if the condition is fulfilled

As seen in the following code snippet, `std::enable_if_t` is used as the return value of the function that it is intended to enable:

```
template <typename T>
auto interpolate(T left, T right, T power)
-> std::enable_if_t<std::is_floating_point_v<T>, T> {
  return left * (1 - power) + right * power;
}
```

If this function is called with a non-floating point type, the code will not compile, as the function only exists for floating points.

The preceding interpolation code can be implemented with only one multiplication, thereby achieving a slightly better performance, as follows:
`auto interpolated = left +(right-left) * power;`
The one used in the examples is just for better readability.

Introspecting class members with std::is_detected

At the time of writing this book, `std::is_detected` is currently located in the standard library extensions, but we think it is far too important to ignore in this chapter. If you are using GCC or Clang, it's currently located in `<experimental/type_traits>` and exists in the `std::experimental` namespace.

The `is_detected` type trait is used to detect if a class contains a particular member. Let's take a look at how it is used to detect whether a class has a particular member function by name. If the member function exists, the value of the returned type is true; otherwise, it's false.

Here are two completely different classes:

```
struct Octopus {
  auto mess_with_arms() {}
};
struct Whale {
  auto blow_a_fountain() {}
};
```

Using `std::is_detected`, we can ask the compiler what operations are achievable on the class, as follows:

```
#include <experimental/type_traits>
template <typename T>
using can_mess_with_arms = decltype(&T::mess_with_arms);
template <typename T>
using can_blow_a_fountain = decltype(&T::blow_a_fountain);

auto fish_tester() {
  namespace exp = std::experimental;
```

```
  // Octopus
  static_assert(exp::is_detected<can_mess_with_arms, Octopus>::value, "");
  static_assert(!exp::is_detected<can_blow_a_fountain, Octopus>::value,"");

  // Whale
  static_assert(!exp::is_detected<can_mess_with_arms, Whale>::value, "");
  static_assert(exp::is_detected<can_blow_a_fountain, Whale>::value, "");
}
```

As you can see in the example, we have to declare `typedef` to the member function we are detecting. The reason for this is that `is_detected` technically looks for a compile-time error, but instead of failing when the function being searched for is missing, it simply returns `false`. This means that `is_detected` can not only check for member functions but can also check for member typedefs or member variables. Here is how we would perform these checks:

```
struct Shark { using fin_type = float; };
struct Eel { int electricity_{}; };

template <typename T> using has_fin_type = typename T::fin_type;
template <typename T> using has_electricity = decltype(T::electricity_);

auto shark_and_shrimp_tester() {
  namespace exp = std::experimental;
  // The shark has a fin type but no electricity
  static_assert(exp::is_detected<has_fin_type, Shark>::value, "");
  static_assert(!exp::is_detected<has_electricity , Shark>::value, "");
  // The eel has electricity but no fins
  static_assert(exp::is_detected<has_electricity , Eel>::value, "");
  static_assert(!exp::is_detected<has_fin_type, Eel>::value, "");
}
```

Usage example of is_detected and enable_if_t combined

As `is_detected::value` is a compile-time Boolean, `is_detected` can be combined with `enable_if_t` to enable a certain function for classes that contain a particular member function.

For example, we can implement a generic print function that can print both the `to_string()` method and the `name_` member variable, depending on what the printed class has implemented:

```
namespace exp = std::experimental;
template<typename T> using has_to_string = decltype(&T::to_string);
template<typename T> using has_name_member = decltype(T::name_);

// Print the to_string() function if it exists in class
template <
 typename T,
 bool HasToString = exp::is_detected<has_to_string,T>::value,
 bool HasNameMember = exp::is_detected<has_name_member,T>::value
>
auto print(const T& v)
-> std::enable_if_t<HasToString && !HasNameMember> {
  std::cout << v.to_string() << '\n';
}

// Print the name_ member variable if it exists in class
template <
 typename T,
 bool HasToString = exp::is_detected<has_to_string, T>::value,
 bool HasNameMember = exp::is_detected<has_name_member, T>::value
>
auto print(const T& v)
-> std::enable_if_t<HasNameMember && !HasToString> {
  std::cout << v.name_ << '\n';
}
```

Test the methods with two classes, where one contains a `to_string()` method and the other one contains a `name_` member variable:

```
struct Squid {
  auto to_string() const { return std::string{"Steve the Squid"}; }
};
struct Salmon {
  Salmon() : name_{"Jeff the Salmon"} {}
  std::string name_{};
};

auto fish_printer() {
  print(Squid{}); // Prints "Steve the Squid"
  print(Salmon{}); // Prints "Jeff the Salmon"
}
```

The constexpr keyword

The `constexpr` keyword tells the compiler that a certain function is intended to be evaluated at compile time if all the conditions allowing for compile-time evaluation are fulfilled. Otherwise, it will execute at runtime, like a regular function.

A `constexpr` function has a few restrictions; it is not allowed to do the following:

- Allocate memory on the heap
- Throw exceptions
- Handle local static variables
- Handle `thread_local` variables
- Call any function, which, in itself, is not a constexpr.

Back in C++11, `constexpr` functions were only allowed to contain a single return statement, requiring the programmer to resort to recursion for more advanced `constexpr` functions; however, in C++14 this restriction has been removed. The `constexpr` functions may now contain several statements, declare variables, and even mutate variables.

With the constexpr keyword, writing a compile-time evaluated function is as easy as writing a regular function, as its parameters are regular parameters instead of template parameters.

Consider the following `constexpr` function:

```
constexpr auto sum(int x, int y, int z) { return x + y + z; }
```

Let's call the function like this:

```
const auto value = sum(3, 4, 5);
```

In this case, the compiler will **generate** the following regular C++ code:

```
const auto value = 12;
```

This is then compiled to machine code as usual. In other words, the compiler evaluates a `constexpr` function and generates regular C++ code where the result is calculated.

Constexpr functions in a runtime context

In the previous example, the summed values, (`3`, `4`, `5`), were known to the compiler at compile time, but how do `constexpr` functions handle variables whose values are not known until runtime? As mentioned in the previous section, constexpr is an indicator to the compiler that a function, under certain conditions, can be evaluated at compile time. If variables with values unknown till runtime are invoked, they will be evaluated just like regular functions.

In the following example, the values of `x`, `y`, and `z` are provided from the user at runtime, and therefore, it would be impossible for the compiler to calculate the sum at compile time:

```
int x, y, z;
std::cin >> x >> y >> z; // Get user input
auto value = sum(x, y, z);
```

Verify compile-time computation using std::integral_constant

To verify that `constexpr` is evaluated at compile time, you can use `std::integral_constant`. The integral constant is a template class that takes an integer type and an integer value as template parameters. From these, it generates a new class representing a number. If the compiler cannot evaluate the integer value at compile time, it won't compile. The value of the class is then accessed via the static field `value` of `std::integral_constant`.

Here is an example of compile-time integral values versus runtime integral values:

```
const auto ksum = std::integral_constant<int, sum(1,2,3)>;

auto func() -> void {
  // This compiles as the value of sum is evaluated at compile time
  const auto sum_compile_time = std::integral_constant<int,sum(1,2,3)>;
  int x, y, z;
  std::cin >> x >> y >> z;
  // Line below will not compile, the compiler cannot determine which value
  // the integral constant has at compile time
  const auto sum_runtime = std::integral_constant<int, sum(x, y, z)>;
}
```

The if constexpr statement

The `if constexpr` statement allows template functions to evaluate different scopes in the same function at compile time (also called compile-time polymorphism). Take a look at the following example, where a template function called `speak()` tries to differentiate member functions depending on the type:

```
struct Bear { auto roar() const { std::cout << "roar"; } };
struct Duck { auto quack() const { std::cout << "quack"; } };

template <typename Animal>
auto speak(const Animal& a) {
  if (std::is_same_v<Animal, Bear>) { a.roar(); }
  else if (std::is_same_v<Animal, Duck>) { a.quack(); }
}
```

Let's say, we compile the following lines:

```
auto bear = Bear{};
speak(bear);
```

The compiler will then generate a `speak()` function similar to this:

```
auto speak(const Bear& a) {
  if (true) { a.roar(); }
  else if (false) { a.quack(); } // This line will not compile
}
```

As you can see, the compiler will keep the call to the member function, `quack()`, which will then fail to compile, as `Bear` does not contain a `quack()` member function. This happens even though the `quack()` member function will never be executed due to the `else if (false)` statement.

In order to make the `speak()` function compile regardless of the type, we need to inform it that we'd like to completely ignore the scope for which the `if` statement is `false`. Conveniently, this is exactly what `if constexpr` does.

Here is how we can write the `speak()` function with the ability to handle both `Bear` and `Duck`, even though they do not have share a common interface:

```
template <typename Animal>
auto speak(const Animal& a) {
  if constexpr (std::is_same_v<Animal, Bear>) { a.roar(); }
  else if constexpr (std::is_same_v<Animal, Duck>) { a.quack(); }
}
```

When `speak()` is invoked with `Animal == Bear`...

```
auto bear = Bear{};
speak(bear);
```

...the compiler generates the following function:

```
auto speak(const Bear& animal) { animal.roar(); }
```

When `speak()` is invoked with `Animal == Duck`...

```
auto duck = Duck{};
speak(duck);
```

...the compiler generates the following function:

```
auto speak(const Duck& animal) { animal.quack(); }
```

If `speak()` is invoked with any other primitive type, such as `Animal == int`...

```
speak(42);
```

...the compiler generates an empty function:

```
auto speak(const int& animal) {}
```

Unlike a regular `if` statement, the compiler will now be able to generate two different functions when invoked; one where `if constexpr` is `true` and another one where it is `false`. Actually, it may be able to generate a third function; if the `Animal` type is neither `Bear` nor `Duck`, it will just be an empty function.

Comparison with runtime polymorphism

As a side note, if we were to implement the previous example with traditional runtime polymorphism, using inheritance and virtual functions to achieve the same functionality, the implementation would look like the code example below:

```
struct AnimalBase {
  virtual ~AnimalBase() {}
  virtual auto speak() const -> void {}
};
struct Bear : public AnimalBase {
  auto roar() const { std::cout << "roar"; }
  auto speak() const override -> void { roar(); }
};
struct Duck : public AnimalBase {
```

```
  auto quack() const { std::cout << "quack"; }
  auto speak() const override -> void { quack(); }
};
auto speak(const AnimalBase* a) {
  a->speak();
}
```

The objects have to be accessed using pointers or references, and the type is inferred at **runtime**, which results in a performance loss compared with the compile-time version, where everything is available when the application executes.

Example of generic modulus function using if constexpr

This example is similar to the previous example, but this time we will see how to distinguish between operators and global functions. In C++, the `%` operator is used to get the modulus of integers while `std::fmod()` is used for floating point types. We'd like to generalize our code base and create a generic modulus function called `generic_mod()`.

If we would implement `generic_mod()` with a regular `if` statement...

```
template <typename T>
auto generic_mod(const T& v, const T& n) -> T {
  assert(n != 0);
  if (std::is_floating_point_v<T>) { return std::fmod(v, n); }
  else { return v % n; }
}
```

... it would fail if invoked with `T == float` as the compiler will generate the following function, which will fail to compile:

```
auto generic_mod(const float& v, const float& n) -> float {
  assert(n != 0);
  if(true) { return std::fmod(v, n); }
  else { return v % n; } // Will not compile
}
```

Even though the application cannot reach it, the compiler will generate the line `return v % n;` , which isn't compliant with `float`. The compiler doesn't care that the application cannot reach it, as it cannot generate an assembly for it, it will fail to compile.

As in the previous example, we change the `if` statement to a `if constexpr` statement:

```
template <typename T>
auto generic_mod(const T& v, const T& n) -> T {
  assert(n != 0);
  if constexpr (std::is_floating_point_v<T>) return std::fmod(v, n);
  else return v % n; // If T is a floating point, this line is eradicated
}
```

Now, when the function is invoked with a floating point type, it will generate the following function where the `v % n` operation is eradicated:

```
auto generic_mod(const float& v, const float& n) -> float {
  assert(n != 0);
  return std::fmod(v, n);
}
```

Heterogeneous containers

Heterogenous containers, as opposed to regular homogenous containers, are containers containing different types; that is, in homogenous containers, such as `std::vector`, `std::list`, `std::set`, and so on, every element is of the same type. A heterogeneous container is a container where elements may have different types.

Static-sized heterogenous containers

C++ comes with two heterogeneous containers, `std::pair` and `std::tuple`. As `std::pair` is a subset of `std::tuple` with only two elements, we will only focus on `std::tuple`.

The std::tuple container

The `std::tuple` is a statically sized heterogeneous container that can be declared to be of any size. In contrast to `std::vector`, for example, its size cannot change at runtime; you cannot add or remove elements.

A tuple is constructed with its member types explicitly declared like this:

```
auto tuple0 = std::tuple<int, std::string, bool>{};
```

This will make the compiler generate a class which can roughly be viewed like this:

```
class Tuple {
public:
  int data0_{};
  std::string data1_{};
  bool data2_{};
};
```

As with many other classes in C++, `std::tuple` also has a corresponding `std::make_tuple` function, which deduces the types automatically from the parameters:

```
auto tuple = std::make_tuple(42, std::string{"hi"}, true);
```

As you can see, using `std::make_tuple`, we can make the code a bit more readable (as stated earlier, from C++17 and onward, many of these `std::make_` functions are superfluous, since C++17 classes can deduce these types from the constructor).

Accessing the members of a tuple

The individual elements of `std::tuple` can be accessed using the global function, `std::get<Index>(tuple)`. You may wonder why the members can't be accessed like a regular container with the `at(size_t index)` member function. The reason is that a member function such as `at()` is only allowed to return one type, whereas a tuple consists of different types at different indices. Instead, the templated global function `std::get` is used with the index as a template parameter:

```
auto number = std::get<0>(tuple);
auto str = std::get<1>(tuple);
auto boolean = std::get<2>(tuple);
```

We can imagine the `std::get()` function being implemented roughly like this:

```
template <size_t Index, typename Tuple>
auto& get(const Tuple& tpl) {
  if constexpr(Index == 0) { return tpl.data0_; }
  else if constexpr(Index == 1) { return tpl.data1_; }
}
```

This means that when we create and access a tuple like this:

```
auto tuple = std::make_tuple(42, true);
auto value = std::get<0>(tuple);
```

The compiler roughly generates the following code:

```
// "make_tuple" and the Tuple class is generated first...
class Tuple {
  int data0_{};
  bool data1_{};
};
auto make_tuple(int v0, bool v1) { return Tuple{v0, v1}; }

// get<0>(Tuple) is then generated to something like this...
auto& get(const Tuple& tpl) { return idata_0; }
// The generated function is then utilized
auto tuple = make_tuple(42, true);
auto value = get(tuple);
```

Note that this example can merely be thought of as a simplistic way to imagine what the compiler generates when constructing `std::tuple`; the interior of `std::tuple` is very complex. Still, it is important to understand that an `std::tuple` class is basically a simple struct whose members can be accessed by a compile-time index.

The `std::get` function can also use the typename as parameter. It is then used like this:

```
auto number = std::get<int>(tuple);
auto str = std::get<std::string>(tuple);
```

This is only possible if the specified type is contained once in the tuple.

Iterating std::tuple

From a programmer's perspective it may seem that `std::tuple` can be iterated with a regular range-based `for` loop, just like any other container, as follows:

```
auto tpl = std::make_tuple(1, true, std::string{"Jedi"});
for(const auto& v: tpl) { std::cout << v << " "; }
```

To be honest, I also think that most C++ programmers (including myself) have tried something like this at some point only to notice that it isn't possible. The reason it is not possible is that the type of `const auto& v` is only evaluated once, and since `std::tuple` contains elements of different types, this code simply does not compile.

The same goes for regular algorithms, as iterators don't mutate the type pointed to; therefore, `std::tuple` does not provide a `begin()` or `end()` member function.

Unrolling the tuple

As tuples cannot be iterated as usual, what we need to do is to use metaprogramming to unroll the loop. From the previous example, we want the compiler to generate something like this:

```
auto tpl = std::make_tuple(1, true, std::string{"Jedi"});
std::cout << std::get<0>(tpl) << " ";
std::cout << std::get<1>(tpl) << " ";
std::cout << std::get<2>(tpl) << " ";
// Prints "1 true Jedi"
```

As you can see, we iterate every index of the tuple, and therefore, we need the number of types/values contained in the tuple. Then, as the tuple contains different types, we need to write a metafunction that generates a new function for every type in the tuple.

If we start with a function that generates the call for a specific index, it will look like this:

```
template <size_t Index, typename Tuple, typename Functor>
auto tuple_at(const Tuple& tpl, const Functor& func) -> void {
  const auto& v = std::get<Index>(tpl);
  func( v );
}
```

We can then combine it with a polymorphic lambda, as you learned in `Chapter 2`, *Modern C++ Concepts*:

```
auto tpl = std::make_tuple(1, true, std:.string{"Jedi"});
auto func = [](const auto& v){ std::cout << v << " "; };
tuple_at<0>(tpl, func);
tuple_at<1>(tpl, func);
tuple_at<2>(tpl, func);
// Prints "1 true Jedi"
```

With the function `tuple_at()` in place, we can then move on to the actual iteration. The first thing we need is the number of values in the tuple as a compile-time constant. Fortunately, this value can be obtained by the type trait, `std::tuple_size_v<Tuple>`. Using `if constexpr`, we can then unfold the iteration by creating a similar function, but which takes different actions depending on the index:

1. If the index is equal to the tuple size, it generates an empty function
2. Otherwise, it executes the lambda at the passed index and generates a new function with `1` added to the index.

This is how the code will look:

```
template <typename Tuple, typename Functor, size_t Index = 0>
auto tuple_for_each(const Tuple& tpl, const Functor& f) -> void {
  constexpr auto tuple_size = std::tuple_size_v<Tuple>;
  if constexpr(Index < tuple_size) {
    tuple_at<Index>(tpl, f);
    tuple_for_each<Tuple, Functor, Index+1>(tpl, f);
  }
}
```

As you can see, the default index is set to zero so that we don't have to specify it when iterating. This `tuple_for_each()` function can then be called like this, with the lambda directly in place:

```
auto tpl = std::make_tuple(1, true, std:.string{"Jedi"});
tuple_for_each(tpl, [](const auto& v){ std::cout << v << " "; });
// Prints "1 true Jedi"
```

Quite nice; syntactically, it looks pretty similar to the `std::for_each()` algorithm.

Implementing other algorithms for tuples

Expanding upon `tuple_for_each()`, different algorithms iterating a tuple can be implemented in a similar manner. Here is an example of how `any_of()` for tuples is implemented:

```
template <typename Tuple, typename Functor, size_t Index = 0>
auto tuple_any_of(const Tuple& tpl, const Functor& f) -> bool {
  constexpr auto tuple_size = std::tuple_size_v<Tuple>;
  if constexpr(Index < tuple_size) {
    bool success = f(std::get<Index>(tpl));
    return success ?
      true:
      tuple_any_of<Tuple, Functor, Index+1>(tpl, f);
  } else {
    return false;
  }
}
```

It can then be used like this:

```
auto tuple = std::make_tuple(42, 43.0f, 44.0);
auto has_44 = tuple_any_of(tuple, [](auto v){ return v == 44; });
```

The `tuple_any_of` tuple iterates through every type in the tuple and generates a lambda function for the element at the current index, which it then compares with `44`. In this case, `has_44` will evaluate to `true`, as the last element, a `double` value, is `44`. If we add an element of a type that is not comparable with `44`, such as `std::string`, we will get a compilation error.

Accessing tuple elements

Prior to C++17, there were two standard ways of accessing elements of a `std::tuple`:

- For accessing single elements, the static function `std::get<N>(tuple)` was used.
- For accessing multiple elements, the static function `std::tie()` was used.

Although they both worked, the syntax was for performing such a simple task was very verbose, as shown in the following example:

```
// Prerequisite
auto make_bond() { return std::make_tuple(std::string{"James"}, 7, true) }

// Using std::get<N>
auto tpl = make_bond();
auto name = std::get<0>(tpl);
auto id = std::get<1>(tpl);
auto kill_license = std::get<2>(tpl);
std::cout << name << ", " << id << ", " << kill_license << '\n';
// Output: James, 7, true

// Using std::tie
auto name = std::string{};
auto id = int{};
auto kill_license = bool{};
std::tie(name, agent_id, kill_license) = make_bond();
std::cout << name << ", " << id << ", " << kill_license << '\n';
// Output: James, 7, true
```

Structured bindings

In order to being able to perform this common task elegantly, structured bindings were introduced in C++17. Using structured bindings, multiple variables can be initialized at once using `auto` and a bracket initializer list. As with the `auto` keyword in general, you can apply control over whether the variables should be mutable references, forward references, const references, or values by using the corresponding modifier. In the following example a structured binding of const references is constructed:

```
const auto& [name, id, kill_license] = make_bond();
std::cout << name << ", " << id << ", " << kill_license << '\n';
// Output: James, 7, true
```

Structured bindings can also be used to extract the individual members of a tuple in a `for` loop, as follows:

```
auto agents = {
  std::make_tuple("James", 7, true),
  std::make_tuple("Nikita", 108, false)
};
for(auto&& [name, id, kill_license]: agents) {
   std::cout << name << ", " << id << ", " << kill_license << '\n';
}

// Output
James, 7, true
Nikita, 108, false
```

Here's a quick hint. If you want to return multiple arguments with named variables instead of tuple indices, it is possible to return a struct defined inside a function and use automatic return type deduction:

```
auto make_bond() {
  struct Agent{std::string name_; int id_; bool kill_license_;}
  return Agent{"James", 7, true};
}
auto b = make_bond();
std::cout
  << b.name_ << ", "
  << b.id_ << ", "
  << b.kill_license_ << '\n';
```

The variadic template parameter pack

The variadic template parameter packs enables programmers to create template functions that can accept any number of arguments.

An example of a function with variadic number of arguments

If we were to create a function that makes a string out of any number of arguments without variadic template parameter packs, we would have to create a separate function for every number of arguments:

```
// Makes a string of by one argument
template <typename T0>
auto make_string(const T0& v0) -> std::string {
  auto sstr = std::ostringstream{};
  sstr << v0;
  return sstr.str();
}
// Makes a string of by two arguments
template <typename T0, typename T1>
auto make_string(const T0& v0, const T1& v1) -> std::string {
   return make_string(v0) + " " + make_string(v1);
}
// Makes a string of by three arguments
template <typename T0, typename T1, typename T2>
auto make_string(const T0& v0, const T1& v1, const T2& v2) -> std::string {
  return make_string(v0, v1) + " " + make_string(v2);
}
// ... and so on for as many parameters we might need
```

This is the intended use of our function:

```
auto str0 = make_string(42);
auto str1 = make_string(42, "hi");
auto str2 = make_string(42, "hi", true);
```

If we require a large number of arguments, this becomes tedious, but with a parameter pack, we can implement this as a function that accepts an arbitrary number of arguments.

How to construct a variadic parameter pack

The parameter pack is identified by putting three dots in front of the type name, and three dots after the variadic argument expands the pack, with a comma in between:

Here's the syntactic explanation:

- `Ts` is a list of types
- The `<typename ...Ts&>` function indicates that the function deals with a list
- The `values...` function expands the pack such that a comma is added between every type

To put it into code, consider this `expand_pack` function:

```
template <typename ...Ts>
auto expand_pack(const Ts& ...values) {
   auto tuple = std::tie(values...);
}
```

Let's call the preceding function like this:

```
expand_pack(42, std::string{"hi"});
```

In that case, the compiler will generate a function similar to this:

```
auto expand_pack(const int& v0, const std::string& v1) {
  auto tuple = std::tie(v0, v1);
}
```

This is what the individual parameter pack parts expand to:

Expression:	**Expands to:**
`template <typename... Ts>`	`template <typename T0, typename T1>`
`expand_pack(const Ts& ...values)`	`expand_pack(const T0& v0, const T1& v1)`
`std::tie(values...)`	`std::tie(v0, v1)`

Now, let's see how we can create a `make_string` function with a variadic parameter pack.

Going further with the initial make_string function, in order to create a string out of every parameter, we need to iterate the pack. There is no way to directly iterate a parameter pack, but a simple workaround would be to make a tuple out of it and, then, iterate it with the tuple_for_each function, as follows:

```
template <typename ...Ts>
auto make_string(const Ts& ...values) {
  auto sstr = std::ostringstream{};
  // Create a tuple of the variadic parameter pack
  auto tuple = std::tie(values...);
  // Iterate the tuple
  tuple_for_each(tuple, [&sstr](const auto& v){ sstr << v; });
  return sstr.str();
}
```

We converted the parameter pack to a tuple with std::tie() and, then, iterated it with tuple_for_each.

Dynamic-sized heterogenous containers

As seen in the preceding section, std::tuple is a heterogenous container with a fixed size and fixed element positions, more or less, like a regular struct but without named member variables.

How can we expand upon this to create a container with a variable size (such as std::vector, std::list, and so on) but with the ability to store different types? As the size of the container changes at runtime, we cannot use compile-time programming to generate code.

Using std::any as the base for a dynamic-size heterogenous container

Note that std::any was added in C++17; if your compiler does not include std::any, you can use boost::any from the Boost Library instead.

The simplest solution is to use `std::any` as the base type. The `std::any` object can store any type of value in it:

```
auto container = std::vector<std::any>{42, "hi", true};
```

It has some drawbacks, though; every time a value in it is accessed, the type must be tested for at runtime. In other words, we completely lose the type information of the stored value at compile time. Rather, we have to rely on runtime type checks for the information.

If we would like to iterate our container, we need to explicitly ask every `std::any` object *if you are an* `int`*, do this, if you are a* `char` *pointer, do that*. This is not desirable, as it requires repeated source code, and it is also less efficient than using other alternatives, which we will describe later in the chapter.

The following example compiles; the type is explicitly tested for and casted upon:

```
for(const auto& a: container) {
  if(a.type() == typeid(int)) {
    const auto& value = std::any_cast<int>(a);
    std::cout << value;
  }
  else if(a.type() == typeid(const char*)) {
    const auto& value = std::any_cast<const char*>(a);
    std::cout << value;
  }
  else if(a.type() == typeid(bool)) {
    const auto& value = std::any_cast<bool>(a);
    std::cout << value;
  }
}
```

We simply cannot print it with a regular stream operator, since the `std::any` object has no idea of how to access its stored value. Therefore, the following code does not compile; the compiler does not know what is in `std::any`:

```
for(const auto& a: container) {
  std::cout << a; // Will not compile
}
```

The std::variant

If we can trade off the ability to store any type in the container and, rather, concentrate on a fixed set of types declared at the container initialization, then `std::variant` is a better choice.

The `std::variant` has two main advantages over `std::any`:

- It does not store its contained type on the heap (unlike `std::any`)
- It can be invoked with a polymorphic lambda, meaning you don't explicitly have to know its currently contained type (more about this in the later sections of this chapter)

The `std::variant` works in a somewhat similar manner to a tuple, except that it only stores one object at a time. The contained type and value is the type and value you assigned it last. Look at the following image:

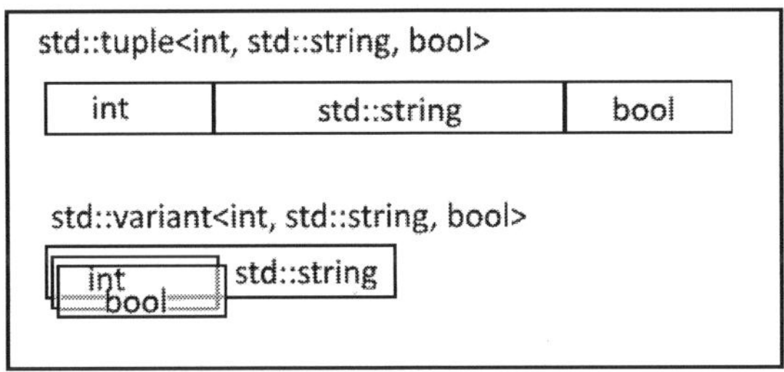

Tuple of types versus variant of types

Here's an example of `std::variant` usage:

```
using VariantType = std::variant<int, std::string, bool>;
auto v = VariantType{}; // The variant is empty
v = 7; // v holds an int
v = std::string{"Bjarne"}; // v holds a std::string, the integer is
overwritten
v = false; // v holds a bool, the std::string is overwritten
```

Visiting variants

When accessing variables in the `std::variant`, we use the global function `std::visit()`. As you might have guessed, we have to use our main companion when dealing with heterogeneous types; the polymorphic lambda:

```
std::visit(
  [](const auto& v){ std::cout << v; },
  my_variant
);
```

The compiler then generates a regular C++ of the lambda, for every type contained in the variant. Thus, when invoking `std::visit()` with the lambda and variant type in the example, the compiler would generate code roughly similar to the following snippet where the polymorphic lambda is converted to a regular class with `operator()` overloads for every type in the variant

Note that as very complex code are involved in expanding both a polymorphic lambda and the `std::visit()`, this piece of code is heavily simplified. Still it gives a clear view of what happens when you invoke `std::visit()`.

```
struct FunctorImpl {
  auto operator()(const int& v) { std::cout << v; }
  auto operator()(const std::string& v) { std::cout << v; }
  auto operator()(const bool& v) { std::cout << v; }
};
```

The `std::visit` function is expanded to an `if...else` chain corresponding to the types in the lambda:

```
auto visit_impl(FunctorImpl f, const VariantType& v) {
  if(std::holds_alternative<int>(v)) {
    return f(std::get<int>(v));
  }
  else if(std::holds_alternative<std::string>(v)) {
    return f(std::get<std::string>(v));
  }
  else if(std::holds_alternative<bool>(v)) {
    return f(std::get<bool>(v));
  }
}
// The actual function call
visit_impl(FunctorImpl(), my_variant);
```

The size of the variant is equal to the largest object type declared as its member, in the preceding example it would be the `sizeof(std::string)`.

Heterogenous container of variants

Now that we have a variant which can store any type of a provided list, we can expand upon this to a heterogeneous container. We do this by simply creating a `std::vector` of our variant.

```
using VariantType = std::variant<int, std::string, bool>;
auto container = std::vector<VariantType>{};
```

We can now push elements of different types to our vector:

```
container.push_back(false);
container.push_back(std::string{"I am a string"});
container.push_back(std::string{"I am also a string"});
container.push_back(13);
```

The vector will now look like this in memory, where every element in the vector has the size of the variant, in this case `sizeof(std::string)`:

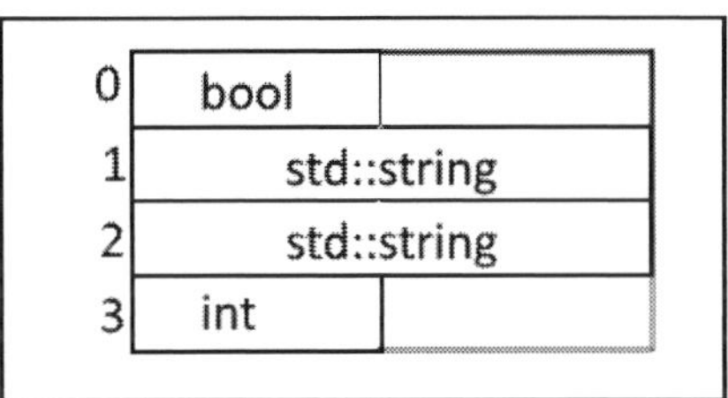

Vector of variants

Of course, we can also `pop_back()`, or modify the container in any other way the container allows.

```
container.pop_back();
std::reverse(container.begin(), container.end());
// etc...
```

Accessing the values in our variant container

Now that we have the boilerplate for a heterogeneous container of dynamic size, let's see how we can use it like a regular `std::vector`:

1. **Construct a heterogeneous container of variants**: Here we construct a `std::vector` with different types, note that the initializer list contains different types:

```
using VariantType = std::variant<int, std::string, bool>;
auto c = std::vector<VariantType> { 42, std::string{"needle"}, true };
```

2. **Print the content by iterating with a regular for loop**: To iterate the container with a regular `for`-loop we utilize `std::visit()` and a polymorphic lambda. The global function `std::visit()` takes care of the type conversion. The example prints each value to `std::cout`, independent of the type:

```
for (const auto& val: c) {
  std::visit([](const auto& v){ std::cout << v << '\n';}, val);
}
```

3. **Inspect what types are in the container**: Here we inspect each element of the container by type. This is achieved by using the global function `std::holds_alternative<type>`, which returns `true` if the variant currently holds the type asked for. The example counts the number of booleans currently contained in the container:

```
auto num_bools = std::count_if(c.begin(), c.end(),
  [](const auto& v){
    return std::holds_alternative<bool>(v);
  }
);
```

4. **Find content by both contained type and value**: In this example we inspect the container both for type and the value by combining `std::holds_alternative` and `std::get`:

   The example inspects if the container contains a `std::string` with the value `"needle"`.

```
auto contains_needle_string = std::any_of(
  c.begin(),
  c.end(),
  [](const auto& v){
```

```
      return
        std::holds_alternative<std::string>(v) &&
        std::get<std::string>(v) == "needle";
    }
  );
```

Global function std::get

The global function `std::get` can be used for all of `std::tuple`, `std::pair`, `std::variant` and `std::array`.

std::get<Index>

When `std::get` is used with an index, as in `std::get<1>(v)` it returns the value at the corresponding index in a `std::tuple`, `std::pair`, or `std::array`.

std::get<Type>

When `std::get` is used with a type, as in `std::get<int>(v)` , the corresponding value in a `std::tuple`, `std::pair` or `std::variant` is returned.
In the case of `std::variant`, an exception is thrown if the variant doesn't currently hold that type. Note that if `v` is a `std::tuple` and `Type` is contained more than once, you have to use the index to access the type.

Real world examples of metaprogramming

Advanced metaprogramming can appear to be very academic, so in order to demonstrate its usefulness we'd like to provide some examples which not only demonstrate the syntax of metaprogramming, but how it can be used in practice.

Example 1 – Reflection

The term *reflection* is the ability to inspect a class without knowing anything about its content.

In this case we are going to limit the reflection to give classes the ability to iterate their members just like we can iterate the members of a tuple. By using reflection we can create generic functions for serialization or logging which automatically works with any class. This reduces large amounts of boiler plate code traditionally required for classes in C++.

Making a class reflect its members

In contrast to many other programming languages, C++ does not have built in reflection, which means we have to write the reflection functionality ourselves. In this case we simply expose the member variables via a member function called `reflect()` which simply returns a tuple of references to the member variables by invoking `std::tie`.

```
class Town {
public:
  Town(size_t houses, size_t settlers, const std::string& name)
  : houses_{houses}, settlers_{settlers}, name_{name} {}
  auto reflect() const {return std::tie(houses_, settlers_, name_);}
private:
  size_t houses_{};
  size_t settlers_{};
  std::string name_{};
};
```

C++ libraries which simplifies reflection

There are quite a few attempts in the C++ library world to simplify the creation of reflection. One example is the meta-programming library *Boost Hana* by *Louis Dionne* which gives classes reflection capabilities via a simple macro. Recently, *Boost* has also added the *Precise and Flat reflection* by *Anthony Polukhin*, which *automatically* reflects public content of classes, as long as all members are simple types.

However, for clarity, in this example we will only use our own `reflect()` member function.

Using the reflection

Now that the `Town` class has the ability to reflect its member variables, we can automate the creation of bulk functionality which would otherwise require us to retype every member variable. As you know, C++ automatically generates constructors and assignment operators, but other common operators, such as equality (`operator==`) and less than (`operator<`) are required to be implemented by the programmer.

```
class Town {
  ...
  auto operator==(const Town& t) const {return reflect()==t.reflect();}
  auto operator<(const Town& t) const {return reflect()<t.reflect();}
  ...
};
```

In addition to member functions, another bulk function in C++ is to print its content to a stream in order to print its content to a file, or more commonly, log it in an application log.

By overloading `operator<<` and using the `tuple_for_each()` function we learned earlier, we can simplify the creation of `std::ostream` output for a class like this:

```
auto& operator<<(std::ostream& ostr, const Town& t) {
  tuple_for_each(t.reflect(), [&ostr](const auto& m){
    ostr << m << " ";
  });
  return ostr;
}
```

Now the class can be used with any `std::ostream` type like this:

```
auto v = Town{34, 68, "Shire"};
std::cout << v;
// Prints "34 68 Shire"
```

Quite neat; by reflecting our class members via a tuple we only have to update our reflect function when members are added/removed from our class, instead of updating every function iterating all member variables.

Evaluating the assembler output of the reflection

To ensure that we do not lose any runtime performance, let's compare the assembler output of our `Town` class with an equal class where the `operator==` operator has been handcrafted like this:

```
auto operator==(const Town& t) const {
  return
    houses_ == t.houses_ &&
    settlers_ == t.settlers_ &&
    name_ == t.name_;
}
```

Then, we create a simple function which takes two towns as references and returns the result of the comparison:

```
auto compare_towns(const Town& t0, const Town& t1) {
  return t0 == t1;
}
```

Inspecting the generated assembler output (in this case from GCC 6.3 with optimization level 3), we see that the generated assembler is exactly the same:

```
compare_reflected
    xor   eax, eax
    mov   rcx, QWORD PTR [rsi]
    cmp   QWORD PTR [rdi], rcx
    je    .L15
.L13:
    rep ret
.L15:
    mov   rdx, QWORD PTR [rsi+8]
    cmp   QWORD PTR [rdi+8], rdx
    jne   .L13
    mov   rdx, QWORD PTR [rdi+24]
    cmp   rdx, QWORD PTR [rsi+24]
    jne   .L13
    test  rdx, rdx
    mov   eax, 1
    je    .L13
    sub   rsp, 8
    mov   rsi, QWORD PTR [rsi+16]
    mov   rdi, QWORD PTR [rdi+16]
    call  memcmp
    test  eax, eax
    sete  al
    add   rsp, 8
    ret
```

```
compare_non_reflected
    xor   eax, eax
    mov   rcx, QWORD PTR [rsi]
    cmp   QWORD PTR [rdi], rcx
    je    .L28
.L27:
    rep ret
.L28:
    mov   rdx, QWORD PTR [rsi+8]
    cmp   QWORD PTR [rdi+8], rdx
    jne   .L27
    mov   rdx, QWORD PTR [rdi+24]
    cmp   rdx, QWORD PTR [rsi+24]
    jne   .L27
    test  rdx, rdx
    mov   eax, 1
    je    .L27
    sub   rsp, 8
    mov   rsi, QWORD PTR [rsi+16]
    mov   rdi, QWORD PTR [rdi+16]
    call  memcmp
    test  eax, eax
    sete  al
    add   rsp, 8
    ret
```

Handcrafted operators and reflected operators results in same assembler

With this in our mind, we can rest assured that the reflection approach doesn't cost us any runtime performance.

Conditionally overloading global functions

Now that we have a mechanism to write bulk functions using reflection rather than manually typing each variable, we still need to type the simplified bulk functions for every type. What if we wanted these functions to be generated for every type which is reflectable?

In other words, every type which has the `reflect()` member function should also have `operator==`, `operator<` and the global `std::stream&` operator. First of all, `operator==` and `operator<` need to be moved from being member functions to global functions; fortunately C++ allows these functions to be member functions or global functions.

Secondly, in order to enable these functions only for classes that have a `reflect()` member function, we need to conditionally enable them using a combination of `std::experimental::is_detected` and `std::enable_if_t`.

First, following the procedure learned with `is_detected`, we create a `typedef` referring to the `reflect()` member function:

```
#include <experimental/type_traits>
template <typename T>
using has_reflect_member = decltype(&T::reflect);
```

Then we create a template based bool called `is_reflectable_v` that is `true` if the class contains the member `reflect()`:

```
namespace exp = std::experimental;
template <typename T>
constexpr bool is_reflectable_v =
  exp::is_detected<has_reflect_member, T>::value;
```

Of course, this test only checks if a class has a member named `reflect()`, it does not assure that it has no parameters, nor that it returns a tuple. Anyhow, we can now overload the three functions in the global namespace, giving all reflectable classes the ability to be compared and printed to a `std::ostream`:

```
// Global equal operator for reflectable types
template <typename T, bool IsReflectable = is_reflectable_v<T>>
auto operator==(const T& a, const T& b)
-> std::enable_if_t<IsReflectable, bool> {
  return a.reflect() == b.reflect();
}

// Global not-equal operator for reflectable types
template <typename T, bool IsReflectable = is_reflectable_v<T>>
auto operator!=(const T& a, const T& b)
-> std::enable_if_t<IsReflectable, bool> {
  return a.reflect() != b.reflect();
}

// Global less-than operator for reflectable types
template <typename T, bool IsReflectable = is_reflectable_v<T>>
auto operator<(const T& a, const T& b)
```

```
-> std::enable_if_t<IsReflectable , bool> {
  return a.reflect() < b.reflect();
}

// Global std::ostream output for reflectable types
template <typename T, bool IsReflectable = is_reflectable_v<T>>
auto operator<<(std::ostream& ostr, const T& v)
-> std::enable_if_t<IsReflectable, std::ostream&> {
  tuple_for_each(v.reflect(), [&ostr](const auto& m) {
    ostr << m << " ";
  });
  return ostr;
}
```

As explained in the section about `std::enable_if_t` , the functions above will only exist for types which contain the `reflect()` member function, and will therefore not collide with any other overload.

Testing reflection capabilities

Now we have everything in place:

- The `Town` class we will test has a reflect member function returning a tuple of references to its members
- The equality and less than comparison functions are enabled for all reflectable types
- The global `std::ostream& operator<<` is overloaded for reflectable types

Here is a simple test which verifies the functionality:

```
auto town_tester() {
  auto shire = Town{100, 200, "Shire"};
  auto mordor = Town{1000, 2000, "Mordor"};
  // Prints "100 200 Shire" using reflection
  std::cout << shire;
  // Prints "1000 2000 Mordor" using reflection
  std::cout << mordor;
  // Compares mordor and shire using reflection
  auto is_same = shire == morder;
  assert(!is_same);
}
```

Quite nice, isn't it? With these capabilities in place we are relieved from writing them for every class in our code base. For the sake of it, let's compare the `Town` class side by side with a `Town` class without reflection capabilities:

Handcrafted operators

```
class Town {
public:
  Town(
    size_t houses,
    size_t settlers,
    std::string name)
  : houses_{houses}
  , settlers_{settlers}
  , name_{name} {}
  auto operator==(const Town&t)const{
    return houses_ == t.houses_ &&
           settlers_ == t.settlers_&&
           name_ == t.name_;
  }
  auto operator!=(const Town&t)const{
    return !(*this == t);
  }
  auto operator<(const Town& t)const{
    auto a = std::tie(houses_,
      settlers_, name_);
    auto b = std::tie(t.houses_,
      t.settlers_, t.name);
    return a < b;
  }
  size_t houses_{};
  size_t settlers_{};
  std::string name_{};
};
auto operator<<(
  std::ostream& ostr, const Town& t
) -> std::ostream& {
  ostr << t.houses_ << " ";
  ostr << t.settlers_ << " ";
  ostr << t.name_ << " ";
  return ostr;
}
```

Rely on reflection for operators

```
class Town {
public:
  Town(
    size_t houses,
    size_t settlers,
    std::string name)
  : houses_{houses}
  , settlers_{settlers}
  , name_{name} {}
  auto reflect()const{
    return std::tie(
      houses_,
      settlers_,
      name_
    );
  }
  size_t houses_{};
  size_t settlers_{};
  std::string name_{};
};
```

As you can see, using reflection reduces a great deal of boiler plate code.

Implementing a less-than operator can be tricky, however, using `std::tie` as in the Town example above makes it easy.

Example 2 – Creating a generic safe cast function

When casting between data types in C++ there is a multitude of different ways things can go wrong:

- You might lose a value if casting to a integer type of lower bit length
- You lose a value if casting a negative value to an unsigned integer
- If casting from a pointer to any other integer than `uintptr_t`, the correct address might become wrong as C++ only guarantees that `uintptr_t` is the only integer type to withhold an address
- If casting from `double` to `float`, the result might be `int` if the `double` value is too large for `float` to withhold
- If casting between pointers with a `static_cast()`, we might get undefined behavior if the types aren't sharing a common base class

In order to make our code more robust we can create a generic checked cast function which verifies our casts in debug mode, and performs the cast as fast as possible if in release mode.

Depending on the types that are being casted, different checks are performed. If we try to cast between types that are not verified, it won't compile.

These are the cases the `safe_cast()` are intended to handle:

- **Same type**: Obviously if we're casting the same type, we just return the input value.
- **Pointer to pointer**: If casting between pointers the `safe_cast()` performs a dynamic cast in debug to verify it is castable.
- **Double to floating point**: The `safe_cast()` accepts precision loss when casting from double to float with one exception: if casting from a double to floating point there is a chance the double is too large for the float to handle resulting.

- **Arithmetic to arithmetic**: if casting between arithmetic types, the value is cast back to its original type to verify no precision are lost.
- **Pointer to non-pointer**: If casting from a pointer to a non-pointer type, `safe_cast()` verifies that the destination type is an `uintptr_t` or `intptr_t`, the only integer type that is guaranteed to hold an address.
- In any other case, the `safe_cast()` function will fail to compile.

Let's see how we can implement this, we start by fetching information about our cast operation to `constexpr` booleans. The reason they are `constexpr` booleans and not const booleans is that we will utilize them later in `if constexpr` expressions, which requires constexpr conditions:

```
template <typename T> constexpr auto make_false() { return false; }
template <typename Dst, typename Src>
auto safe_cast(const Src& v) -> Dst{
  using namespace std;
  constexpr auto is_same_type = is_same_v<Src, Dst>;
  constexpr auto is_pointer_to_pointer =
    is_pointer_v<Src> && is_pointer_v<Dst>;
  constexpr auto is_float_to_float =
    is_floating_point_v<Src> && is_floating_point_v<Dst>;
  constexpr auto is_number_to_number =
    is_arithmetic_v<Src> && is_arithmetic_v<Dst>;
  constexpr auto is_intptr_to_ptr = (
    (is_same_v<uintptr_t,Src> || is_same_v<intptr_t,Src>)
    && is_pointer_v<To>;
  constexpr auto is_ptr_to_intptr =
    is_pointer_v<Src> &&
    (is_same_v<uintptr_t,Dst> || is_same_v<intptr_t,Dst>);
```

So now that we have all the information about the cast as `constexpr` booleans, we assert at compile time that we can perform the cast. As said before, a `static_assert()` will fail to compile if the condition is not satisfied (unlike a regular assert, which verifies conditions at runtime).

Note the usage of `static_assert()` and `make_false<T>` at the end of the if/else chain. We cannot just type `static_assert(false, "")` as that would prevent the `safe_cast()` from compiling at all; instead we utilize the template function `make_false<T>()` to delay the generation until required.

When that actual `static_cast()` is performed, we cast back to the original type and verify that the result is equal to the un-casted argument using a regular runtime assert. This way we can make sure the `static_cast()` has not lost any data:

```
  if constexpr(is_same_type) {
    return v;
  }
  else if constexpr(is_intptr_to_ptr || is_ptr_to_intptr){
    return reinterpret_cast<Dst>(v);
  }
  else if constexpr(is_pointer_to_pointer) {
    assert(dynamic_cast<Dst>(v) != nullptr);
    return static_cast<Dst>(v);
  }
  else if constexpr (is_float_to_float) {
    auto casted = static_cast<Dst>(v);
    auto casted_back = static_cast<Src>(v);
    assert(!isnan(casted_back) && !isinf(casted_back));
    return casted;
  }
  else if constexpr (is_number_to_number) {
    auto casted = static_cast<Dst>(v);
    auto casted_back = static_cast<Src>(casted);
    assert(casted == casted_back);
    return casted;
  }
  else {
    static_assert(make_false<Src>(),"CastError");
    return Dst{}; // This can never happen,
    // the static_assert should have failed
  }
}
```

Note how we use the `if constexpr` in order for the function to conditionally compile. If we used a regular `if` statement, the function would fail to compile.

This would fail to compile with a regular `if` statement:

```
auto x = safe_cast<int>(42.0f);
```

This is because the compiler would try to compile the following line and `dynamic_cast` only accepts pointers:

```
// type To is an integer
assert(dynamic_cast<int>(v) != nullptr); // Does not compile
```

However, thanks to the `if constexpr` and `safe_cast<int>(42.0f)` constructs, the following function compiles properly:

```
auto safe_cast(const float& v) -> int {
  constexpr auto is_same_type = false;
  constexpr auto is_pointer_to_pointer = false;
  constexpr auto is_float_to_float = false;
  constexpr auto is_number_to_number = true;
  constexpr auto is_intptr_to_ptr = false;
  constexpr auto is_ptr_to_intptr = false
  if constexpr(is_same_type) { /*Eradicated*/ }
  else if constexpr(is_intptr_to_ptr||is_ptr_to_intptr){/*Eradicated*/}
  else if constexpr(is_pointer_to_pointer) {/*Eradicated*/}
  else if constexpr(is_float_to_float) {/*Eradicated*/}
  else if constexpr(is_number_to_number) {
    auto casted = static_cast<int>(v);
    auto casted_back = static_cast<float>(casted);
    assert(casted == casted_back);
    return casted;
  }
  else { /*Eradicated*/ }
}
```

As you can see, except for the `is_number_to_number` clause, everything in between the `if constexpr` statements has been completely eradicated, allowing the function to compile.

Example 3 – Hash strings at compile time

Let's say you have a resource system consisting of an unordered map of strings which identify bitmaps. If the bitmap is already loaded, it returns the loaded bitmap; otherwise it loads the bitmap and returns it.

```
// External function which loads a bitmap from the filesystem
auto load_bitmap_from_filesystem(const char* path) -> Bitmap {...}

// Bitmap cache
auto get_bitmap_resource(const std::string& path) -> const Bitmap& {
  // Static storage of all loaded bitmaps
  static auto loaded = std::unordered_map<std::string, Bitmap>{};
  // If the bitmap is already in loaded_bitmaps, return it
  if (loaded.count(path) > 0) {
    return loaded.at(path);
  }
  // The bitmap isn't already loaded, load and return it
  auto bitmap = load_bitmap_from_filesystem(path.c_str());
```

```
    loaded.emplace(path, std::move(bitmap));
    return loaded.at(path);
  }
```

The bitmap cache is then utilized wherever a bitmap resource is needed.

- If it's not loaded yet, the `get_bitmap_resource()` function will load and return it
- If it's already loaded somewhere else, the `get_bitmap_resource()` will simply return the loaded function

So independently of which of these draw functions is executed first, the second one will not have to load the bitmap from disc.

```
auto draw_something() {
  const auto& bm = get_bitmap_resource("my_bitmap.png");
  draw_bitmap(bm);
}
auto draw_something_again() {
  const auto& bm = get_bitmap_resource("my_bitmap.png");
  draw_bitmap(bm);
}
```

The advantages of compile-time hash sum calculation

The problem which we will try to solve is that every time the line `get_bitmap_resource("my_bitmap.png")` is executed, the application will compute the hash sum of the string `"my_bitmap.png"` at runtime. What we would like to do is to perform this calculation already at compile time, so that when the application executes, the hash sum is already calculated. In other words, just as we have learned to use metaprogramming to generate functions and classes at compile time, we will now have it generate the hash sum at compile time.

One might come to the conclusion already that this is a so called *micro-optimization*: calculating the hash sum of a small string won't affect the application performance at all, as it is such a tiny operation. That is probably completely true; this is just an example of how to move a calculation from run time to compile-time, and there might be other instances where this can make a significant performance impact.
As a side note, when writing software for weak hardware, string hashing is pure luxury, but hashing strings at compile gives us this luxury on any platform, as everything is computed at compile time.

Implement and verify a compile-time hash function

In order to enable the compiler to calculate the hash-sum at compile time, we rewrite the `hash_function()` to take a raw null-terminated `char` string as parameter as an advanced class like `std::string` cannot be evaluated at compile time. Now, we can mark the `hash_function()` a `constexpr`:

```
constexpr auto hash_function(const char* str) -> size_t {
  auto sum = size_t{0};
  for(auto ptr = str; *ptr != '\0'; ++ptr)
    sum += *ptr;
  return sum;
}
```

Now, let's invoke this with a raw literal string known at compile time:

```
auto hash = hash_function("abc");
```

Then, the compiler will generate the following piece of code, which is the sum of the ASCII values corresponding to `a`, `b`, and `c` (`97`, `98`, and `99`):

```
auto hash = size_t{294};
```

Just accumulating the individual values is a very bad hash function, do not do this in a real-world application. It's only here because it's easy to grasp. A better hash function would be to combine all the individual characters with a `boost::hash_combine()` as explained in `Chapter 4`, *Data Structures*.

The `hash_function()` will only evaluate at compile time if the compiler knows the string at compile time; if not, the compiler will execute the `constexpr` at runtime, just as any other expression.

Constructing a PrehashedString class

Now that we have the hash function we create a class for pre-hashed strings. It consists of the following:

- A constructor which takes raw string as parameter and calculates the hash at construction.
- Comparison operators.
- A `get_hash()` member function which returns the hash.

- An overload of `std::hash()` which simply returns the hash value. This overload is used by `std::unordered_map`, `std::unordered_set` or any other STL class which uses hash values. To put it simply, this makes the STL container aware that it exists a hash function for the `PrehashedString`.

Here is a basic implementation of a `PrehashedString` class:

```
class PrehashedString {
public:
  template <size_t N>
  constexpr PrehashedString(const char(&str)[N])
  : hash_{hash_function(&str[0])}
  , size_{N - 1} // The subtraction is to avoid null at end
  , strptr_{&str[0]}
  {}
  auto operator==(const PrehashedString& s) const {
    return
      size_ == s.size_ &&
      std::equal(c_str(), c_str() + size_, s.c_str());
  }
  auto operator!=(const PrehashedString& s) const {
    return !(*this == s); }
  constexpr auto size()const{ return size_; }
  constexpr auto get_hash()const{ return hash_; }
  constexpr auto c_str()const->const char*{ return strptr_; }
private:
  size_t hash_{};
  size_t size_{};
  const char* strptr_{nullptr};
};

namespace std {
template <>
struct hash<PrehashedString> {
  constexpr auto operator()(const PrehashedString& s) const {
    return s.get_hash();
  }
};
}
```

Forcing PrehashedString to only accept compile time string literals

Note the template trick in the constructor. This forces the `PrehashedString` to only accept compile time string literals. The reason for this is that the `PrehashedString` class does not own the `const char* ptr` and therefore we may only use it with string literals created at compile time:

```
// This compiles
auto prehashed_string = PrehashedString{"my_string"};

// This does not compile
// The prehashed_string object would be broken if the str is modified
auto str = std::string{"my_string"};
auto prehashed_string = PrehashedString{str.c_str()};

// This does not compile.
// The prehashed_string object would be broken if the strptr is deleted
auto* strptr = new char[5];
auto prehashed_string = PrehashedString{strptr};
```

Evaluating PrehashedString

So now that we have everything in place, let's see how the compiler handles the `PrehashedString`. Here is a simple test function which returns the hash value for the string `"abc"`:

```
auto test_prehashed_string() {
  const auto& hash_fn = std::hash<PrehashedString>{};
  const auto& str = PrehashedString("abc");
  return hash_fn(str);
}
```

For simplicity, we used the string `"abc"`. As our hash function simply sum the values, and the letters in `"abc"` have the following ASCII values: $a = 97$, $b = 98$, and $c = 99$, the assembler (generated by Clang 4.0) ought to output the sum $97+98+99 = 294$ somewhere. Inspecting the assembler we can see that the `test_prehashed_string()` function compiles to exactly one return statement which returns `294`:

```
mov     eax, 294
ret
```

This means that the whole `test_prehashed_string()` function has been executed at compile time; when the application executes, the hash sum is already calculated!

Evaluating get_bitmap_resource() with PrehashedString

Let's return to our original `get_bitmap_resource()` function, the `std::string` originally used is exchanged to a `PrehashedString`:

```
// Bitmap cache
auto get_bitmap_resource(const PrehashedString& path) -> const Bitmap& {
  // Static storage of all loaded bitmaps
  static auto loaded_bitmaps =
    std::unordered_map<PrehashedString, Bitmap>{};
  // If the bitmap is already in loaded_bitmaps, return it
  if (loaded_bitmaps.count(path) > 0) {
    return loaded_bitmaps.at(path).second;
  }
  // The bitmap isn't already loaded, load and return it
  auto bitmap = load_bitmap_from_filesystem(path.c_str());
  loaded_bitmaps.emplace(path, std::move(bitmap));
  return loaded_bitmaps.at(path);
}
```

We also need a function to test with:

```
auto test_get_bitmap_resource() { return get_bitmap_resource("abc"); }
```

What we would like to know is if even this function precalculated the hash sum. As the `get_bitmap_resource()` does quite a lot (constructing a static `std::unordered_map`, inspecting the map), the resulting assembly is about five hundred lines. Nevertheless, if our magic hash sum is found in the assembler, it means that we have succeeded.

Inspecting the assembler generated by Clang 4.0 we find a line which corresponds to our hash sum, `294`:

```
.quad    294                    # 0x126
```

Just to be even more sure, we change the string from `"abc"` to `"aaa"`, which ought to change this line in assembler to *97*3 = 291*, but everything else should be exactly the same.

We do this to make sure this wasn't just some other magic number which popped up, totally unrelated to the hash sum.

Inspecting the resulting assembler, we find the desired result:

```
.quad   291                     # 0x123
```

Everything, except this line, is the same, and we can therefore safely assume that the hash is calculated at compile time.

Summary

In this chapter you have learned how to use metaprogramming to generate functions and values at compile time instead of runtime. You also learned how to do this in a modern C++ way by using templates, `constexpr`, `static_assert()`, `if constexpr` and type traits. Moreover, with the constant string hashing, you also learned how to use compile time evaluation in a practical context. In the next chapter we will learn how to further expand our C++ toolbox for creating libraries by learning how to construct hidden proxy objects.

9
Proxy Objects and Lazy Evaluation

In this chapter, you will learn how to use proxy objects and lazy evaluation in order to postpone the execution of certain code until required. Using proxy objects enables optimizations to occur under the hood, thereby leaving the exposed interfaces intact.

An introduction to lazy evaluation and proxy objects

First and foremost, the techniques used in this chapter are used to hide optimizations in a library from the user of that library. This is useful because exposing every single optimization technique as a separate function requires a lot of attention and education from the user of the library.

It also bloats the code base with a multitude of specific functions, making it hard to read and understand. By using proxy objects, you can achieve optimizations under the hood; hence, the resultant code is, both, optimized and readable.

Lazy versus eager evaluation

Lazy evaluation is a technique used to postpone an operation until its result is really required. The opposite, where operations are performed right away, is called eager evaluation. In some situations eager evaluation is undesired as we might end up constructing a value which is not utilized.

Take a look at the following function class corresponding to an audio library. It consists of two functions for retrieving an audio file by name, `get_eager()` in which we pass an audio file if the name cannot be found, and `get_lazy()` in which we pass a function which returns an audio file if the name cannot be found:

```
struct Audio {};
auto load_audio(const std::string& path) -> Audio {...};

class AudioLibrary {
public:
 auto get_eager(std::string id, const Audio& otherwise)const{
   return map_.count(id) ? map.at(id) : otherwise;
 }
 auto get_lazy(std::string id, std::function<Audio> otherwise)const{
   return map_.count(id) ? map.at(id) : otherwise();
 }
private:
 std::map<std::string, Audio> map_{};
};
```

If we were to utilize the `get_eager()` function the `load_audio("default_fox.wav")` file would be executed even if the returned value is unused:

```
auto library = AudioLibrary{};
auto red_fox_sound = library.get_eager(
  "red_fox",
  load_audio("default_fox.wav")
);
```

However using the `get_lazy()` member function, where a function returning an audio file when invoked is passed, the `load_audio("default_fox.wav")` is only executed when necessary:

```
auto library = AudioLibrary{};
auto red_fox_sound = library.get_lazy(
  "red_fox",
  [](){ return load_audio("default_fox.wav"); }
);
```

This is a very simple example, but the idea is that your code gets expressed almost exactly in the same way as if it were declared eagerly. You will now learn how to use proxy objects in order to evaluate more advanced expressions lazily.

Proxy objects

Proxy objects are internal library objects that aren't intended to be visible to the user of the library. Their task is to postpone operations until required and to collect the data of an expression until it can be evaluated and optimized. However, proxy objects act in the dark; the user of the library should be able to handle the expressions as if the proxy objects were not there.

In other words, using proxy objects, you can encapsulate optimizations in your libraries while leaving the syntax intact—more or less, a free lunch.

Comparing concatenated strings using a proxy

Take a look at this code snippet, which concatenates two strings and compares the result:

```
auto func_a() {
  auto a = std::string{"Cole"};
  auto b = std::string{"Porter"};
  auto c = std::string{"ColePorter"};
  auto is_cole_porter = (a + b) == c;
  // is_cole_porter is true
}
```

Here is a visual representation of the preceding code snippet:

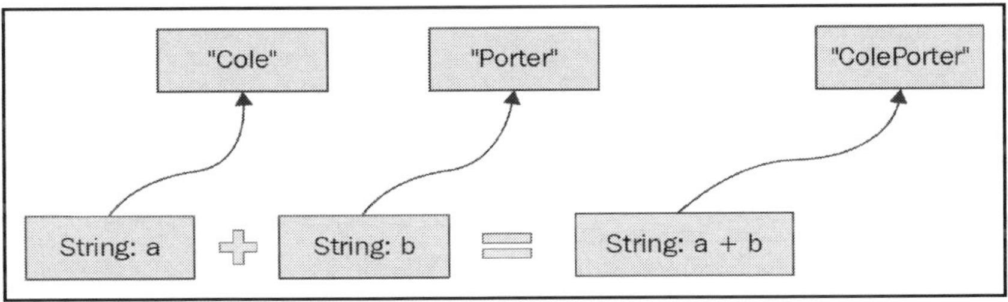

Accumulating two strings into a new string

The problem, here, is that `(a + b)` constructs a new temporary string in order to compare it with `c`. Instead of constructing a new string, we could just compare the concatenation right away, like this:

```
auto is_concat_equal(
 const std::string& a,const std::string& b,const std::string& c
) {
  return
    a.size() + b.size() == c.size() &&
    std::equal(a.begin(), a.end(), c.begin()) &&
    std::equal(b.begin(), b.end(), c.begin() + a.size());
}
```

We can then use it like this:

```
auto func_b() {
  auto a = std::string{"Cole"};
  auto b = std::string{"Porter"};
  auto c = std::string{"ColePorter"};
  auto is_cole_porter = is_concat_equal(a, b, c);
}
```

Performance wise, we've achieved a bit of a win, but syntactically, a code base littered with special-case convenience functions like this is not realistic. So, let's see how this optimization can be achieved with the original syntax still intact.

Implementing the proxy

First, we'll create a proxy class representing the concatenation of two strings:

```
struct ConcatProxy {
  const std::string& a;
  const std::string& b;
};
```

Then, we'll construct our own `String` class, simply consisting of `std::string` and an overloaded `operator+` method. Note that this is an example of how to make and use proxy objects; creating your own `String` class is not something we recommend:

```
class String {
public:
  String() = default;
  String(std::string istr) : str_{std::move(istr)}{}
  std::string str_{};
};
```

```
auto operator+(const String& a, const String& b) {
   return ConcatProxy{ a.str_, b.str_ };
}
```

Here's a visual representation of the preceding code snippet:

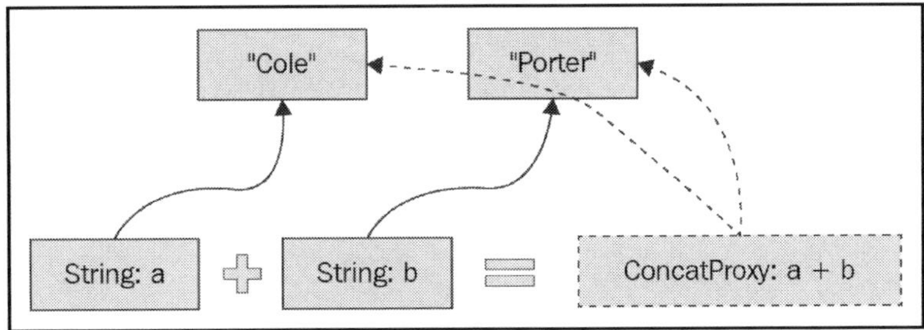

Proxy object representing an accumulation of two strings

Lastly, we'll create a global `operator==` method, which will utilize the `is_concat_equal()` function. Note that `ConcatProxy` is an explicit r-value; we will talk about this later in this chapter:

```
auto operator==(ConcatProxy&& concat, const String& str) -> bool {
  return is_concat_equal(concat.a, concat.b, str.str_);
}
```

Now that we have everything in place, we can get the best of both worlds:

```
auto func_c() {
  auto a = String{"Cole"};
  auto b = String{"Porter"};
  auto c = String{"ColePorter"};
  auto is_cole_porter = (a + b) == c;
  // is_cole_porter is true
}
```

In other words, we gained the performance of `func_b()` while preserving the expressive syntax of `func_a()`.

Performance evaluation

To evaluate the performance benefits, we'll utilize the following code, which compares `100'000'000` strings:

```
auto n = size_t{100'000'000};
auto a = std::vector<String>{};
auto b = std::vector<String>{};
auto c = std::vector<String>{};
a.resize(n);
b.resize(n);
c.resize(n);
// {Fill the vectors with random strings...}
auto num_equal = 0;
for(size_t i = 0; i < n; ++i) {
  num_equal += (a[i] + b[i] == c[i]) ? 1 : 0;
}
```

When executing this on an Intel i7 7700k CPU, we get the following results:

Comparison type	**Time (milliseconds)**	**Speed up**
No proxy object	675	1.00 x
With a proxy object	62	10.7 x

In other words, the speed up with a proxy object is almost eleven times as fast, when we got rid of the temporary string and the allocation that comes with it.

The r-value modifier

In the preceding code, the global `operator==` method only accepts r-values. If we were to accept an l-value, we could end up accidentally misusing the proxy, like this:

```
auto fail() {
  auto concat = String("Cole") + String("Porter");
  auto is_cole_porter = concat == String("ColePorter");
}
```

The problem here is that both the `Cole` and `Porter` strings are destructed when the comparison is executed, leading to a failure. As we force the `concat` object to be an r-value, the code will not compile when used like in the preceding code. Of course, you could brute-force it to compile using `std::move(concat) == String("ColePorter")`, but that wouldn't be a realistic case.

Assigning a concatenated proxy

Now you might be thinking, what if we actually want to store the concatenated string as a new string rather than just compare it? What we do is simply overload an `operator String()` method so that the concatenation of the strings can implicitly convert itself to a string, like this:

```
struct ConcatProxy {
  const std::string& a;
  const std::string& b;
  operator String() const && { return String{a + b}; }
};

auto func() {
  String c = String{"Marc"} + String{"Chagall"};
}
```

There is one little snag though; we cannot initialize the new `String` object with the `auto` keyword, as this would result in `ConcatProxy`:

```
auto c = String{"Marc"} + String{"Chagall"};
// c is a ConcatProxy due to the auto
```

Unfortunately, we have no way to get around this; the result must be explicitly cast to `String`.

Postponing an sqrt computation when comparing distances

In this example, we will show you how to use a proxy object in order to postpone, or even avoid, using the computationally heavy `std::sqrt()` method when comparing the distance between two dimensional points.

A simple two-dimensional point class

Let's start with a simple point class in 2D. It has x and y coordinates and a member function, which calculates the distance to another point:

```
class Point{
public:
  Point(float x, float y) : x_{x}, y_{y} {}
```

```
    auto distance(const Point& p) const {
      auto dist_sqrd = std::pow(x_-p.x_, 2) + std::pow(y_-p.y_, 2)
      return std::sqrt(dist_sqrd);
    }
  private:
    float x_{};
    float y_{};
  };
```

A simple usage example would be as follows:

```
auto target = Point{3, 5};
auto a = Point{6, 9};
auto b = Point{7, 4};
auto nearest_target =
  target.distance(a) < target.distance(b) ?
  a : b;
auto a_to_b_distance = a.distance(b);
```

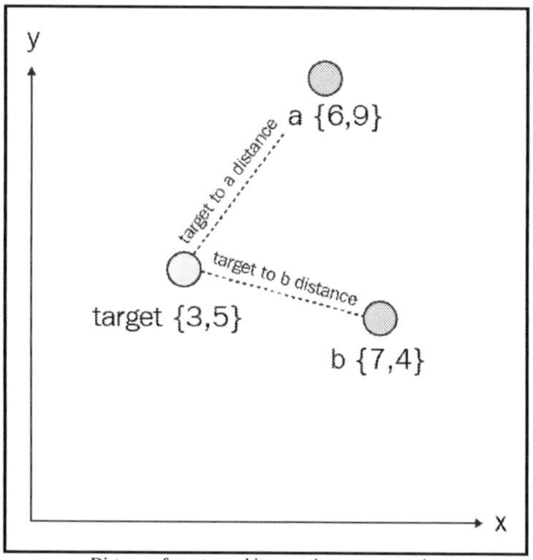

Distances from two arbitrary points to target point

The underlying mathematics

Looking into the mathematics of the distance calculation, you may notice something interesting. The formula used for distance is as follows:

$$distance = \sqrt{(x_0 - x_1)^2 + (y_0 - y_1)^2}$$

However, if we only need to compare the distance between points, the squared distance is all we need, as the following formula shows:

$$distance^2 = (x_0 - x_1)^2 + (y_0 - y_1)^2$$

As the `std::sqrt()` operation is not required if we just want to compare distances to each other, we can omit it. The nice thing is, `std::sqrt()` is a relatively slow operation, meaning that if we compare a lot of distances between points, we can gain some performance.

The question is, how can we do this while preserving a clean syntax? Let's see how we can use a proxy object to make a simple library perform this optimization under the hood when comparing distances.

Using the squared distance also has better precision on floating point values, as `std::sqrt()` loses precision and, thus, two very similar values might result in the same square root. That is, `std::sqrt(56.999999999999)` might result in the same value as `std::sqrt(57)` due to lost precision.

For clarity, we start with the original `Point` class but we split the `distance()` function into two—the `distance_squared()` and `distance()` functions:

```
class Point {
public:
  Point(float x, float y) : x_{x}, y_{y} {}
  auto distance_squared(const Point& p) const {
    return std::pow(x_-p.x_, 2) + std::pow(y_-p.y_, 2);
  }
  auto distance(const Point& p) const {
    return std::sqrt(distance_squared(p));
  }
private:
  float x_{};
  float y_{};
};
```

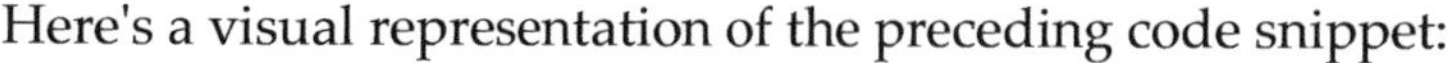

Here's a visual representation of the preceding code snippet:

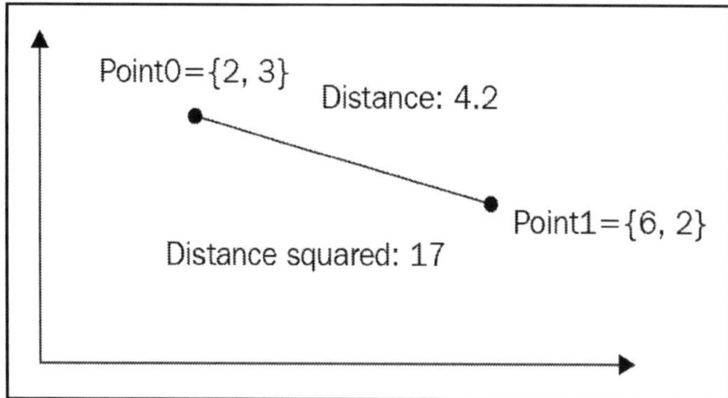

Distance, and squared distance between two points

Let's say a user of the `Point` class is implementing a convenient function that determines if two points are nearer to each other than a specific threshold. She now has two options, either use the `distance()` function or the `distance_squared()` function. Their corresponding implementations are shown in the following table:

Using the distance() member function	Using the distance_squared() member function

`auto is_near0(Point a, Point b,`
`float th) {`
`  auto dist = a.distance(b);`
`  return dist < th;`
`}`
	`auto is_near1(Point a, Point b, float th) {`
	` auto th_sqrd = std::pow(th, 2);`
	` auto dist_sqrd = a.distance_squared(b);`
	` return dist_sqrd < th_sqrd;`
	`}`

The `is_near0()` method has the advantage of being more readable, whereas the `is_near1()` method has the advantage of being faster, since `std::pow(th, 2)` is much faster than the `std::sqrt(th)` method invoked inside the `a.distance(b)` call of `is_near0`.

The optimal solution would be to have the syntax of `is_near0` and the performance of `is_near1`.

In order to achieve this, instead of returning a `float` value from the `distance()` member function, we return an intermediate object hidden to the user. Depending on how the user uses the hidden object, it should not perform the `std::sqrt()` operation until it is really required. This object will be referred to as `DistProxy`.

Implementing the DistProxy object

Now, let's create the proxy object for distances between points: `DistProxy`. A point distance simply consists of the squared distance between two points and a comparison to a distance. The actual squared distance is never exposed in order to prevent the library user from mixing the squared distance with the regular distance. That is, if we do not take precaution, the user of the code might accidentally write the following:

```
auto a = Point{23, 45};
auto b = Point{55, 66};
auto spot = Point{34, 55};
// Subtle bug below as distance is compared to distance_squared
bool a_is_nearest = a.distance(spot) < b.distance_squared(spot);
```

Thus, he may end up accidentally comparing the squared distance with the real distance, yielding hard-to-track bugs.

The proxy object, `DistProxy`, is implemented as follows, taking the coordinates of the two points as input and a method that compares it with a regular distance:

```
class DistProxy{
public:
  DistProxy(float x0, float y0, float x1, float y1)
  : dist_sqrd_{ std::pow(x0-x1, 2) + std::pow(y0-y1, 2) } {}
  auto operator<(float dist) const { return dist_sqrd_ < dist*dist; }
private:
  float dist_sqrd_{};
};
```

Then, we rewrite the `Point` class to return `DistProxy` instead of the actual distance as `float`:

```
class Point {
public:
  Point(float x, float y) : x_{x}, y_{y} {}
  auto distance(const Point& p) const {
    return DistProxy{x_, y_, p.x_, p.y_}; }
  float x_{};
  float y_{};
};
```

The `is_near0()` method now performs its comparison much faster, as the `std::sqrt()` operation is omitted in favor of `std::pow(x, 2)`, which is a much faster operation, especially when the second parameter is an integer (`2`).

Moreover, the nicest thing is that it all happens under the hood; the implementor of the `is_near0()` function can compare the result of the distance function with a floating point value, as if the distance function returned a floating point value right away.

Expanding DistProxy to something more useful

Now that we have the basis, we want to make the `DistProxy` class more useful. For example, the user might actually want to utilize the received distance or compare it with other distances.

Let's expand the `DistProxy` class accordingly, with a comparator to another `DistProxy` class and an implicit cast to `float`:

```
class DistProxy{
public:
  DistProxy(float x0, float y0, float x1, float y1)
  : dist_sqrd_{std::pow(x0 - x1, 2) + std::pow(y0 - y1, 2)}
  {}
  auto operator==(const DistProxy& dp) const {
    return dist_sqrd_ == dp.dist_sqrd_; }
  auto operator<(const DistProxy& dp) const {
    return dist_sqrd_ < dp.dist_sqrd_; }
  auto operator<(float dist) const {
    return dist_sqrd_ < dist*dist; }
  // Implicit cast to float
  operator float() const { return std::sqrt(dist_sqrd_); }
private:
  float dist_sqrd_{};
};
```

Comparing distances with DistProxy

So let's see how the `PointDistance` proxy class looks in action. In this example, we'll determine which of the points, `a` or `b`, that are closest to `bingo`. Note how the code syntactically looks exactly the same as had we not utilized a `PointDistance` proxy class:

```
auto bingo = Point{31, 11};
auto a = Point{23, 42};
auto b = Point{33, 12};
bool a_is_nearest = a.distance(bingo) < b.distance(bingo);
```

Under the hood, the final statement is expanded to something similar to this:

```
// These "DistProxy" proxy objects are never visible from the outside
DistProxy a_to_bingo = a.distance(bingo);
DistProxy b_to_bingo = b.distance(bingo);
// Member operator< on DistProxy is invoked, which compares member
dist_sqrd_
auto a_is_nearest = a_to_bingo < b_to_bingo;
```

Sweet! The `std::sqrt()` operation is omitted while the interface of the `Point` class is still intact. Let's see how it looks if we need the actual distance.

Calculating distances with DistProxy

When requesting the actual distance, the calling code changes a teeny-weeny bit; we have to explicitly parse the `DistProxy` object to `float`; that is, we can't just use `auto` as usual:

```
auto a = Point{23, 42};
auto b = Point{33, 12};
float dist = a.distance(b); // Note that we cannot use auto here
```

If we were to just write `auto`, the `dist` object would be of the `DistProxy` type rather than `float`. We do not want the users of our code base to explicitly handle `DistProxy` objects; proxy objects should operate in the dark and only their results should be utilized (in this case, the comparison result or the actual distance value is `float`). Even though we cannot hide proxy objects completely, let's see how we can tighten them to prevent misuse.

Preventing the misuse of DistProxy

You may have noted that there can be a case where using the `DistProxy` class might lead to worse performance—if the user of the class were to use the `Point` class like this, that is, if the `std::sqrt()` method were invoked multiple times according to the programmer's requests for the distance value:

```
auto a = Point{23, 42};
auto b = Point{33, 12};
auto dist = a.distance(b);
float dist_float0 = dist; // Assignment invoked std::sqrt()
float dist_float1 = dist; // std::sqrt() of dist is invoked again
```

Although a stupid example, there can be real-world cases where this might happen, and we want to force the user to only invoke `operator float()` once per `DistProxy` object. In order to prevent this we make the `operator float()` member function invocable only on r-values; that is, the `DistProxy` object can only be converted to a floating point if it is not tied to a variable.

We force this behavior by using `&&` as a modifier on the `operator float()` member function. The `&&` modifier works just like a `const` modifier, but where a `const` modifier forces the member function to not modify the class, the `&&` modifier forces the function to only invoke on temporary classes.

The modification looks like this:

```
operator float() const && { return std::sqrt(dist_sqrd_); }
```

If we were to invoke `operator float()` on a `DistProxy` object that is tied to a variable, such as the `dist` object in the following example, the compiler will refuse to compile:

```
auto a = Point{23, 42};
auto b = Point{33, 12};
auto dist = a.distance(b); // "dist" is of type DistProxy
float dist_float = dist;
```

However, we can still invoke `operator float()` directly on the `a.distance(b)` operation, like this:

```
auto a = Point{23, 42};
auto b = Point{33, 12};
float dist_float = a.distance(b);
```

A temporary `DistProxy` class will still be created in the background, but since it is not tied to a variable, we are allowed to implicitly convert it to `float`. This will prevent such misuse as invoking `operator float()` several times on a `DistProxy` object.

Performance evaluation

For the sake of it, let's see how much performance we've actually gained. Here is a function that finds the distance to a specified point in a vector of randomly generated points:

```
// Generate 10000 random points
auto points = std::vector<Point>{};
for(size_t i = 0; i < 10000; ++i) {
  auto x = static_cast<float>(std::rand());
  auto y = static_cast<float>(std::rand());
  points.emplace_back(x, y);
}
// Find the distance to the nearest point
auto needle = Point{135.0f, 246.0f};
auto nearest_point = *std::min_element(
  points.begin(),
  points.end(),
  [&needle](const Point& a, const Point& b) {
    return a.distance(needle) < b.distance(needle);
  });
float dist = nearest_point.distance(needle);
```

Using `DistProxy`, this piece of code is executed twice as fast (measured using an Intel i7 7700k CPU). And, as you can see, the syntax is exactly the same as if we did not implement any optimization.

Creative operator overloading and proxy objects

As you know, C++ has the ability to overload operators that are usually utilized to make custom math objects that can be used with standard math operators, such as plus, minus, and so on, in order to make the code more readable. Another example is the stream operator, which in the standard library is overloaded in order to convert the objects to streams, as shown below:

```
std::cout << "iostream " << "uses " << "overloaded " << "operators.";
```

Some libraries, however, use the overloading in other contexts. The Range V3 library, as discussed earlier, uses overloading to compose views like this:

```
namespace rv = ranges::view;
auto odd_positive_numbers =
  std::vector<int>{-5, -4, -3, -2, -1, 0, 1, 2, 3, 4, 5}
  | rv::filtered([](auto v){ return v > 0; }
  | rv::filtered([](auto v){ return (v % 2) == 1; }
  ;
```

Other libraries have used it to create an infix operator so that we can emulate the Python keyword, `in`, like this:

```
bool has_three = 3 <in> {1, 2, 3, 4, 5};
```

Although most people would probably argue against creative operator overloading, it can be educational to learn how it's implemented.

The pipe operator as an extension method

Compared to other languages, for example, C# and JavaScript, C++ does not support extension methods, that is, you cannot extend a class locally with a new member function.

For example, you cannot extend `std::vector` with a `contains(T val)` function to be used like this:

```
auto numbers = std::vector<int>{1,2,3,4};
auto has_two = numbers.contains(2);
```

However, you can overload the pipe operator to achieve this, almost equivalent, syntax:

```
auto has_two = numbers | contains(2);
```

The pipe operator

Let's see how we can implement a simple pipe operator so that we can write the following:

```
auto numbers = std::vector<int>{1, 3, 5, 7, 9};
auto seven = 7;
bool has_seven = numbers | contains(seven);
```

The `contains` function used with a pipeable syntax has two arguments: `numbers` and `seven`. As the left argument, `numbers` could be anything; we need the overload to contain something unique on the right side.

So, we create a struct named `ContainsProxy`, which holds onto the right argument; this way, the overloaded pipe operator can recognize the overload:

```
template <typename T>
struct ContainsProxy { const T& value_; };

template <typename Range, typename T>
auto operator|(const Range& r, const ContainsProxy<T>& proxy) {
  const auto& v = proxy.value_;
  return std::find(r.begin(), r.end(), v) != r.end();
}
```

Now we can use it like this; the pipe operator works, although the syntax is still ugly as we need to specify the type:

```
auto numbers = std::vector<int>{1,3,5,7,9};
auto seven = 7;
auto proxy = ContainsProxy<decltype(seven)>{seven};
bool has_seven = numbers | proxy;
```

In order to make the syntax neater, we can simply make a convenience function take the value and create a proxy containing the type:

```
template <typename T>
auto contains(const T& v) { return ContainsProxy<T>{v}; }
```

That's all we need; we can now use it for any type or container:

```
auto penguins = std::vector<std::string>{"Ping","Roy","Silo"};
bool has_silo = penguins | contains("Silo");
```

The infix operator

First of all, adding an infix operator is both a hack and, more or less, an abuse of operator overloading. What you actually do is overload both the less than (`operator<`) and greater than (`operator>`) operators in order to make something that looks like an infix operator.

If nothing less, it can be used to show to your Python-fan friends, who praise the `in` keyword in Python, that you can implement something similar in C++.

Essentially, we want to see whether an object is contained in a list with the following syntax:

```
auto asia = std::vector<std::string>{"Korea","Philippines","Macau"};
auto africa = std::vector<std::string>{"Senegal","Botswana","Guinea"};
auto is_botswana_in_asia = "Botswana" <in> asia;
auto is_botswana_in_africa = "Botswana" <in> africa;
// is_botswana_in_asia is false
// is_botswana_in_africa is true
```

As with the pipe overload, we create a proxy, but in this case, the proxy holds the left value of the operation:

```
template <typename T> struct InProxy { const T& val_; };
```

We then define an empty struct called `in_tag` and instantiate a static object called `in` like this. Note that the `in` object is only a convenience in order to invoke the infix operator using `<in>` rather than `<in_tag{}>`, that is, to remove the curly braces:

```
struct InTag{};
constexpr static auto in = InTag{};
```

The `InTag` type is then used for `operator<`, so it can recognize the overload:

```
template <typename T>
auto operator<(const T& v, const InTag&) { return InProxy<T>{v}; }
```

Finally, we overload the greater than operator to take `in_proxy` as the first argument and the right side as its second argument. It also holds the actual function:

```
template <typename T, typename Range>
auto operator>(const InProxy<T>& p, const Range& r) {
  return std::find(r.begin(), r.end(), p.val_) != r.end();
}
```

Now we can use it like this:

```
auto africa = std::vector<std::string>{ "Kenya", "Ethiopia", "Kongo"};
auto sweden = std::string{"Sweden"};
auto is_sweden_in_africa = sweden <in> africa;
// is_sweden_in_africa is false
```

Under the hood, the code expands to the following code:

```
auto africa = std::vector<std::string>{ "Kenya", "Ethiopia", "Kongo"};
auto sweden = std::string{"Sweden"};
InTag in_tag{};
InProxy<std::string> p = sweden < in_tag;
bool is_sweden_in_africa = p > africa; // is_sweden_in_africa is false
```

Further reading

The examples covered in this section show a rudimentary approach to implementing the pipe and infix operators. Libraries such as Range V3 and the *Fit* library by *Paul Fultz*, available at `https://github.com/pfultz2/Fit`, implement adapters that take a regular function and give them the ability to be invoked using the pipe syntax.

Summary

In this chapter, you learned the difference between lazy evaluation and eager evaluation. You also learned how to use hidden proxy objects to implement lazy evaluation behind the scenes, meaning that you understood how to implement lazy evaluation optimizations while preserving an easy-to-use interface for your classes.

This makes writing optimized code much more readable and less error-prone, as the complex optimizations can be kept inside your library classes instead of having it exposed in the application code.

10
Concurrency

In this chapter, we are going to explore how to write concurrent programs in C++ using threads with shared memory. We will look at ways to make concurrent programs correct by writing programs that are free from data races and deadlocks. This chapter will also contain some pieces of advice on how to make concurrent programs run with low latency and high throughput.

Before we go any further, it should be said that this chapter is not a complete introduction to concurrent programming, nor will it cover all the details of concurrency in C++. Instead, this chapter is an introduction to the core building blocks of writing concurrent programs in C++, mixed with some performance-related guidelines. If you haven't been writing concurrent programs before, it is probably wise to go through some introduction texts to cover the theoretical aspects of concurrent programming first. Concepts such as deadlocks, critical sections, monitors, condition variables, and mutexes, will be very briefly discussed, but that serves more as a refresher than a thorough introduction to the concepts.

The chapter includes the following:

- The fundamentals of concurrent programming, including parallel execution, shared memory, data races, and deadlocks
- An introduction to the C++ thread support library, the atomic library, and the C++ memory model
- A short example of lock-free programming
- Performance guidelines

Understanding the basics of concurrency

A concurrent program can execute multiple tasks at the same time. Concurrent programming is, in general, a lot harder than sequential programming, but there are several reasons why a program may benefit from being concurrent:

- **Efficiency**: Smartphones and desktop computers of today have multiple CPU cores that can execute multiple tasks in parallel if your program allows it to. If you manage to split a big task into subtasks that can be run in parallel, it is theoretically possible to divide the running time of the big task by the number of CPU cores. For programs that run on machines with one single core, there can still be a gain in performance if a task is I/O bound. While one subtask is waiting for I/O, other subtasks can still perform useful work on the CPU.
- **Responsiveness and low latency contexts**: For applications with a graphical user interface, it is important to never block the UI so that the application becomes unresponsive. To prevent unresponsiveness, it is common to let long-running tasks execute in separate background threads so that the thread responsible for the UI is never blocked by long-running tasks. Another example where low latency matters is real-time audio. The function responsible for producing buffers of audio data is being executed in a separate high-priority thread, while the rest of the program can run in lower-priority threads to handle the UI and so on.
- **Simulation**: Concurrency can make it easier to simulate systems that are concurrent in the real world. After all, most things around us happen concurrently, and sometimes it is very hard to model concurrent flows with a sequential programming model. We will not focus on simulation in this book, but instead focus on performance-related aspects of concurrency.

What makes concurrent programming hard?

There are a couple of reasons why concurrent programming is hard, and, if you have been writing concurrent programs before, you have most likely already encountered the ones listed here:

1. Sharing state between multiple threads in a safe manner is hard. Whenever we have data that can be read and written to at the same time, we need some way of protecting that data from *data races*. We will see a lot of examples of this later on.

2. Concurrent programs are usually more complicated to reason about because of the multiple parallel execution flows.
3. Concurrency complicates debugging. Bugs that occur because of data races can be very hard to debug since they are dependent on how threads are being scheduled. These kinds of bugs can be hard to reproduce and in the worst case, they cease to exist when running the program using a debugger. Sometimes an innocent debug trace to the console could change the way a multithreaded program behaves and make the bug temporarily disappear. You have been warned!

Concurrency and parallelism

Concurrency and parallelism are two terms that are sometimes used interchangeably. However, they are not the same and it is important to understand the difference. A program is said to run *concurrently* if it has multiple individual control flows running during overlapping time periods. In C++, each individual control flow is represented by a *thread*. The threads may or may not execute at the exact same time, though. If they do, they are said to execute in *parallel*. For a concurrent program to run in parallel, it needs to be executed on a machine that has support for parallel execution of instructions: that is, machines with multiple CPU cores.

At first glance, it might seem obvious that we always want concurrent programs to run in parallel if possible, for efficiency reasons. However, that is not necessarily always true. A lot of synchronization primitives we will cover in this chapter are required only to support the parallel execution of threads. Concurrent tasks that are not run in parallel do not require the same locking mechanisms and can be a lot easier to reason about.

Time slicing

"How are concurrent threads executed on machines with only a single CPU core?" you might ask. The answer is *time slicing*. It is the same mechanism that is being used by the operating system to support concurrent execution of processes. In order to understand time slicing, let's assume we have two separate sequences of instructions that should be executed concurrently, as shown in the following figure:

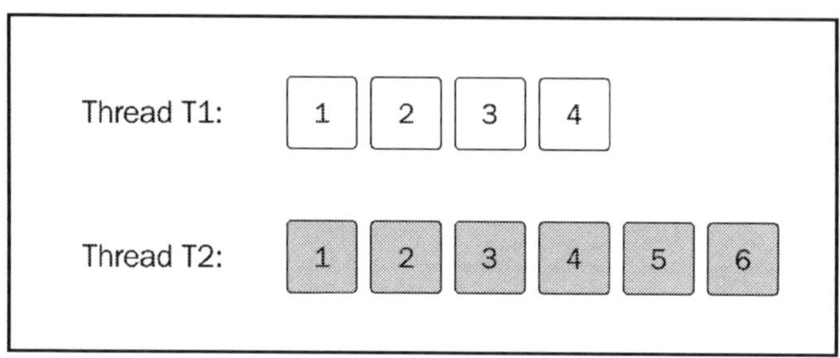

Two separate sequences of instructions executed in two threads labeled T1 and T2

The numbered boxes represent instructions. Each sequence of instructions is executed in separate threads labeled T1 and T2. The operating system will schedule each thread to have some limited time on the CPU and then perform a *context switch*. The context switch stores the current state of the running thread and loads the state of the thread that should be executed. This is done often enough so that it appears as if the threads are running at the same time. A context switch is time-consuming though, and most likely generates a lot of cache misses each time a new thread gets to execute on a CPU core. Therefore, you don't want context switches to happen too often.

The following figure shows a possible execution sequence of the two threads that are being scheduled on a single CPU:

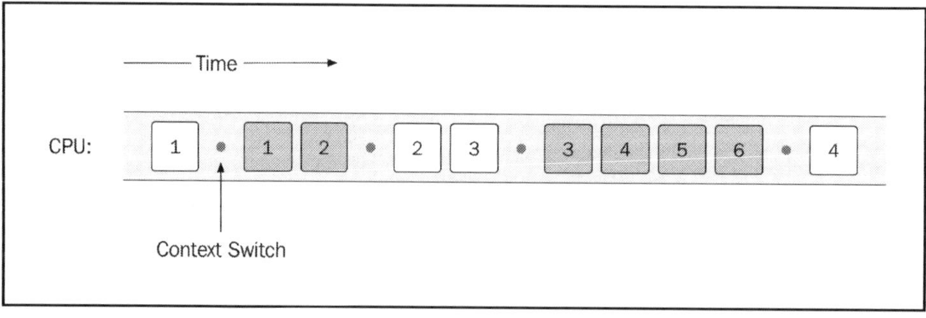

A possible execution of two threads which are being scheduled on a single core. The red dots indicate context switches

The first instruction of thread T1 is starting, and is then followed by a context switch to let the other thread (T2) execute the first two instructions. As programmers, we must make sure that the program can run as expected, regardless of how the operating system scheduler is scheduling the tasks. If a sequence, for some reason, should be illegal, there are ways to control the order in which the instructions get executed by using locks—more on that in the sections to come.

If a machine has multiple CPU cores, it is possible to execute the two threads in parallel. However, there is no guarantee (it's even unlikely) that the two threads will execute on one core each throughout the lifetime of the program. The entire system is sharing time on the CPU so the scheduler will let other processes execute as well. This is one of the reasons why the threads are not scheduled on dedicated cores.

The following figure shows the execution of the same two threads, but now they are running on a machine with two CPU cores. As can be seen, the second and third instructions of the first thread (white boxes) are being executed at the exact same time as the other thread is executing—the two threads are executing in parallel:

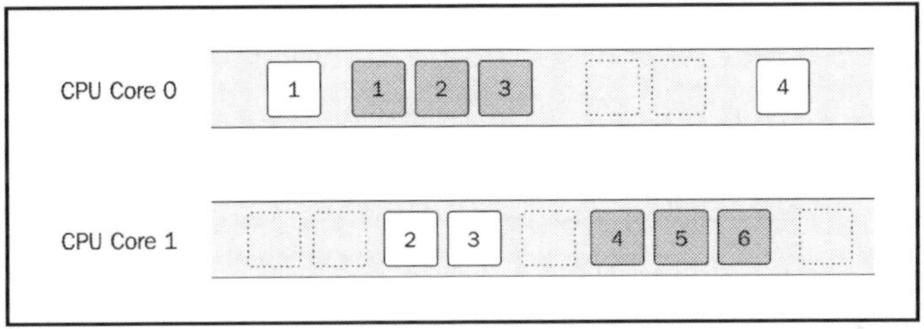

Two threads are executing on a multicore machine. This makes it possible to execute the two threads in parallel

Shared memory

Threads created in the same process share the same virtual memory. This means that a thread can access any data that is addressable within the process. The operating system, which protects memory between processes using virtual memory, does nothing to protect us from accidentally accessing memory inside a process that was not intended to be shared among different threads. Virtual memory only protects us from accessing memory allocated in other processes than our own.

Sharing memory between multiple threads can be a very efficient way to handle communication between threads. However, sharing memory in a safe way between threads is one of the major challenges when writing concurrent programs in C++. You should always strive to minimize the number of shared resources between threads.

Fortunately, not all memory is shared by default. Each thread has its own stack for storing local variables and other data necessary for handling function calls. Unless a thread passes references or pointers to local variables to other threads, no other thread will be able to access the stack from that thread. This is one more reason to use the stack as much as possible (if you are not already convinced that the stack is a good place for your data after reading `Chapter 7`, *Memory Management*).

There is also *thread local storage,* sometimes abbreviated to TLS, which can be used for storing variables that are global in the context of a thread but which are not shared between threads. A thread local variable can be thought of as a global variable where each thread has its own copy.

Everything else is shared by default: that is, dynamic memory allocated on the heap, global variables, and static local variables. Whenever you have shared data that is mutated by some thread, you need to ensure that no other thread is accessing that data at the same time or you will have a data race.

Remember the figure from the *Process memory* section of `Chapter 7`, *Memory Management,* which illustrated the virtual address space of a process? Here it is again, but modified to show how it looks when a process contains multiple threads. As you can see in the following figure, each thread has its own stack memory, but there is only one heap for all threads:

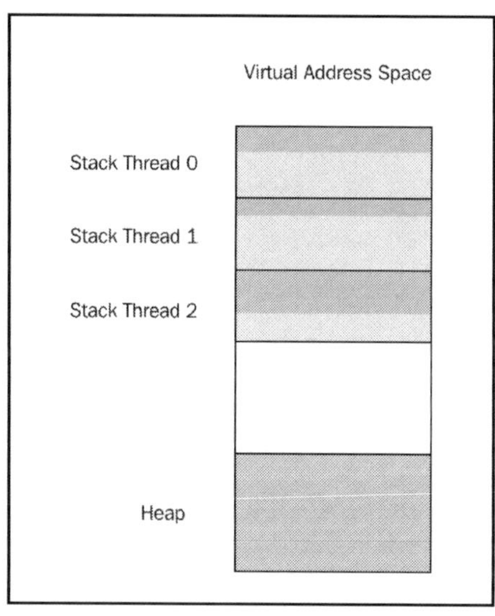

A possible layout of the virtual address space for a process

The process contains three threads in this example, and each thread has its own dedicated stack memory. The heap memory is by default shared by all threads.

Data races

A *data race* happens when two threads are accessing the same memory at the same time and at least one of the threads is mutating the data. If your program has a data race, it means that your program has *undefined behavior*. In other words, you can under no circumstances allow data races in your program. The compiler usually doesn't warn you about data races since they are hard to detect at compile time.

The following image shows two threads that are going to update an integer called `counter`. Imagine that we have two threads that are both incrementing a global *counter* variable by the instruction `++counter`. It turns out that incrementing an `int` might involve multiple CPU instructions. This can be done in different ways on different CPUs, but let's pretend that `++counter` generates the following made-up machine instructions:

```
 R:  Read counter from memory
+1:  Increment counter
 W:  Write new counter value to memory
```

Now, if we have two threads that are going to update the `counter` value that initially is 42, we would expect it to become 44 after both threads have run. However, as we can see in the following figure, there is no guarantee that the instructions will be executed sequentially to guarantee a correct increment of the `counter` variable:

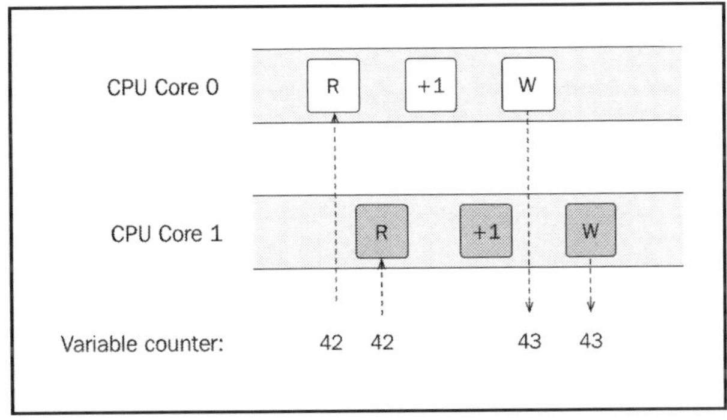

The two threads are both incrementing the same shared variable

Without a data race, the counter would have reached the value 44, but instead, it only reaches 43.

In this example, both threads read the value 42 and incremented that value to 43. Then, they both write the new value, 43, which means that we never reached the correct answer of 44. Had the first thread been able to write the value 43 before the next thread started to read, we would have ended up with 44 instead. Note also that this would have been possible even if there was only one CPU core. The scheduler could have scheduled the two threads in a similar way so that both read instructions were executed before any writes.

Again, this is one possible scenario, but the important thing is that the behavior is undefined. Anything could happen when your program has a data race.

How can we avoid data races? There are two main options:

- Use an atomic data type instead of the `int`. This will tell the compiler to execute the read, increment, and write atomically. In general, this approach works if the size of the data type we are modifying is less than or equal to the word size of the machine. We will spend more time discussing atomic data types later in this chapter.
- Use a mutually exclusive lock (mutex) that guarantees that multiple threads never execute a critical section at the same time. A critical section is a place in the code that must not be executed simultaneously since it updates or reads shared memory that potentially could generate data races.

It is also worth emphasizing that immutable data structures—data structures that are never being changed—can be accessed by multiple threads without any risk of data races. Minimizing the use of mutable objects is good for many reasons, but it becomes even more important when writing concurrent programs. A common pattern is to always create new immutable objects instead of mutating existing objects. When the new object is fully constructed and represents the new state, it can be swapped with the old object. In that way, we can minimize the critical sections of our code. Only the swap is a critical section, and hence needs to be protected by an atomic operation or a mutex.

Mutex

A **mutex**, short for mutual exclusion lock, is a synchronization primitive for avoiding data races. A thread that needs to enter a critical section is first *locking* the mutex (locking is sometimes also called acquiring a mutex lock). This means that no other thread can lock the same mutex until the first thread that holds the lock has unlocked the mutex. In that way, the mutex guarantees that only one thread at a time is inside a critical section.

In the following figure, we can see how the example of the race condition can be avoided by using a mutex. The instruction labeled *L* is a lock instruction and the instruction labeled *U* is an unlock instruction. The first thread executing on Core 0 reaches the critical section first and locks the mutex before reading the value of the counter. It then adds one to the counter and writes it back to memory. After that, it releases the lock.

The second thread, executing on Core 1, reaches the critical section just after the first thread has acquired the mutex lock. Since the mutex is already locked, the thread is blocked until the first thread has updated the counter undisturbed and released the mutex:

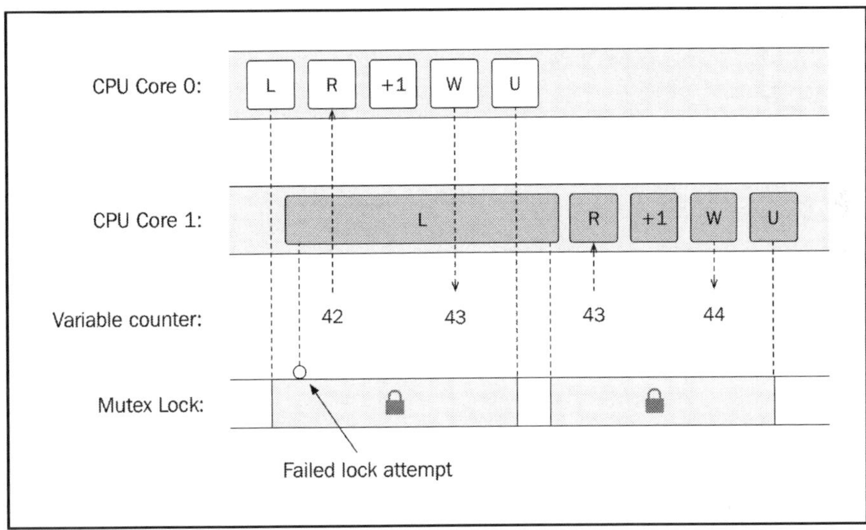

The mutex lock is protecting the critical section and avoids the data races on the counter variable

The net result is that the two threads can update the mutable shared variable in a safe and correct way. But, it also means that the two threads can no longer be run in parallel. If most of the work a thread does cannot be done without serializing the work, there is, from a performance perspective, no point in using threads.

The state where the second thread is blocked by the first thread to finish its work is called **contention**. This is something we strive to minimize, because it hurts the scalability of a concurrent program. Adding more CPU cores will not improve performance if the degree of contention is high.

Deadlock

When using mutex locks to protect shared resources, there is a risk of getting stuck in a state called **deadlock**. A deadlock can happen when two threads are waiting for each other to release their locks. None of the threads can proceed and are stuck in a deadlock state. One condition that needs to be fulfilled for a deadlock to occur is that one thread that already holds a lock tries to acquire an additional lock. When a system grows and gets larger, it becomes more and more difficult to track all locks that might be used by all threads running in a system. This is one reason for always trying to minimize the use of shared resources, and this demonstrates the need for exclusive locking.

The following figure shows how two threads are in a waiting state, trying to acquire the lock held by the other thread:

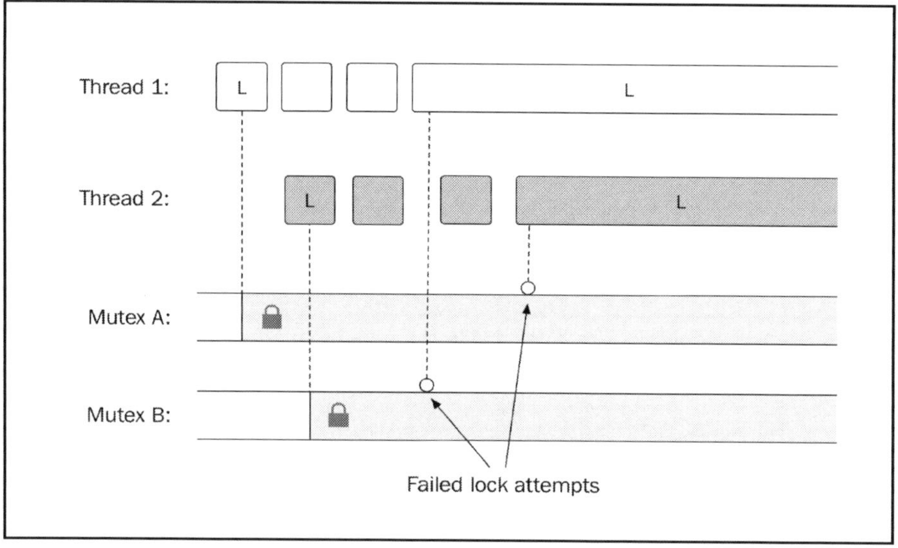

Example of a deadlock state. Thread 1 and Thread 2 are waiting for each other to release their locks, respectively

Synchronous and asynchronous tasks

We will refer to *synchronous* and *asynchronous tasks* or *function calls* in this chapter. Synchronous tasks are like the ordinary functions that we are used to in a C++ program. When a synchronous task is finished doing whatever it is supposed to do, it will return the control to the caller of the task. The caller of the task is waiting or blocked until the synchronous task has finished.

An asynchronous task, on the other hand, will return the control back to the caller immediately and instead perform its work concurrently. The sequence in the following diagram shows the difference between calling a synchronous and asynchronous task, respectively:

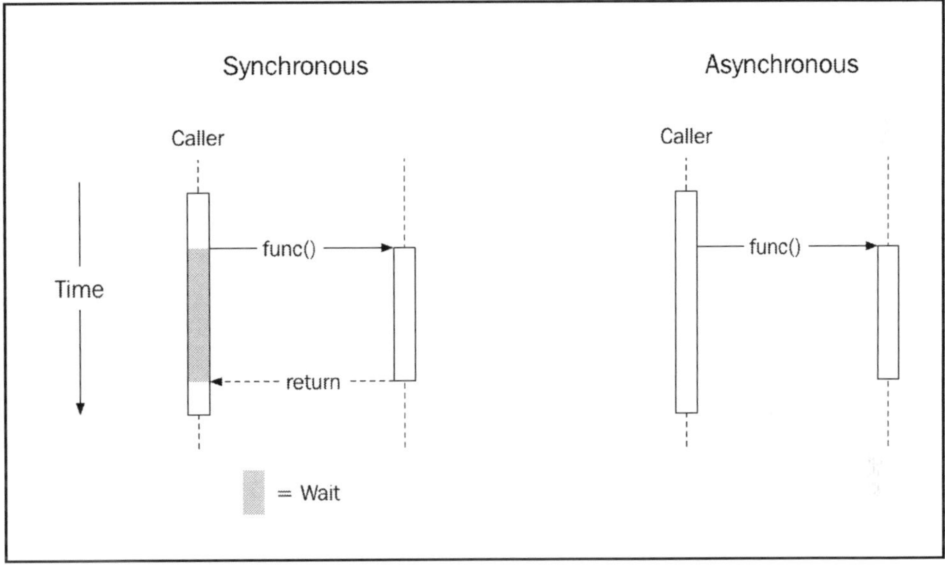

Synchronous versus asynchronous calls. The asynchronous task returns immediately but continue to work after the caller has regained control.

If you haven't seen asynchronous tasks before, it might look strange at first, since ordinary functions in C++ always stop executing when they encounter a return statement or reach the end of the function body. Asynchronous APIs are getting more and more common though, and it is likely that you have encountered them before, for example, when working with asynchronous JavaScript.

Sometimes, we use the term blocking of operations that blocks the caller—that is, it makes the caller wait until the operation has finished.

Concurrent programming in C++

The concurrency support in C++ makes it possible for a program to execute multiple tasks concurrently. As mentioned earlier, writing a correct concurrent C++ program is, in general, a lot harder than writing a program that executes all tasks sequentially in one thread. This section will also demonstrate some common pitfalls to make you aware of all the difficulties involved in writing concurrent programs.

Concurrency support was first introduced in C++11 and has since then been extended into both C++14 and C++17. Before concurrency was part of the language, concurrency was implemented with native concurrency support from the operating system, **POSIX Threads** (**pthreads**), or some other library. With concurrency support directly in the C++ language, we can now write cross-platform concurrent programs, which is great! However, since the concurrency support in C++ is rather new, don't be surprised if you have to reach for platform-specific functionality when dealing with concurrency on your platform. It should also be said that the thread support library is likely to be extended quite a bit in the next few releases of C++. The need for good concurrency support is increasing because of the way hardware is being developed, and there is a lot yet to be discovered when it comes to the efficiency, scalability, and correctness of highly concurrent programs.

The thread support library

We will here take a tour through the C++ thread support library and cover the most important components of the library.

Threads

A running program contains at least one thread. When your main function is being called, it is executed on a thread usually referred to as the **main thread**. Each thread has an identifier, which can be useful when debugging a concurrent program. The following program prints the thread identifier of the main thread:

```
auto main() -> int {
  std::cout << "Thread ID: " <<  std::this_thread::get_id() << '\n';
}
```

Running the preceding program might produce something like this:

```
Thread ID: 0x1001553c0
```

It is possible to make a thread sleep. Sleep is rarely used in production code but can be very useful during debugging. For example, if you have a data race that only occurs under rare circumstances, adding sleep to your code might make it appear more often. Here is how you make the currently running thread sleep for a second:

```
std::this_thread::sleep_for(std::chrono::seconds{1});
```

Your program should never expose any data races after inserting random sleeps in your code. Your program may not work satisfactorily after adding sleeps: buffers may become full, the UI lags, and so on, but it should always behave in a predictable and defined way. We don't have control over the scheduling of the threads, and random sleeps simulate unlikely but possible scheduling scenarios.

Now, let us create an additional thread using the `std::thread` class from the `<thread>` header. It represents a single thread of execution and is usually a wrapper around an operating system thread. The `print` function will be invoked from a thread created by us explicitly:

```
auto print() {
  std::this_thread::sleep_for(std::chrono::seconds{1});
  std::cout << "Thread ID: "<<  std::this_thread::get_id() << '\n';
}

auto main() -> int {
  auto t1 = std::thread{print};
  t1.join();
  std::cout << "Thread ID: "<<  std::this_thread::get_id() << '\n';
}
```

When creating the thread, we pass in a callable object (a function, lambda, or a functor) that the thread will begin to execute whenever it gets scheduled time on the CPU. We have added a call to sleep to make it obvious why we need to call join on the thread. When a `std::thread` object is destructed, it must have been *joined* or *detached* or it will cause the program to call `std::terminate()`, which by default will call `std::abort()` if you haven't installed a custom `std::terminate_handler`.

If we forget to call either join or detach on a `std::thread` object before it is destructed, the program will abort, as demonstrated in the following example:

```
auto main() -> int {
   auto t1 = std::thread{print};
   // Error: forgot to detach or join t1, program will abort
}
```

Always remember that you have to call either join or detach on a thread object before it is destructed, or the program will abort.

In the preceding example, the `join()` function is blocking—it waits until the thread has finished running. So, in the preceding example, the `main` function will not return until thread `t1` has finished running. Consider the following line:

```
t1.join();
```

Suppose we detach the thread `t1` by replacing the preceding line with the following line:

```
t1.detach();
```

In such a case, our main function will end before thread `t1` wakes up to print the message, and as a result, the program will (most likely) only output the thread ID of the main thread. Remember, we have no control of the scheduling of the threads and it is possible but very unlikely that the main thread will output its message *after* the `print()` function has had time to sleep, wake up, and print its thread ID.

Using `detach()` instead of `join()` in this example also introduces another problem. We are using `std::cout` from both threads without any synchronization, and since `main()` is no longer waiting for thread `t1` to finish, they both could theoretically use `std::cout` in parallel. Fortunately, `std::cout` is thread-safe and can be used from multiple threads without introducing data races, so there is no undefined behavior. However, it is still possible that the output generated by the threads are interleaved, resulting in something like:

```
Thread ID: Thread ID: 0x1003a93400x700004fd4000
```

If we want to avoid the interleaved output, we need to treat the outputting of characters as a critical section and synchronize access to `std::cout`. We will talk more about critical sections and race conditions in a while, but first, some details about `std::thread`.

Thread states

Before we go any further, we should make sure that we have a good understanding of what a `std::thread` object really represents and in what states it can be. We haven't yet talked about what sort of threads there normally are in a system executing a C++ program. In the following figure, we have captured a snapshot of a hypothetical running system:

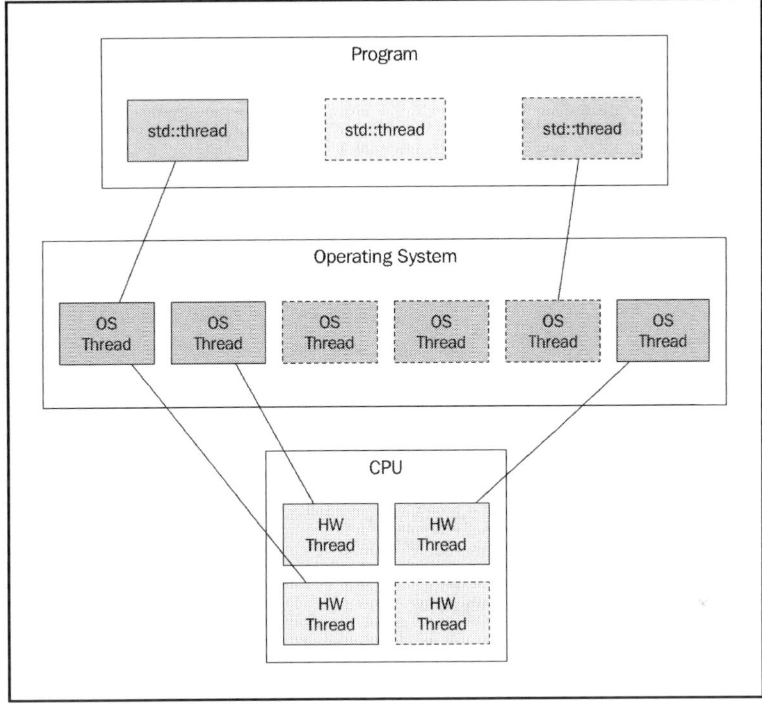

Snapshot of a hypothetical running system

Starting from the bottom, the figure shows the CPU and its hardware threads. Those are the execution units on the CPU. In this example, the CPU provides four hardware threads; usually that means it has four cores, but it could be some other configuration. Some cores can execute two hardware threads, for example. The total number of hardware threads can be printed at runtime with this:

```
std::cout << std::thread::hardware_concurrency() << '\n';
// Possible output: 4
```

The preceding code might also output `0` if the number of hardware threads cannot be determined on the running platform.

The layer above the hardware threads contains the operating system threads. These are the actual software threads. The OS scheduler determines when and how long an OS thread is executed by a hardware thread. In the preceding figure, there are currently three out of six software threads executing.

The topmost layer in the figure contains the `std::thread` objects. A `std::thread` object is nothing more (or nothing less) than an ordinary C++ object that may or may not be associated with an underlying OS thread. Two instances of `std::thread` cannot be associated with the same underlying thread. In the figure, we can see that the program currently has three instances of `std::thread`, whereas two are associated with threads and one is not. It is possible to query a `std::thread` object in what state it is by using the `std::thread::joinable` property. A thread is *not* joinable if it has been:

- Default constructed; that is, if it has nothing to execute
- Moved from (its associated running thread has been transferred to another `std::thread` object)
- Detached by a call to `detach()`
- Already joined by a call to `join()`

Otherwise, the `std::thread` object is in the joinable state. Remember, when a `std::thread` object is destructed, it must no longer be in the joinable state or the program will terminate.

Protecting critical sections

As already mentioned, our code must not contain any data races. Unfortunately, writing code with data races is very easy. Finding the critical sections and protecting them with locks is something we constantly need to think about when writing concurrent programs in this style using threads.

C++ provides us with a `std::mutex` class that can be used for protecting critical sections and avoiding data races. We will demonstrate how to use a mutex with a classic example using a shared mutable counter variable updated by multiple threads.

First, we define a global mutable variable and the function incrementing the counter:

```
auto counter = 0; // Warning! Global mutable variable

auto increment_counter(int n) {
  for (int i = 0; i < n; ++i)
    ++counter;
}
```

The `main()` function below creates two threads that will both execute the `increment_counter()` function. Note also in this example how we can pass arguments to the function invoked by the thread. We can pass an arbitrary number of arguments to the thread constructor in order to match the parameters in the signature of the function to be called. Finally, we assert that the counter has the value we expect it to have if the program was free from race conditions:

```
auto main() -> int {
  constexpr auto n_times = int{1000000};
  auto t1 = std::thread{increment_counter, n_times};
  auto t2 = std::thread{increment_counter, n_times};
  t1.join();
  t2.join();
  std::cout << counter << '\n';
  // If we don't have a data race, this assert should hold:
  assert(counter == (n_times * 2));
}
```

This program will most likely fail. The `assert()` function doesn't hold since the program currently contains a race condition. When I repeatedly run the program, I end up with different values of the counter. Instead of reaching the value 2000000, I once ended up with no more than 1032304. This example is very similar to the data race example that was illustrated earlier in this chapter.

The line with the expression `++counter` is a critical section—it uses a shared mutable variable and is executed by multiple threads. In order to protect the critical section, we will now use the `std::mutex` included in the `<mutex>` header. Later on, we will see how we can avoid data races in this example by using atomics, but for now we will use a lock.

First, add the global `std::mutex` object next to the `counter`:

```
auto counter = 0; // Counter will be protected by counter_mutex
auto counter_mutex = std::mutex{};
```

Isn't the `std::mutex` object itself a mutable shared variable that can generate data races if used by multiple threads? Yes, it is a mutable shared variable, but no, it will not generate data races. The synchronization primitives from the C++ thread such as `std::mutex` are designed for this particular purpose. In that respect, they are very special and use hardware instructions or whatever is necessary on your platform to guarantee that they don't generate data races themselves.

Now we need to use the mutex in our critical section that reads and updates the counter variable. We could use the `lock()` and `unlock()` member functions on the `counter_mutex`, but the preferred and safer way is to always use RAII for handling the mutex. Think of the mutex as a resource that always needs to be unlocked when we are done using it. The thread library provides us with some useful RAII class templates for handling locking. Here, we will use the `std::lock_guard<Mutex>` template to ensure that we release the mutex safely. The following is the updated `increment_counter` function now protected with a mutex lock:

```
auto increment_counter(int n) {
  for (int i = 0; i < n; ++i) {
    auto lock = std::lock_guard<std::mutex>{counter_mutex};
    ++counter;
  }
}
```

The program now works as expected, free from data races, and if we run it again, the condition in the `assert()` function, it will now hold true.

Avoiding deadlocks

As long as a thread never acquires more than one lock at a time, there is no risk of deadlocks. Sometimes, though, it is necessary to acquire another lock while already holding on to a previously acquired lock. The risk of deadlocks in those situations can be avoided by grabbing both locks at the exact same time. C++ has a way to do this by using the `std::lock()` function, which takes an arbitrary number of locks, and blocks until all locks have been acquired.

The following is an example of transferring money between accounts. Both accounts need to be protected during the transaction, and therefore we need to acquire two locks at the same time. Here is how it works:

```
struct Account {
  Account() {}
  int balance_ = 0;
  std::mutex m_{};
```

```
};

void transfer_money(Account& from, Account& to, int amount) {
   auto lock1 = std::unique_lock<std::mutex>{from.m_, std::defer_lock};
   auto lock2 = std::unique_lock<std::mutex>{to.m_, std::defer_lock};
   // Lock both unique_locks at the same time
   std::lock(lock1, lock2);
   from.balance_ -= amount;
   to.balance_ += amount;
}
```

We are again using a RAII class template to ensure that we release the lock whenever this function returns. In this case, we are using `std::unique_lock`, which provides us with the possibility to defer the locking of the mutex. Then, we explicitly lock both mutexes at the same time by using the `std::lock()` function.

Condition variables

A *condition variable* makes it possible for threads to wait until some specific condition has been met. Threads can also use the condition variable to signal to other threads that the condition has changed.

A common pattern in a concurrent program is to have one or many threads that are waiting for data to be consumed somehow. These threads are usually called **consumers**. Another group of threads are then responsible for producing data that is ready to be consumed. The group of threads that are producing data are called **producers**, or **producer** if it is only one thread.

The producer and consumer pattern can be implemented using a condition variable. We can use a combination of `std::condition_variable` and `std::unique_lock` for this purpose. Let's have a look at an example of a producer and consumer to make it less abstract:

```
auto cv = std::condition_variable{};
auto q = std::queue<int>{};
auto mtx = std::mutex{}; // Protects the shared queue
constexpr int done = -1; // Special value to signal that we are done

void print_ints() {
  auto i = int{0};
  while (i != done) {
    {
      auto lock = std::unique_lock<std::mutex>{mtx};
      while (q.empty())
```

```
      cv.wait(lock); // The lock is released while waiting

    i = q.front();
    q.pop();
  }
  if (i != done) {
    std::cout << "Got: " << i << '\n';
  }
 }
}

auto generate_ints() {
  for (auto i : {1, 2, 3, done}) {
    std::this_thread::sleep_for(std::chrono::seconds(1));
    {
      std::lock_guard<std::mutex> lock(mtx);
      q.push(i);
    }
    cv.notify_one();
  }
}
auto main() -> int {
   auto producer = std::thread{generate_ints};
   auto consumer = std::thread{print_ints};
   producer.join();
   consumer.join();
}
```

We are creating two threads: one `consumer` thread and one `producer` thread. The producer thread is generating a sequence of integers and pushes them to a global `std::queue<int>` once every second. Whenever it adds an element to the queue, it signals that the condition has changed. The condition in this program is whether there is data in the queue available for consumption by the consumer thread. Note also that it is not required to hold the lock while notifying the condition variable.

The consumer thread is responsible for printing the data (that is, the integers) to the console. It uses the condition variable to wait for the empty queue to change. When the consumer calls `cv.wait(lock)`, the thread goes to sleep and will leave the CPU for other threads to execute. It is important to understand why we need to pass the variable lock when calling `wait()`. Apart from putting the thread to sleep, `wait()` also unlocks the mutex while sleeping and then acquires the mutex before it returns. If `wait()` didn't release the mutex, the producer would not be able to add elements to the queue.

Why is the consumer waiting on the condition variable with a `while`-loop around it and not an `if` statement? This is a common pattern, and sometimes we need to do that since there might be other consumers that were also woken up and emptied the queue before us. In our program, we only have one consumer thread though, so that cannot happen. However, it is possible for the consumer to be awoken from its wait even though the producer thread did not signal. This phenomenon is called **spurious wakeup**, and the reasons for why this can happen are beyond the scope of this book. We now at least know how to handle situations where spurious wakeups can happen: *always check the condition in a* `while`*-loop*.

Returning data and handling errors

The examples presented so far in this chapter have used shared variables to communicate state between threads. We have used mutex locks to ensure that we avoid data races. Using shared data with mutexes, as we have been doing, can be very hard to do correctly when the size of a program increases. There is also a lot of work in maintaining code that uses explicit locking spread out over a code base. Keeping track of shared memory and explicit locking moves us farther away from what we really want to accomplish and spend time on when writing a program.

In addition, we haven't dealt with error handling at all yet. What if a thread needs to report an error to some other thread? How do we do that using exceptions, as we are used to do when a function needs to report a runtime error?

In the standard library `<future>` header, we can find some class templates that help us writing concurrent code without global variables and locks, and, in addition, can communicate exceptions between threads for handling errors. We will here present *futures* and *promises*, which represent two sides of a value. The future is the receiving side of the value and the promise is the returning side of the value.

The following is an example of using `std::promise` to return the result to the caller:

```
auto divide(int a, int b, std::promise<int>& p) {
  if (b == 0) {
    auto e = std::runtime_error{"Divide by zero exception"};
    p.set_exception(std::make_exception_ptr(e));
  }
  else {
    const auto result = a / b;
    p.set_value(result);
  }
}

auto main() -> int {
```

```
    auto p = std::promise<int>{};
    std::thread(divide, 45, 5, std::ref(p)).detach();
    auto f = p.get_future();
    try {
      const auto& result = f.get(); // Blocks until ready
      std::cout << "Result: " << result << '\n';
    }
    catch (const std::exception& e) {
      std::cout << "Caught exception: " << e.what() << '\n';
    }
}
```

The caller (the `main()` function) creates the `std::promise` object and passes it to the `divide()` function. We need to use `std::ref` from `<functional>` so that a reference can be correctly forwarded through the `std::thread` to `compute()`.

When the `divide()` function has computed the result, it passes the return value through the promise by calling the `set_value()` function. If an error occurred in the `divide()` function, it would have called the `set_exception()` function on the promise instead.

The future represents the value of the computation that may or may not be computed yet. Since the future is an ordinary object, we can, for example, pass it around to other objects that need the computed value. Finally, when the value is needed by some client, it calls `get()` to get hold of the actual value. If it is not computed at that point in time, the call to `get()` will block until it is finished.

Note also how we managed to pass data back and forth with proper error handling without using any shared global data and no explicit locking. The promise takes care of that for us, and we can focus on implementing the essential logic of the program instead.

Tasks

With futures and promises, we managed to get away from explicit locks and shared global data. Our code will benefit from using higher level abstractions when possible, especially when the code base grows. Here, we will go further and explore classes that make us have the futures and promises automatically set up for us. We will also see how we can get rid of the manual administration of threads and leave that to the library.

In many cases, we don't have any need for managing threads—instead, what we really need is to be able to execute a *task* asynchronously and have that task execute on its own concurrently with the rest of the program, and then eventually get the result or error communicated to the parts of the program that need it. The task should be done in isolation to minimize contention and the risk of data races.

We begin by rewriting our previous example that divided two numbers. This time, we will use the `std::packaged_task` from `<future>`, which makes all the work of setting up the promise correct for us:

```
auto divide(int a, int b) -> int { // No need to pass a promise ref here!
  if (b == 0) {
    throw std::runtime_error{"Divide by zero exception"};
  }
  return a / b;
}

auto main() -> int {
  auto task = std::packaged_task<decltype(divide)>{divide};
  auto f = task.get_future();
  std::thread{std::move(task), 45, 5}.detach();
  // The code below is unchanged from the previous example
  try {
    const auto& result = f.get(); // Blocks until ready
    std::cout << "Result: " << result << '\n';
  }
  catch (const std::exception& e) {
    std::cout << "Caught exception: " << e.what() << '\n';
  }
  return 0;
}
```

`std::packaged_task` is itself a callable object that can be moved to the `std::thread` object we are creating. As you can see, `std::packaged_task` now does most of the work for us: we don't have to create the promise ourselves. But, more importantly, we can write our `divide()` function just like a normal function, without the need for explicitly returning values or exceptions through the promise; the `std::packaged_task` will do that for us.

As a last step in this section, we would also like to get rid of the manual thread management. Creating threads is not free, and we will see later on that the number of threads in a program can affect performance. It seems like the question of whether we should create a new thread for our divide function is not necessarily up to the caller of `divide()`. The library again helps us here by providing another useful function template called `std::async()`. The only thing we need to do in our `divide()` example is replace the code creating the `std::packaged_task` and the `std::thread` object with a simple call to `std::async()`:

```
auto f = std::async(divide, 45, 5);
```

We have now switched from a thread-based programming model to a task-based model. The complete task-based example now looks like this:

```
auto divide(int a, int b) -> int {
  if (b == 0) {
    throw std::runtime_error{"Divide by zero exception"};
  }
  return a / b;
}

auto main() -> int {
  auto future = std::async(divide, 45, 5);
  try {
    const auto& result = future.get();
    std::cout << "Result: " << result << '\n';
  }
  catch (const std::exception& e) {
    std::cout << "Caught exception: " << e.what() << '\n';
  }
}
```

There is really a minimal amount of code left here for handling concurrency. The recommended way to call functions asynchronously is to use `std::async()`. For a deeper discussion about why and when `std::async()` is to be preferred, I highly recommend the *Concurrency* chapter in *Effective Modern C++* by Scott Meyers.

Atomic support in C++

The standard library contains support for *atomic variables,* sometimes called **atomics**. An atomic variable is a variable that can safely be used and mutated from multiple threads without introducing data races. An atomic variable may or may not use a lock to protect the data, this depends on the type of the variable and the platform. If the atomic does not use a lock, it is said to be *lock-free*. You can query the variable in runtime (or compile time since C++17) to be certain that it is lock-free if, for some reason, you need to ensure that it does not use locks internally.

Do you remember the data race example we looked at earlier where two threads updated a global counter? We solved it by adding a mutex lock together with the counter. Instead of using an explicit lock, we could have used a `std::atomic<int>` instead:

```
std::atomic<int> counter;

auto increment_counter(int n) {
  for (int i = 0; i < n; ++i)
    ++counter; // Safe, counter is now an atomic<int>
}
```

The `++counter` is a convenient way of saying `counter.fetch_add(1)`. All member functions that can be invoked on an atomic are safe to call from multiple threads concurrently.

The atomic types are from the `<atomic>` header. There are typedefs for all the scalar data types named on the `std::atomic_int` form. This is identical to saying `std::atomic<int>`. It is possible to wrap a custom type in a `std::atomic` template, as long as the custom type is trivially copyable. Basically, this means that an object of a class is fully described by the bits of its data members. In that way, an object can be copied with, for example, `std::memcpy()`, by only copying the raw bytes. So, if a class contains virtual functions, pointers to dynamic memory, and so on, it's no longer possible to just copy the raw bits of the object and expect it to work, and hence it is not trivially copyable. This can be checked at compile time, so you will get a compilation error if you try to create an atomic of a type that is not trivially copyable:

```
struct Point {
  int y{};
  int x{};
};

auto p = std::atomic<Point>{};       // OK: Point is trivially copyable
auto s = std::atomic<std::string>{}; // Error: cannot be trivially copied
```

It's also possible to create atomic pointers. This makes the pointer itself atomic, but not the object it points at.

Using shared_ptr in a multithreaded environment

What about the `std::shared_ptr`? Can it be used in a multithreaded environment, and how is the reference counting handled when multiple threads are accessing an object referenced by multiple shared pointers?

To understand shared pointers and thread safety, we need to recall how `std::shared_ptr` is typically implemented (see also `Chapter 7`, *Memory Management*). Consider the following code:

```
// Thread 1
auto p1 = std::make_shared<int>(int{42});
```

The code creates an `int` on the heap and a reference-counted smart pointer pointing at the `int` object. When creating the shared pointer with `std::make_shared()`, a control block will be created next to the `int`. The control block contains, among other things, a variable for the reference count, which is incremented whenever a new pointer to the `int` is created and decremented whenever a pointer to the `int` is destroyed. To summarize, when the preceding code line is executed, three separate entities are being created:

- The actual `std::shared_ptr` object `p1` (local variable on the stack)
- A control block (heap object)
- An `int` (heap object)

The following figure shows the three objects:

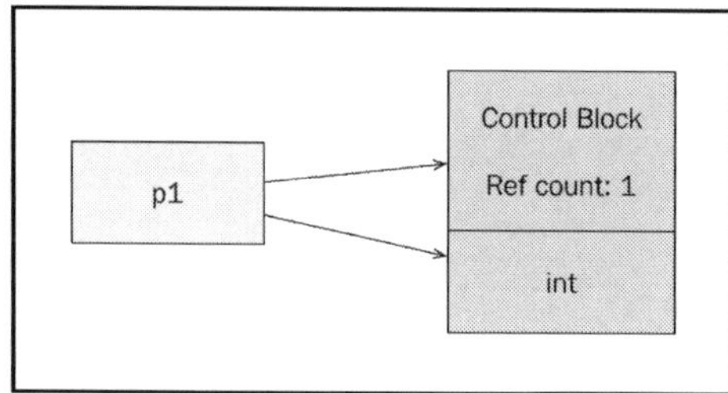

A shared_ptr instance p1 which points to the integer object and a control block which contains the reference counting. In this case, there is only one shared pointer using the int, and hence the ref count is 1.

Now, consider what would happen if the following code is executed by a second thread:

```
// Thread 2
auto p2 = p1;
```

We are creating a new pointer pointing at the `int` (and the control block). When creating the `p2` pointer, we read `p1`, but we also need to mutate the control block when updating the ref counter. The control block lives on the heap and is shared among the two threads, so it needs synchronization to avoid data races. Since the control block is an implementation detail hidden behind the `std::shared_ptr` interface, there is no way for us to know how to protect it, and it turns out that it has already been taken care of by the implementation. Typically, it would use a mutable atomic counter. In other words, the ref counter update is thread-safe so that we can use multiple shared pointers from different threads without worrying about synchronizing the ref counter. This is good practice and something to think of when designing classes: if you are mutating variables in methods that appear to be semantically read-only (`const`) from the client's perspective, you should make the mutating variable thread-safe. On the other hand, everything that can be detected by the client as mutating functions should be left to the client of the class to synchronize.

The following figure shows two `std::shared_ptrs`, `p1` and `p2`, that have access to the same object. The `int` is the shared object and the control block is an internally shared object between the `std::shared_ptr` instances. The control block is thread-safe by default:

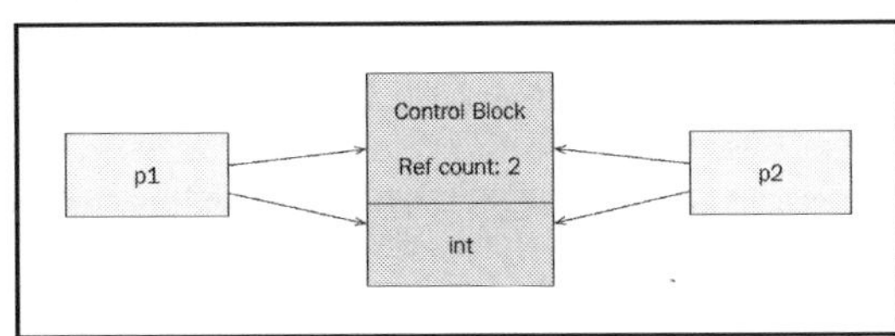

Two shared_ptrs accessing the same object

To summarize:

- The shared object, the `int` in this example, is not thread-safe and needs explicit locking if accessed from multiple threads
- The control block is already thread-safe, so the reference counting mechanism works in multi-threaded environments

Now there is only one part remaining: what about the actual `std::shared_ptr` objects, `p1` and `p2`, in the previous example? To understand this, let's turn to an example using only one global `std::shared_ptr` object called `p`:

```
// Global
auto p = std::shared_ptr<int>{};
```

How can we mutate `p` from multiple threads without introducing a data race?

Of course, we could protect p with a mutex lock whenever we use p. Or, we could use functions from the atomic library. There is no way to say std::atomic<shared_ptr<T>> at the time of writing, but we can instead use overloads of the atomic functions for mutating a std::shared_ptr atomically. The following example demonstrates how to load and store a shared pointer object atomically from multiple threads:

```
// Thread T1 calls this function
auto f1() {
  auto new_p = std::make_shared<int>(std::rand());
  // ...
  std::atomic_store(&p, new_p);
}

// Thread T2 calls this function
auto f2() {
  auto local_p = std::shared_ptr<int>{std::atomic_load(&p)};
  // Use local_p...
}
```

In the example above we assume that there are two threads, T1 and T2 , which call functions f1() and f2(), respectively. New heap-allocated int objects are created from the thread T1 with the call to std::make_shared<int>().

There is one subtle detail to consider in this example: in which thread is the heap-allocated int deleted? When local_p goes out of scope in the f2() function, it might be the last reference to the int (the reference count reaches zero). In that case, the deletion of the heap-allocated int will happen from thread T2. Otherwise, the deletion will happen from thread T1 when std::atomic_store() is called. So, the answer is that the deletion of the int can happen from both threads.

C++ memory model

Why are we talking about the memory model of C++ in a chapter about concurrency?

The memory model is closely related to concurrency since it defines how the reads and writes to the memory should be visible among threads. This is a rather complicated subject which touches on both compiler optimizations and multicore computer architecture. The good news, though, is that if your program is free from data races and you use the memory order that the atomics library provides by default, your concurrent program will behave according to an intuitive memory model that is easy to understand. Still, it is important to at least have an understanding of what the memory model is and what the default memory order guarantees.

The concepts covered in this section are thoroughly explained by Herb Sutter in his talks, *Atomic Weapons: The C++ Memory Model and Modern Hardware 1 & 2*. The talks are freely available at `https://herbsutter.com/2013/02/11/atomic-weapons-the-c-memory-model-and-modern-hardware/` and are highly recommended if you need more depth on this subject.

Instruction reordering

To understand the importance of the memory model, we first need some background about how programs we write are actually being executed.

When we write and run a program, it would be reasonable to assume that the instructions in the source code are being executed in the same order as they appear in the source code. This is not true though—the code we write will be optimized in multiple stages before it is finally executed. Both the compiler and the hardware will reorder instructions with the goal of executing the program more efficiently. This is not new technology: compilers have done this for a long time, and this is one reason why an optimized build runs faster than a non-optimized build. The compiler (and hardware) are free to reorder instructions as long as the reordering is not observable when running the program. The program runs *as if* everything happens in program order.

Let's look at an example code snippet to clarify:

```
int a = 10; // 1
cout << a;  // 2
int b = a;  // 3
cout << b;  // 4
// Observed output: 1010
```

Here, it is obvious that line number two and line number three could be swapped without introducing any observable effect:

```
int a = 10; // 1
int b = a;  // 3 This line moved up
cout << a;  // 2 This line moved down
cout << b;  // 4
// Observed output: 1010
```

Here is another example, similar, but not identical, to the example from `Chapter 4`, *Data Structures*, where the compiler can optimize a cache-unfriendly version when iterating over a two-dimensional matrix:

```
constexpr auto ksize = size_t{100};
using MatrixType = std::array<std::array<int, ksize>, ksize>;
```

```
auto cache_thrashing(MatrixType& matrix, int v) { // 1
  for (size_t i = 0; i < ksize; ++i)              // 2
    for (size_t j = 0; j < ksize; ++j)            // 3
      matrix[j][i] = v;                           // 4
}
```

We saw in `Chapter 4`, *Data Structures*, that code similar to this produces a lot of cache misses, which hurts performance. A compiler is free to optimize this by reordering the `for` statements, like this:

```
auto cache_thrashing(MatrixType& matrix, int v) { // 1
  for (size_t j = 0; j < ksize; ++j)              // 3 This line moved up
    for (size_t i = 0; i < ksize; ++i)            // 2 This line moved down
      matrix[j][i] = v;                           // 4
}
```

There is no way to observe the difference between the two versions when executing the program, but the latter will run faster.

Optimizations performed by the compiler and the hardware (including instruction pipelining, branch prediction, and cache hierarchies) are very complicated and constantly-evolving technologies. Fortunately, all these transformations of the original program can be seen as reorderings of reads and writes in the source code. This also means that it doesn't matter whether it is the compiler or some part of the hardware that performs the transformations. The important thing for C++ programmers to know is that the instructions can be reordered but without any observable effect.

If you have been trying to debug an optimized build of your program, you have probably noticed that it can be hard to step through it because of the reorderings. So, by using a debugger, the reorderings are in some sense observable, but they are not observable when running the program in a normal way.

Atomics and memory orders

When writing single-threaded programs in C++, there is no risk of data races occurring. We can write our programs happily without being aware of instruction reorderings. However, when it comes to shared variables in multi-threaded programs, it is a completely different story. The compiler (and hardware) does all its optimizations based on what is true and observable for *one* thread only. The compiler cannot know what other threads are able to observe by shared variables, so it is our job as programmers to inform the compiler of what reorderings are allowed. In fact, that is exactly what we are doing when we are using an atomic variable or a mutex to protect us from data races.

When protecting a critical section with a mutex, it is guaranteed that only the thread that currently owns the lock can execute the critical section. But, the mutex is also creating memory fences around the critical section to inform the system that certain reorderings are not allowed at the critical section boundaries. When acquiring the lock, an acquire fence is added, and when releasing the lock, a release fence is added.

We will demonstrate this with an example. Imagine that we have four instructions: i1, i2, i3, and i4. There is no dependency between each other, so the system could reorder the instructions arbitrarily without any observable effect. The instructions i2 and i3 are using shared data and are, therefore, critical sections that needs to be protected by a mutex. After adding the acquire and release of the mutex lock, there are now some reorderings that are no longer valid. Obviously, we cannot move the instructions that are part of the critical section outside of the critical section, or they will no longer be protected by the mutex. The one-way fences ensure that no instructions can move out from the critical section. The i1 instruction could be moved inside the critical section by passing the acquire fence, but not beyond the release fence. The i4 instruction could also be moved inside the critical section by passing the release fence, but not beyond the acquire fence.

The following figure shows how one-way fences limit the reordering of instructions. No read or write instructions can pass above the acquire fence, and nothing can pass below the release fence:

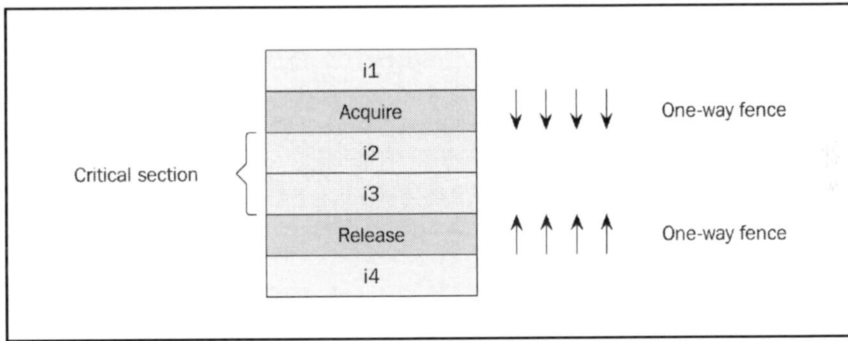

The one-way fences limit the reordering of the instructions

When acquiring a mutex, we are creating an acquire memory fence. It tells the system that no memory accesses (reads or writes) can be moved above the line where the acquire fence is located. It is possible for the system to move the i4 instruction above the release fence beyond the i3 and i2 instructions, but no longer than that because of the acquire fence.

Now, let's have a look at atomic variables instead of mutexes. When we use a shared atomic variable in our program, it gives us two things:

- **Protection against torn writes**: The atomic variable is always updated atomically so there is no way a reader can read a partially written value.
- **Synchronization of memory by adding sufficient memory fences**: This prevents certain instruction reorderings to guarantee a certain memory order specified by the atomic operations.

The C++ memory model guarantees *sequential consistency* if your program is free from data races and you use the default memory order when using atomics. So, what is *sequential consistency*? Sequential consistency guarantees that the result of the execution is the same as if the operations were executed in the order specified by the original program. The interleaving of instructions among threads is arbitrary; that is, we have no control over the scheduling of the threads. This may sound complicated at first, but it is probably the way you already think about how a concurrent program is executed.

The downside with sequential consistency is that it can hurt performance. It is, therefore, possible to use atomics with a relaxed memory model instead. This means that you only get the protection against torn writes, but not the strong sequential consistency memory order guarantees. We strongly advise you against using anything else except the default sequential consistency memory order, unless you have a very thorough understanding of the effects a weaker memory model can introduce. We will not discuss relaxed memory order any further here because it is beyond the scope of this book. But as a side note, it can be interesting to know that the reference counter in a `std::shared_ptr` uses a relaxed model when incrementing the counter (but not when decrementing the counter). This is the reason why the `std::shared_ptr` member function `use_count()` only reports the approximate number of actual references when being used in a multi-threaded environment.

Lock-free programming

Lock-free programming is hard. We will not spend a lot of time discussing lock-free programming in this book, but instead provide you with an example of how a very simple lock-free data structure could be implemented. There is a great wealth of resources—on the web and in books—dedicated to lock-free programming that will explain the concepts you need to understand before writing your own lock-free data structures. Some concepts you might have heard of, related to lock-free programming, such as Compare-And-Swap (CAS) and the ABA-problem will not be further discussed in this book.

Lock-free queue example

Here, we are going to show an example of a lock-free queue, which is a relatively simple but useful lock-free data structure. Lock-free queues can be used for one-way communication with threads that cannot use locks to synchronize access to shared data.

Its implementation is straightforward because of the limited requirements: it only supports one reader thread and one writer thread. The capacity of the queue is also fixed and cannot change during runtime.

The writer thread is allowed to call:

- `push()`: adds an element to the queue

The reader thread is allowed to call:

- `front()`: returns the front element of the queue
- `pop()`: removes the front element from the queue

Both threads can call:

- `size()`: returns the current size of the queue

The following is the complete implementation of the queue:

```
template <class T, size_t N>
class LockFreeQueue {
public:
  LockFreeQueue() : read_pos_{0}, write_pos_{0}, size_{0} {
    assert(size_.is_lock_free());
  }
  auto size() const { return size_.load(); }
  // Writer thread
  auto push(const T& t) {
    if (size_.load() >= N) {
      throw std::overflow_error("Queue is full");
    }
    buffer_[write_pos_] = t;
    write_pos_ = (write_pos_ + 1) % N;
    size_.fetch_add(1);
  }
  // Reader thread
  auto& front() const {
    auto s = size_.load();
    if (s == 0) {
```

```
      throw std::underflow_error("Queue is empty");
    }
    return buffer_[read_pos_];
  }
  // Reader thread
  auto pop() {
    if (size_.load() == 0) {
      throw std::underflow_error("Queue is empty");
    }
    read_pos_ = (read_pos_ + 1) % N;
    size_.fetch_sub(1);
  }
private:
  std::array<T, N> buffer_{};  // Used by both threads
  std::atomic<size_t> size_{}; // Used by both threads
  size_t read_pos_ = 0;        // Used by reader thread
  size_t write_pos_ = 0;       // Used by writer thread
};
```

The only data member that needs atomic access is the `size_` variable. The `read_pos_` member is only used by the reader thread, and the `write_pos_` is only used by writer thread. So what about the buffer of type `std::array`? It is mutable and accessed by both threads—doesn't that require synchronization? Since the algorithm ensures that the two threads are never accessing the same element in the array concurrently, C++ guarantees that individual elements in an array can be accessed without data races. It doesn't matter how small the elements are, even a `char` array holds this guarantee.

When can a non-blocking queue like this be useful? One example is in audio programming, when there is a UI running on the main thread that needs to send or receive data from a real-time audio thread, which cannot block under any circumstances. The real-time thread cannot use mutex locks, allocate/free memory, or anything else that may cause the thread to wait on threads with lower priority. Lock-free data structures are required for scenarios like these.

Both the reader and the writer are lock-free in `LockFreeQueue`, so we could have two instances of the queue to communicate in both directions between the main thread and the audio thread, as the following figure demonstrates:

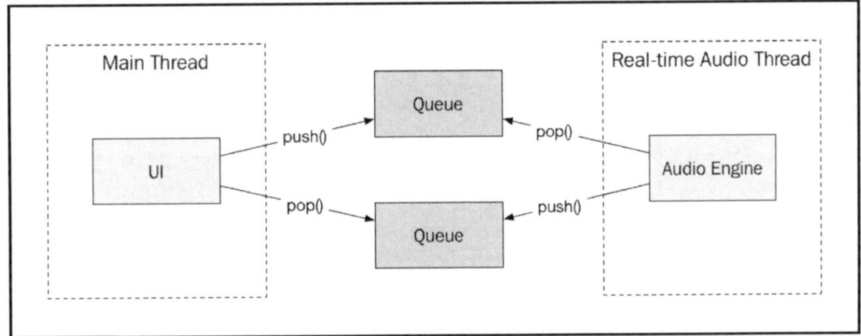

Using two lock-free queues to pass state between the main thread and a real-time audio thread

Performance guidelines

This chapter will end with some guidelines related to performance. We cannot stress enough the importance of having a concurrent program running *correctly* before trying to improve the performance. Also, before applying any of these guidelines related to performance, you first need to set up a reliable way of measuring what you are trying to improve.

Avoid contention

Whenever multiple threads are using shared data, there will be contention. Contention hurts performance and sometimes the overhead caused by contention can make a parallel algorithm work slower than a single-threaded alternative.

Using a lock that causes a wait and a context switch is an obvious performance penalty, but what is not equally obvious is that both locks and atomics disable optimizations in the code generated by the compiler, and they do so at runtime when the CPU executes the code. This is necessary in order to guarantee sequential consistency. But remember, the solution to such problems is never to ignore synchronization and therefore introduce data races. Data races mean undefined behavior, and having a fast incorrect program makes nobody happy.

Instead, we need to minimize the time spent in critical sections. We can do that by entering critical sections less often, and by minimizing the critical section itself so that once we are in a critical section we will leave it as soon as possible.

Avoid blocking operations

To write a modern responsive UI application that always runs smoothly, it is absolutely necessary to never block the main thread for more than a few milliseconds. A smooth running app is updating its interface 60 times a second. This means that if you are doing something that blocks the UI thread for more than 16 ms, the FPS will drop.

You can design your internal APIs in an application with this in mind. Whenever you write a function that performs I/O or something else that might take more than a few milliseconds, it needs to be implemented as an asynchronous function. This pattern has become very common in iOS and Windows where, for example, all network APIs have become asynchronous.

Number of threads/CPU cores

The more CPU cores a machine has, the more active running threads you can have. If you manage to split a sequential CPU-bound task into a parallel version, you can gain performance by having multiple cores working on the task in parallel.

Going from a single-threaded algorithm to an algorithm that can be run by two threads can, in the best case, double the performance. But, after adding more and more threads, you will eventually reach a limit when there is no more performance gain. Adding more threads beyond that limit will actually degrade performance since the overhead caused by context switching becomes more significant the more threads you add.

For I/O intensive tasks, for example, a web crawler that will spend a lot of time waiting for network data, it would require a lot of threads before reaching the limit where the CPU is oversubscribed. A thread that is waiting for I/O will most likely be switched out from the CPU to make room for other threads that are ready to execute.

For CPU-bound tasks, there is usually no point in using more threads than there are cores on the machine.

Controlling the total number of threads in a big program can be hard. A good way of controlling the number of threads is to use a thread pool that can be sized to match the current hardware.

In the next chapter, we will see examples of how to parallelize algorithms and how to tweak the amount of concurrency based on the number of CPU cores.

Thread priorities

The priority of a thread affects how the thread is being scheduled. A thread with high priority is likely to be scheduled more often than threads with lower priorities. Thread priorities are important for lowering the latency of tasks.

Threads provided by the operating system usually have priorities. There is currently no way of setting the priority on a thread with the current C++ thread APIs. However, by using `std::thread::native_handle`, one can get a handle to the underlying operating system thread and use native APIs for setting priorities.

One phenomenon related to thread priorities that can hurt the performance and should be avoided is called *priority inversion*. It happens when a thread with high priority is waiting to acquire a lock that is currently held by a low priority thread. Such dependencies hurt the high priority thread, which is blocked until the next time the low priority thread gets scheduled so that it can release the lock. For real-time applications, this is a big problem. In practice, it means that you cannot use locks to protect any shared resources that need to be accessed by real-time threads. A thread that produces real-time audio, for example, runs with the highest possible priority, and in order to avoid priority inversion, it is not possible for the audio thread to call any functions (including `std::malloc()`) that might block and cause a context switch.

Thread affinity

Thread affinity makes it possible to give the scheduler hints about which threads could benefit from sharing the same CPU caches. In other words, this is a request to the scheduler that some threads should be executed on a particular core if possible, to minimize cache misses.

Why would you want one thread to be executed on a particular core? The answer is (again) caching. Threads that operate on the same memory could benefit from running on the same core, and hence take advantage of warm caches. For the scheduler, this is just one of many parameters to take into account when assigning a thread to a core, so this is hardly any guarantee, but again the behavior is very different among operating systems. Thread priorities, and even utilization of all cores (to avoid overheating), are some of the requirements that need to be taken into account by a modern scheduler.

It is not possible to set thread affinity in a portable way with the current C++ APIs, but most platforms support some way of setting an affinity mask on a thread. In order to access platform-specific functionality, you need to get a handle on the native thread. The example ahead demonstrates how to set the thread affinity mask on Linux:

```
#include <pthreads> // Non-portable header

auto set_affinity(const std::thread& t, int cpu) {
  cpu_set_t cpuset;
  CPU_ZERO(&cpuset);
  CPU_SET(cpu, &cpuset);
  pthread_t native_thread = t.native_handle();
  pthread_set_affinity(native_thread, sizeof(cpu_set_t), &cpuset);
}
```

Note, this is not portable C++, but it is likely that you need to do some non-portable configuration of threads if you are doing performance-critical concurrency programming.

False sharing

False sharing, or destructive interference, can degrade performance. It occurs when two threads use some data (that is not logically shared between the threads) but happen to be located in the same cache line. Imagine what would happen if the two threads are executing on different cores and constantly update the variable that resides on the shared cache line. The threads will invalidate the cache line for each other although there is no true sharing of data between the threads.

False sharing will most likely occur when using global data or dynamically-allocated data that is shared between threads. An example where false sharing is likely to occur is when allocating an array that is shared between threads, but each thread is only using a single element of the array.

The solution to this problem is to pad each element in the array so that two adjacent elements cannot reside on the same cache line. Since C++17, there is a portable way of doing this using the `std::hardware_destructive_interference_size` constant defined in `<new>` in combination with the `alignas` specifier. The following example demonstrates how to create an element that prevents false sharing:

```
struct alignas(std::hardware_destructive_interference_size) Element {
   int counter_{};
};

auto elements = std::vector<Element>(num_threads);
```

The elements in the vector are now guaranteed to reside on separate cache lines.

Summary

In this chapter, we have seen how to create programs that can execute multiple threads concurrently. We have seen how to avoid data races by protecting critical sections with locks or by using atomics. We have looked into execution order and the C++ memory model, which becomes important to understand when writing lock-free programs. We have seen that immutable data structures are thread-safe. The chapter ended with some guidelines for improving the performance in concurrent applications.

11
Parallel STL

In this chapter, you will learn how to use the computer's graphical processing unit for computationally heavy tasks. We will use the excellent *Boost Compute* library, which exposes the GPU via an interface that resembles the STL, meaning that you will move your standard C++ code almost seamlessly from the CPU to the GPU.

This chapter is not going to go in depth into theories of parallelizing algorithms or parallel programming in general, as these subjects are far too complex to cover in a single chapter. Also, there is a multitude of books on this subject. Instead, this chapter is going to take a more practical approach and demonstrate how to extend a current C++ code base to utilize parallelism while preserving the readability of the code base.

In other words, we do not want the parallelism to get in the way of readability; rather, we want the parallelism to be abstracted away so that parallelizing the code is only a matter of changing a parameter to an algorithm.

In earlier chapters, we have stressed that we prefer STL algorithms over handcrafted `for`-loops; in this chapter, we will see some great advantages of using algorithms.

We will start this chapter off by looking at a few parallel implementations of standard algorithms, and the added complexity of writing parallel versions of them. We will then go on to see how we can adapt a code base to use the parallel extensions of STL, and finally we will take a brief look at how we can use the capabilities of the GPU in a simple way by using Boost Compute and OpenCL.

Importance of parallelism

From a programmer's perspective, it would have been very convenient if the computer hardware of today had been a 100 GHz single core CPU rather than a three gigahertz multi-core CPU, and we wouldn't need to care about parallelism. But, as the evolution of computer hardware is going in the direction of multi-core CPUs, programmers have to use efficient parallel patterns in order to make the most out of the hardware.

Parallel algorithms

As mentioned in `Chapter 10`, *Concurrency*, with parallelism we refer to programming that takes advantage of hardware with multiple cores. It makes no sense to parallelize algorithms if the hardware does not provide any of the benefits of it.

Therefore, a parallel algorithm equivalent of a sequential algorithm is algorithmically slower than the sequential. Its benefits come from the ability to spread the algorithms onto several processing units.

With that in mind, it's also notable that not all algorithms gain the same performance increase when run in parallel. As a simple measurement of how well an algorithm scales, we can measure:

- **A**: The time it takes to execute sequentially at one CPU core
- **B**: The time it takes to execute in parallel, multiplied by the number of cores

If A and B are equal, the algorithm parallelizes perfectly, and the larger B is compared to A, the worse the algorithm parallelizes.

How well an algorithm parallelizes depends on how independently each element can be processed. For example, `std::transform()` is trivial to parallelize in the sense that each element is processed completely independent of every other. This means that theoretically, for *n* number of cores, it would execute *n* times as fast as a sequential execution. In practice, though, there are a multitude of parameters that limit parallel execution such as creating threads, context switches, and so on, as mentioned in `Chapter 10`, *Concurrency in C++*.

As parallel algorithms always have a higher computational cost than their sequential equivalent, there are some cases where you may want a sequential version even though it's slower. An example of such a case is if you are optimizing for low energy consumption rather than low computational time. Even though this is probably a very rare case (perhaps a solar-powered galaxy-exploring spacecraft), it might be worth noting.

Implementing parallel std::transform()

Although algorithmically `std::transform()` is easy to implement, in practice implementing even a rudimentary parallel version is more complex than it might appear at first sight.

A naive parallel implementation of `std::transform()` would probably look something like this:

- Divide the elements into chunks corresponding to the number of cores in the computer
- Execute each chunk in a separate task in parallel
- Wait for all tasks to finish

Naive implementation

Using `std::thread::hardware_concurrency()` to determine the number of supported hardware threads, a naive implementation could look like this. Note that `hardware_concurrency()` might return `0` if it for some reason is undetermined, and therefore it is clamped to be at least one:

```
template <typename SrcIt, typename DstIt, typename Func>
auto par_transform_naive(SrcIt first, SrcIt last, DstIt dst, Func f) {
  auto n = static_cast<size_t>(std::distance(first, last));
  auto num_tasks = std::max(std::thread::hardware_concurrency(), 1);
  auto chunk_sz = std::max(n / num_tasks, 1);
  auto futures = std::vector<std::future<void>>{};
  futures.reserve(num_tasks); // Invoke each chunk on a separate
                              // task, to be executed in parallel
  for (size_t task_idx = 0; task_idx < num_tasks; ++task_idx) {
    auto start_idx = chunk_sz * task_idx;
    auto stop_idx = std::min(chunk_sz * (task_idx + 1), n);
    auto fut = std::async([first, dst, start_idx, stop_idx, &f](){
```

```
      std::transform(first+start_idx, first+stop_idx, dst+start_idx, f);
    });
    futures.emplace_back(std::move(fut));
  }
  // Wait for each task to finish
  for (auto& fut : futures) { fut.wait();}
}
```

Performance evaluation

Continuing the naive implementation, let's measure its performance with a naive performance evaluation compared to `std::transform()` at a single CPU core.

We measure two scenarios:

1. Process 32 elements with an expensive function called `heavy_f`
2. Process 100,000,000 elements with an inexpensive function called `light_f`

The following code processes a low number of elements with the expensive `heavy_f` transform function:

```
// Low number of elements - heavy transform function
auto heavy_f = [](float v) {
  auto sum = v;
  for (size_t i = 0; i < 100'000'000; ++i) { sum += (i*i*i*sum); }
  return sum;
};
auto measure_heavy() {
  auto n = 32;
  auto src = std::vector<float>(n);
  auto dst = std::vector<float>(n);
  std::transform(src.begin(), src.end(), dst.begin(), heavy_f);
  par_transform_naive(src.begin(), src.end(), dst.begin(), heavy_f);
}
```

The following code processes a high number of elements with the inexpensive `light_f` transform function:

```
// High number of elements - light transform function
auto light_f = [](float v) {
  auto sum = v;
  for (size_t i = 0; i < 10; ++i) { sum += (i*i*i*sum); }
  return sum;
};
auto measure_light() {
  auto n = 100'000'000;
```

```
    auto src = std::vector<float>(n);
    auto dst = std::vector<float>(n);
    std::transform(src.begin(), src.end(), dst.begin(), light_f);
    par_transform_naive(src.begin(), src.end(), dst.begin(), light_f);
}
```

The following table shows the results for low number of elements with the expensive `heavy_f` function:

Algorithm	Time (lower is better)	Speed up (higher is better)
`std::transform()`	2913914 microseconds	1.00 x
`par_transform_naive()`	364596 microseconds	7.99 x

The parallelization is perfect as it is approximately eight times as fast at an eight-core CPU. Perfect parallelization like this is very rare, but under certain conditions where memory access is not a bottle neck, it is possible.

Here are the results for a high number of elements with the inexpensive `light_f` function:

Algorithm	Time (lower is better)	Speed up (higher is better)
`std::transform()`	407859 microseconds	1.00 x
`par_transform_naive()`	88887 microseconds	4.60 x

The parallel version is five times as fast, which is roughly what a parallelization of `std::transform()` at eight cores usually ends up at, as the parallelization is affected by a lot of external parameters such as memory bandwidth, as discussed in `Chapter 10`, *Concurrency*.

Shortcomings of the naive implementation

The naive implementation might do a good job if we are the only application utilizing the hardware, and transforming each chunk has the same computational cost. However, this is rarely the case; rather, we want a good general purpose parallel implementation.

The following illustrations show the problems we want to avoid. If the computational cost is not equivalent for each chunk, the implementation is limited to the chunk that takes the most time:

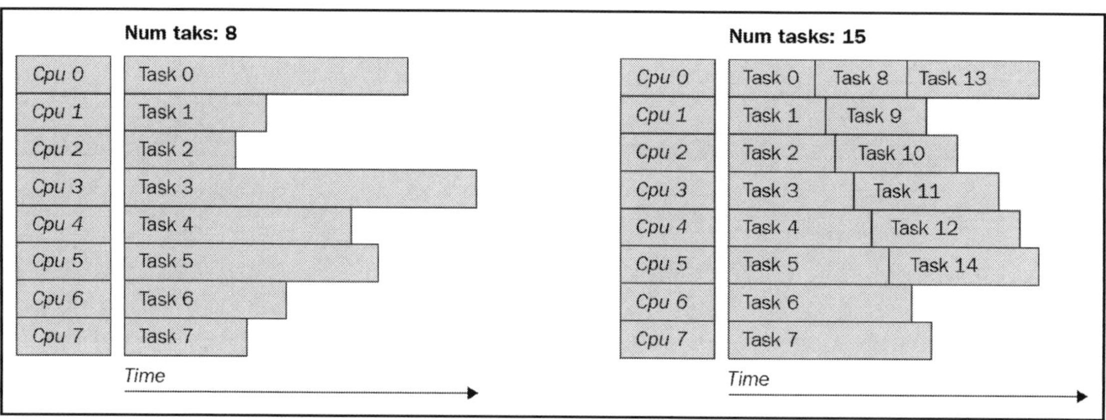

Possible scenarios where computation time is not proportional to chunk size

If the application and/or the operating system has other processes to handle, the operation will not process all chunks in parallel:

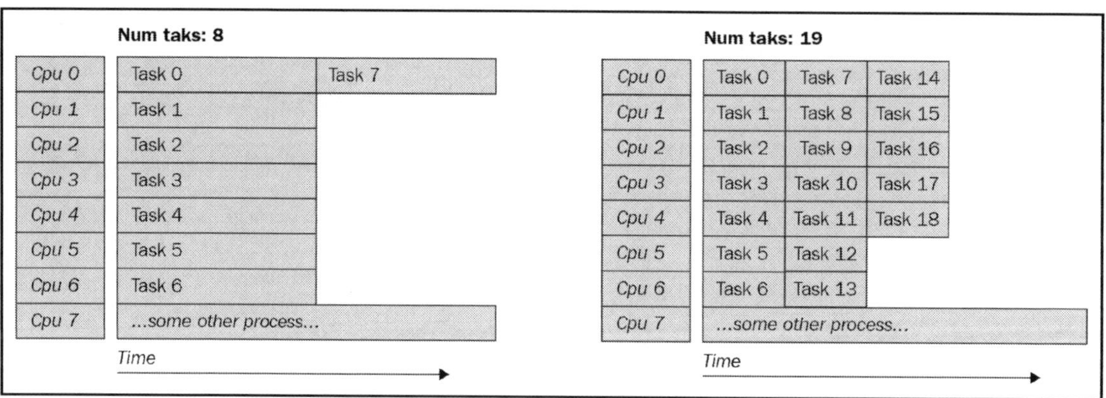

Possible scenarios where computation time is proportional to chunk size

As you can see, splitting the operation into smaller chunks makes the parallelization adjust to the current condition, avoiding single tasks that stall the whole operation.

Divide and conquer

In order to get a good general purpose implementation of the parallel transformation, we divide the range recursively into smaller ranges, sometimes referred to as "*divide and conquer*".

It works as follows:

1. The input range is divided into two ranges; if the input range is smaller than a specified threshold, the range is processed, or else the range is split into two parts:
    - One part is branched to another task recursively processed at that task
    - One part is recursively processed at the calling thread

The following illustration shows how it would recursively transform a range with the following properties:

- **Range size**: 16
- **Chunk size**: 4
- **Transformation function**: `[](const auto& v){ return v*v; }`

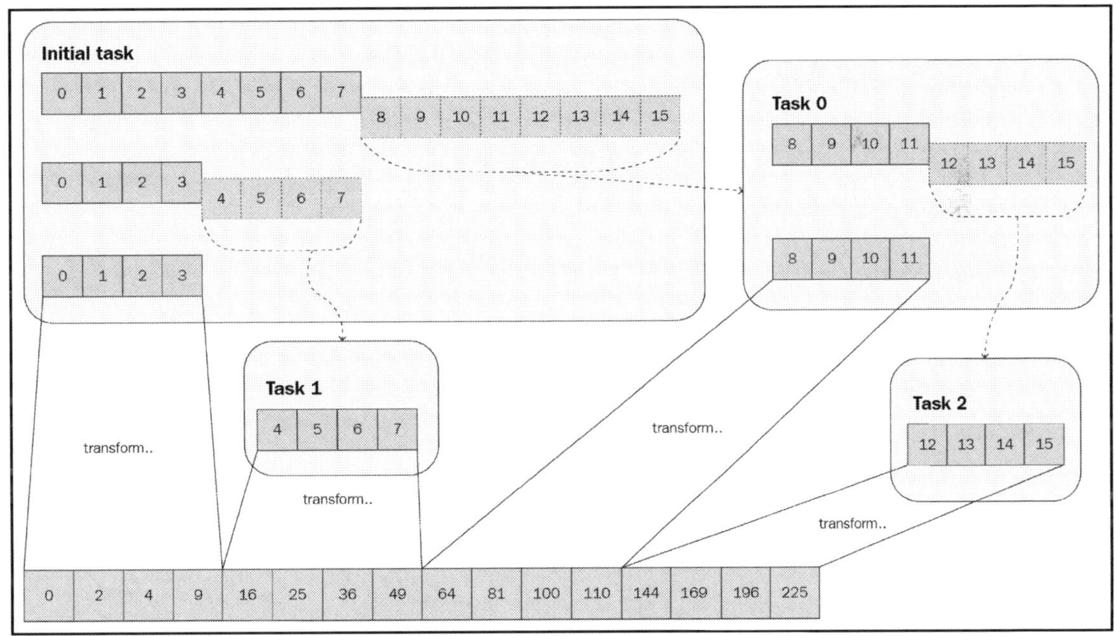

A range is divided recursively for parallel processing

Implementation

Implementation-wise, it's quite a small bit of code. The incoming range is recursively split into two chunks; the first chunk is recursively invoked as a new task, and the second chunk is processed on the same task:

```
template <typename SrcIt, typename DstIt, typename Func>
auto par_transform(SrcIt first,SrcIt last,DstIt dst,Func f,size_t chunk_sz)
{
  const auto n = static_cast<size_t>(std::distance(first, last));
  if (n <= chunk_sz) {
    std::transform(first, last, dst, f);
    return;
  }
  const auto src_middle = std::next(first, n/2);
  // Branch of first part to another task
  auto future = std::async([=, &func]{
    par_transform(first, src_middle, dst, f, chunk_sz);
  });
  // Recursively handle the second part
  const auto dst_middle = std::next(dst, n/2);
  par_transform(src_middle, last, dst_middle, f, chunk_sz);
  future.wait();
}
```

Performance evaluation

Now we create another, rather stupid, `transform_func` that takes more time depending on the input value, and a range of increasing values using `std::iota()` like this:

```
const auto transform_func = [](float v) {
  auto sum = v;
  auto i_max = v / 100'000;  // The larger "v" is, the more to compute
  for (size_t i = 0; i < i_max; ++i) { sum += (i*i*i*sum); }
  return sum;
};
auto n = size_t{ 10'000'000 };
auto src = std::vector<float>(n);
std::iota(src.begin(), src.end(), 0.0f); // "src" goes from 0 to n
```

If we evaluate them with different chunk sizes, as well as `std::transform()` and the old `par_transform_naive()`, we get the following computation times:

Function	**Chunk size**	**Number of tasks**	**Microseconds**	**Speed up**
`std::transform()`	10000000 (= n)	1	844629	1.00x
`par_transform_naive()`	1250000 (= n / 8)	8	222933	3.79x
`par_transform()`	1000000	10	210942	4.00x
`par_transform()`	100000	100	148066	5.70x
`par_transform()`	10000	1000	**144189**	**5.86x**
`par_transform()`	1000	10000	152123	5.55x
`par_transform()`	100	100000	208969	4.04x
`par_transform()`	10	1000000	**1536680**	**0.55x**

Computation time using different chunk sizes

As the table illustrates, the best performance in this case lies around chunk sizes of 10000 elements. With larger chunks, the performance is bottlenecked in the time it takes to process the final chunks, whereas too small chunks results in too much overhead in creating and invoking tasks compared to the computation. As mentioned earlier, this implementation is rather rudimentary as it simply allocates all the tasks in one big list, but the outcome is still worth pointing out.

As noted, a chunk size around 10'000 elements seems most optimal, but how much would this affect a transformation where each computation takes the same amount of time?

If we change the `transform_func` to have a fixed computation cost, regardless of its argument, like this:

```
auto transform_func = [](float v) {
  auto sum = v;
  auto end = 60
  for (size_t i = 0; i < end; ++i) {
    sum += (i*i*i*sum);
  }
  return sum;
};
```

...and execute the code as in the previous example, we get the following table:

Function	Chunk size	Number of tasks	Microseconds	Speed up
`std::transform()`	10000000 (= n)	1	815498	1.00 x
`par_transform_naive()`	1250000 (= n / 8)	8	**129403**	**6.30 x**
`par_transform_chunks()`	1000000	10	184041	4.43 x
`par_transform_chunks()`	100000	100	132248	6.17 x
`par_transform_chunks()`	10000	1000	**131812**	**6.19 x**
`par_transform_chunks()`	1000	10000	141705	5.75 x
`par_transform_chunks()`	100	100000	179279	4.50 x
`par_transform_chunks()`	10	1000000	**1542512**	**0.53 x**

Computation time using different chunk sizes

The fastest version, although marginally, is the `par_transform_naive()` function where the number of chunks corresponds to the number of cores in the computer. This is expected though, as this code is executed in a *clinical* environment where the CPU does more or less nothing more than perform this calculation.

The important takeaway from this example, though, is that the performance penalty of scheduling 1000 smaller tasks rather than eight big ones is marginal enough to draw the conclusion that a generic implementation would be wise to use a large number of tasks rather than trying to figure out the correct number of tasks based on the number of CPU cores on the machine. In other words, let the scheduler involved in launching an asynchronous task do the scheduling.

Implementing parallel std::count_if

We can easily use the same divide and conquer concept to implement a parallel version of `std::count_if()`, with the difference that we need to accumulate the returned value like this:

```
template <typename It, typename Pred>
auto par_count_if(It first, It last, Pred pred, size_t chunk_sz) {
  auto n = static_cast<size_t>(std::distance(first, last));
  if (n <= chunk_sz)
    return std::count_if(first, last, pred);
  auto middle = std::next(first, n/2);
```

```
  auto future = std::async([=, &pred]{
    return par_count_if(first, middle, pred, chunk_sz);
  });
  auto num = par_count_if(middle, last, pred, chunk_sz);
  return num + future.get();
}
```

Implementing parallel std::copy_if

We've had a look at `std::transform()` and `std::count_if()`, which are quite easy to implement both sequentially and in parallel. If we take another algorithm that is easily implemented sequentially, `std::copy_if()`, things get a lot harder to perform in parallel.

Sequentially, implementing `std::copy_if()` is as easy as this:

```
template <typename SrcIt, typename DstIt, typename Pred>
auto copy_if(SrcIt first, SrcIt last, DstIt dst, Pred pred) {
  for(auto it = first; it != last; ++it) {
    if( pred(*it) ) {
      *dst = *it;
      ++dst;
    }
  }
  return dst;
}
```

... and used like this:

```
auto vals = {0,1,2,3,4,5,6,7,8,9,10,11,12,13,14,15};
auto odd_vals = std::vector<int>(vals.size(), -1);
auto is_odd = [](int v){ return (v % 2) == 1;};
auto new_end = copy_if(vals.begin(), vals.end(), odd_vals.begin(), is_odd);
// odd_vals is {1,3,5,7,9,11,13,15,-1,-1,-1,-1,-1,-1,-1,-1}
// new_end points to the first -1
odd_vals.erase(new_end, odd_vals.end());
// odd_vals is {1,3,5,7,9,11,13,15}
```

However, if we were to parallelize this, we immediately run into problems as we cannot write to the destination iterator concurrently:

```
// This is pure undefined behavior,
// both tasks will write to the same position
template <typename SrcIt, typename DstIt, typename Func>
auto par_copy_if(SrcIt first, SrcIt last, DstIt dst, Func func) {
  auto n = std::distance(first, last);
  auto middle = std::next(first, n / 2);
  auto fut0 = std::async([=](){
    return std::copy_if(first, middle, dst, func); } );
  auto fut1 = std::async([=](){
    return std::copy_if(middle, last, dst, func); } );
  auto dst0 = fut0.get();
  auto dst1 = fut1.get();
  return *std::max(dst0, dst1); // Just to return something...
}
```

We now have two simple approaches; either we synchronize the index which we write to (by using an atomic/lock-free variable), or we split the algorithm into two parts.

Approach one – Use a synchronized write position

The first approach one might consider is to synchronize the write position by using an atomic `size_t` and the `fetch_add()` member function, as learned in `Chapter 10`, *Concurrency*. Whenever a thread tries to write a new element, it fetches the current index and adds one atomically, thus each value is written to a unique index.

In code, we will split the function into two functions: an inner function and an outer function. The atomic write index is defined in the outer function, and the actual implementation in the inner function which we call `_inner_par_copy_if_sync()`.

Inner function

The inner function requires an atomic `size_t` that synchronizes the write positions. As the algorithm is recursive, it cannot store the atomic `size_t` itself; it requires an outer function to invoke the algorithm:

```
template <typename SrcIt, typename DstIt, typename Pred>
auto _inner_par_copy_if_sync(
  SrcIt first,
  SrcIt last,
  DstIt dst,
  std::atomic_size_t& dst_idx,
```

```
    Pred pred,
    size_t chunk_sz
  ) -> void {
    auto n = std::distance(first, last);
    if (n <= chunk_sz) {
      std::for_each(first, last, [&](const auto& v) {
        if (pred(v)) {
          auto write_idx = dst_idx.fetch_add(1);
          *std::next(dst, write_idx) = v;
        }
      });
      return;
    }
    auto middle = std::next(first, n / 2);
    auto future = std::async(
      [first, middle, dst, chunk_sz, &pred, &dst_idx] {
        return _inner_par_copy_if_sync(
          first, middle, dst, dst_idx, pred, chunk_sz
        );
      });
    _inner_par_copy_if_sync(middle, last, dst, dst_idx, pred, chunk_sz);
    future.wait();
  }
```

Outer function

The outer function, called from the user code, is simply a placeholder for the atomic `size_t`, which is initialized to zero. It then initializes the first inner function, which parallelizes the code further:

```
  template <typename SrcIt, typename DstIt, typename Pred>
  auto par_copy_if_sync(SrcIt first,SrcIt last,DstIt dst,Pred p,size_t
  chunk_sz){
    auto dst_write_idx = std::atomic_size_t{ 0 };
    _inner_par_copy_if_sync(first, last, dst, dst_write_idx, p,
      chunk_sz);
    return std::next(dst, dst_write_idx);
  }
```

Approach two – Split algorithm into two parts

The second approach is to split the algorithm into two parts. First, the conditional copying is performed in parallel chunks, then the resulting sparse range is squeezed to a continuous range.

Part one – Copy elements in parallel into the destination range

The first part copies the elements in chunks, resulting in the sparse destination illustrated in the following figure. Each chunk is conditionally copied in parallel, and the resulting range iterators are stored in the future for later retrieval:

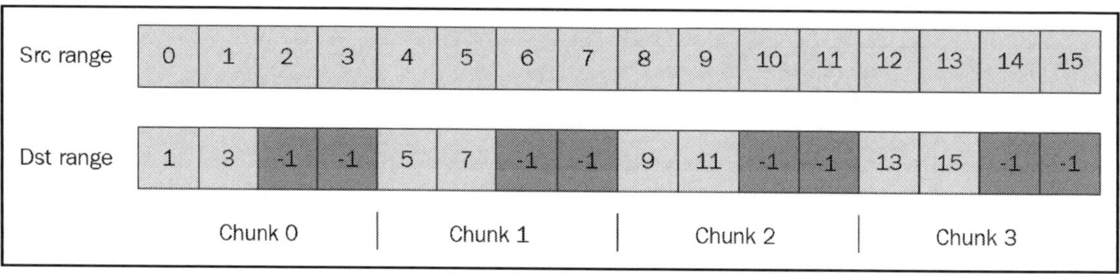

Sparse destination range after first step of conditional copy

The following code implements the algorithm:

```
template <typename SrcIt, typename DstIt, typename Pred>
auto par_copy_if_split(SrcIt first,SrcIt last,DstIt dst,Pred pred,size_t
chunk_sz){
  // Part #1: Perform conditional copy in parallel
  auto n = static_cast<size_t>(std::distance(first, last));
  using CopiedRange = std::pair<DstIt, DstIt>;
  using FutureType = std::future< CopiedRange >;
  auto futures = std::vector<FutureType>{};
  futures.reserve(n / chunk_sz);
  for (size_t start_idx = 0; start_idx < n; start_idx += chunk_sz) {
    auto stop_idx = std::min(start_idx + chunk_sz, n);
    auto future = std::async([=, &pred] {
      auto dst_first = dst + start_idx;
      auto dst_last = std::copy_if(first + start_idx, first + stop_idx,
        dst_first, pred);
      return std::make_pair(dst_first, dst_last);
    });
    futures.emplace_back(std::move(future));
  }
  // To be continued...
```

Part two – Move the sparse range sequentially into a continuous range

When the sparse range is created, it is merged sequentially using the resulting value from each `std::future`, as illustrated in the following figure. This is performed sequentially as the parts overlap. Note that `std::move` is used instead of copying to avoid unnecessary copying:

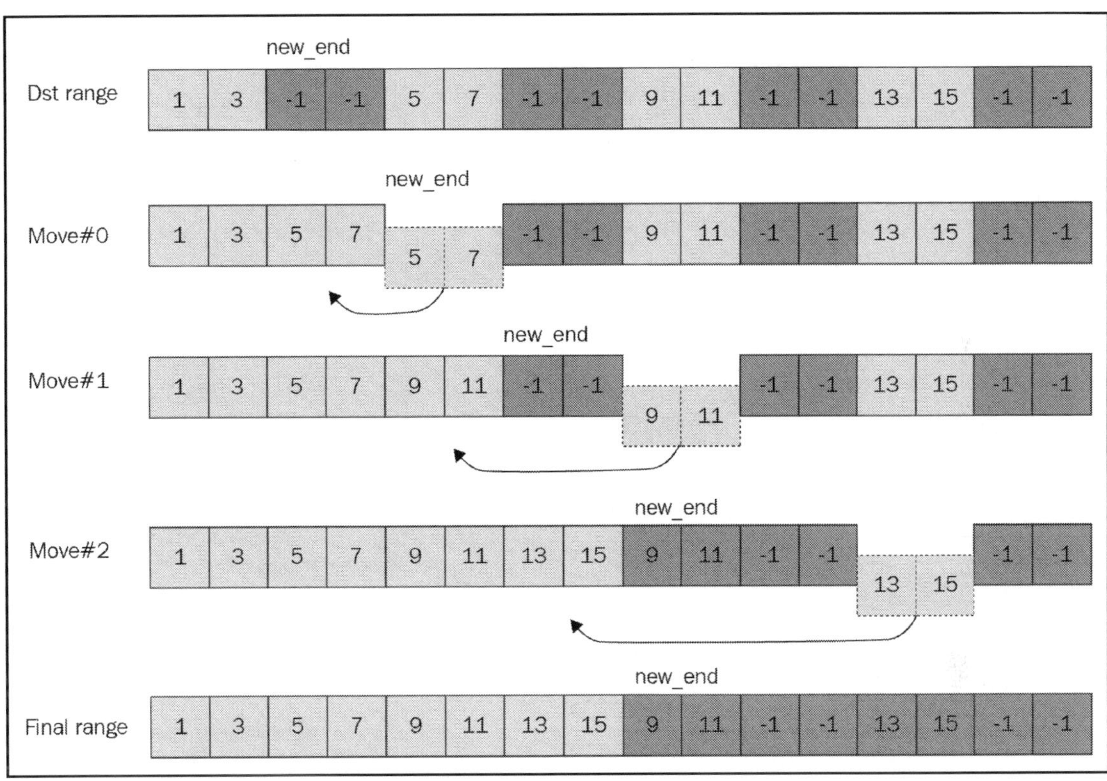

Merge sparse range into a continuous range

```
  // ...continued from above...
  // Part #2: Perform merge of resulting sparse range sequentially
  auto new_end = futures.front().get().second;
  for(auto it = std::next(futures.begin()); it != futures.end(); ++it) {
    auto chunk_rng = it->get();
    new_end=std::move(chunk_rng.first, chunk_rng.second, new_end);
  }
  return new_end;
} // end of par_copy_if_split
```

Performance evaluation

Now that we have two different implementations, let's see how they measure up. The performance boost from using this parallelized version of `copy_if` is heavily dependent on how expensive the predicate is. Therefore, we measure with two predicates; `is_odd`, which is very inexpensive and `is_prime`, which is expensive.

<table>
<tr><th>The light <code>is_odd</code> predicate:</th><th>The heavy <code>is_prime</code> predicate:</th></tr>
<tr><td><pre>auto is_odd = [](unsigned v) {
  return (v % 2) == 1;
};</pre></td><td><pre>auto is_prime = [](unsigned v) {
  if (v < 2) return false;
  if (v == 2) return true;
  if (v % 2 == 0) return false;
  for (unsigned i=3; (i*i)<=v; i+=2) {
    if ((v % i) == 0) {return false; }
  }
  return true;
};</pre></td></tr>
</table>

The following table shows the performance as measured using an Intel i7 7700k CPU. Note that for the algorithms which is split into chunks, the chunk size is set to 100'000.

Predicate	**Algorithm**	**Number of elements**	**Milliseconds**	**Speed up**
`is_odd`	`std::copy_if`	100,000,000	64	1.00 x
`is_odd`	`par_copy_if_split`	100,000,000	58	**1.10 x**
`is_odd`	`par_copy_if_sync`	100,000,000	871	0.07 x (disaster)
`is_prime`	`std::copy_if`	10,000,000	1630	1.00 x
`is_prime`	`par_copy_if_split`	10,000,000	320	**5.09 x**
`is_prime`	`par_copy_if_sync`	10,000,000	321	5.08 x

Conditional copy strategies versus computation time

The most obvious observation when measuring the performance is how ridiculously slow the synchronized version is with the lightweight `is_odd` predicate, *it's not even one tenth as fast as the serial version*. The disastrous performance is actually not due to the atomic write index; rather it is because the cache mechanism of the hardware is trashed due to several threads writing to the same cache line (as learned in `Chapter 7`, *Memory Management*).

So, with that knowledge, let's focus on the `par_copy_if_split` implementation instead. On the lightweight predicate it is just slightly faster than the sequential version, but with the heavyweight `is_prime` predicate, the performance is vastly increased.

The increased performance is a result of spending most of the computations in the first part, which executes in parallel.

Parallel STL

As of C++17, the STL library has been extended with parallel versions of most, but not all, algorithms. Changing your algorithms to execute in parallel is only a matter of adding a parameter that tells the algorithm which parallel execution policy to use.

As stressed earlier in this book, if your code base is based upon STL algorithms, or at least if you have the habit of writing C++ by using algorithms, you get an instant performance boost almost for free by adding an execution policy where suitable.

```
auto roller_coasters = std::vector<std::string>{
  "woody", "steely", "loopy", "upside_down"
};
```

Sequential version	Parallel version

`auto loopy_coaster = *std::find(`
`  roller_coasters.begin(),`
`  roller_coasters.end(),`
`  "loopy"`
`);`
	`auto loopy_coaster = *std::find(`
	`  `**`std::execution::par,`**
	`  roller_coasters.begin(),`
	`  roller_coasters.end(),`
	`  "loopy"`
	`);`

Execution policies

The execution policy informs the algorithms of how they are allowed to parallelize the algorithm; there are three default execution policies included in the STL parallel extensions. In the future, there will probably be libraries extending these policies for certain hardware and conditions. This would make it possible to seamlessly use the parallel power of modern graphics card from STL algorithms.

The execution policies are defined in the header `<execution>` and reside in the namespace `std::execution`.

Sequenced policy

The sequenced execution policy, `std::execution::seq`, makes the algorithm execute sequentially with no parallelism, just as the algorithm would execute if invoked without any execution policy at all. It might seem odd that this policy is even provided, but it allows the programmer to specify an algorithm to execute sequentially if the number of elements is below a certain threshold where executing an algorithm in parallel is slower:

```
auto find_largest(const std::vector<int>& v) {
  auto threshold = 2048;
  return v.size() < threshold ?
    *std::max_element(std::execution::seq, v.begin(), v.end()) :
    *std::max_element(std::execution::par, v.begin(), v.end());
}
```

Parallel policy

The parallel execution policy, `std::execution::par`, can be considered the standard execution policy for parallel algorithms. In contrast with the parallel unsequenced policy described later, it handles exceptions, meaning that if an exception is thrown during the execution of the algorithm, the exception will be thrown out back on the main thread and the algorithm will break at an unspecified position:

```
auto inv_numbers(const std::vector<float>& c, std::vector<float>& out) {
  out.resize(c.size(), -1.0f);
  auto inversef = [](float denominator){
    if(denominator != 0.0f) { return 1.0f/denominator; }
    else throw std::runtime_error{"Division by zero};}
  };
  auto p = std::execution::par;
  std::transform(p, c.begin(), c.end(), out.begin(), inversef);
}

auto test_inverse_numbers() {
  auto numbers = std::vector<float>{3.0f, 4.0f, 0.0f, 8.0f, 2.0f};
  auto inversed = std::vector<float>{};
  try {
    inv_numbers(numbers, inversed);
  }
  catch (const std::exception& e) {
    std::cout << "Exception thrown, " << e.what() << '\n';
  }
  for(auto v: inversed) { std::cout << v << ", "; }
}
```

Executing the previous code would result in the following output, where it is undetermined which of the elements has actually been divided:

```
// Possible output
Exception thrown, division by zero
0.33, -1.0, -1.0, 0.125, -1.0,
```

Parallel unsequenced policy

The parallel unsequenced policy, `std::execution::par_unseq`, executes the algorithm in parallel like the parallel policy, but with the addition that it may also vectorize the loop using, for example, SIMD instructions if plausible.

In addition to the vectorization, it has stricter conditions for the predicates than `std::execution::par`:

- Predicates may not throw, doing so will cause undefined behavior or an instant crash
- Predicates may not use a mutex for synchronization, doing so might cause a deadlock

The following example might cause a deadlock as the `std::execution::par_unseq` might execute concurrently on the same thread:

```
auto trees = std::vector<std::string>{"Pine", "Birch", "Oak"};
auto m = std::mutex{};
auto p = std::execution::par_unseq;
std::for_each(p, trees.begin(), trees.end(), [&m](const auto& t){
  auto guard = std::lock_guard<std::mutex>{m};
  std::cout << t << '\n';
});
```

In other words, when using the `std::execution::par_unseq` policy you must make sure that the predicate does not throw or acquire a lock.

Parallel modifications of algorithm

Most algorithms in STL are available as parallel versions straight out the box, but there are some noteworthy changes to `std::accumulate` and `std::for_each`, as their original requirements required in-order execution.

std::accumulate and std::reduce

The `std::accumulate` algorithm cannot be parallelized as it requires to be executed in order of the elements, which is not possible to parallelize. Instead, a new algorithm called `std::reduce` has been added, which works just like `std::accumulate` with the exception that it is executed un-ordered.

With commutative operations their result is the same, as the order of accumulation doesn't matter.

In other words, given a range of integers:

```
auto c = std::vector<int>{1, 2, 3, 4, 5};
```

Accumulating them by addition or multiplication:

```
auto sum = std::accumulate(c.begin(), c.end(), 0,
  [](int a, int b) { return a + b; }
);
auto product = std::accumulate(c.begin(), c.end(), 1,
  [](int a, int b) { return a * b; }
);
```

Would yield the same result if invoked with `std::reduce()` instead of `std::accumulate`, as both addition and multiplication of integers are commutative:

$$(1+2+3+4+5) = (3+1+2+5+4) \text{ and } (1 \cdot 2 \cdot 3 \cdot 4 \cdot 5) = (3 \cdot 1 \cdot 2 \cdot 5 \cdot 4)$$

But, if the operation is not commutative, the result is dependent on the order of arguments. For example, if we were to accumulate a list of strings like this:

```
auto mice = std::vector<std::string>{"Mickey", "Minnie", "Jerry"};
auto acc = std::accumulate(mice.begin(), mice.end(), {});
std::cout << acc << '\n';
// Prints "MickeyMinnieJerry"
```

But, using `std::reduce`, the resulting string could be any order of names, as:

```
std::string{"Mickey"} + std::string{"Jerry"} == std::string{"MickeyJerry"};
std::string{"Jerry"} + std::string{"Mickey"} == std::string{"JerryMickey"};
```

Therefore, the following code might produce different results:

```
auto red = std::reduce(mice.begin(), mice.end(), {});
std::cout << red << '\n';
// Possible output "MinnieJerryMickey" or "MickeyMinnieJerry" etc
```

std::transform_reduce

As an addition to the STL algorithms, `std::transform_reduce` has also been added. It does exactly what it says; it transforms a range of elements as `std::transform` and then applies a functor. This accumulates them out of order, like `std::reduce`:

```
auto mice = std::vector<std::string>{"Mickey","Minnie","Jerry"};
auto num_chars = std::transform_reduce(
  mice.begin(),
  mice.end(),
  size_t{0},
  [](const std::string& m) { return m.size(); }, // Transform
  [](size_t a, size_t b) { return a + b; }       // Reduce
);
// num_chars is 17
```

std::for_each

Although `std::for_each` is mainly used for applying a functor to a range of elements, it is quite similar to `std::transform()` although it only processes elements, like this:

```
auto peruvians = std::vector<std::string>{
  "Mario", "Claudio", "Sofia", "Gaston", "Alberto"};
std::for_each(peruvians.begin(), peruvians.end(), [](std::string& s) {
  s.resize(1);
});
// Peruvians is now {"M", "C", "S", "G", "A"}
```

It actually also returns the functor passed into it, which means it can be used like this:

```
auto result_func = std::for_each(
  peruvians.begin(),
  peruvians.end(),
  [all_names = std::string{}](const std::string& name) mutable {
```

```
      all_names += name + " ";
      return all_names;
    }
  );
  auto all_names = result_func("");
  // all_names is now "Mario Claudio Sofia Gaston Alberto ";
```

To be honest, this is quite a weird example, as `std::accumulate` is better suited for the job, and I've actually never seen anyone use the returned functor in a real-world code base. However, as with `std::accumulate`, executing it out of order would yield different results every time it is executed as the invocation order is undefined.

Therefore, the parallel version of `std::for_each` simply just returns void.

Parallelizing an index-based for-loop

Even though we recommend using algorithms, sometimes a raw, index-based `for`-loop is required for a specific task. The STL algorithms do provide an equivalent of a range-based `for`-loop, but there is no equivalent of a regular index-based `for`-loop.

In other words, a range based `for`-loop is equal to the STL algorithm `for_each`...

```
auto mice = std::vector<std::string>{"Mickey", "Minnie", "Jerry"};
// Range based for loop
for(auto m: mice) {
  std::cout << m << '\n';
}
// STL algorithm std::for_each
std::for_each(mice.begin(), mice.end(), [](auto m){
  std::cout << m << '\n';
});
```

...but, there is no STL algorithm equivalent of an index-based `for`-loop:

```
for(size_t i = 0; i < mice.size(); ++i) {
  std::cout << i << " " << mice[i] << '\n';
}
```

Therefore, we cannot parallelize an index-based `for`-loop by simply adding a parallel policy like with other STL-algorithms. Let's see how we can build one.

As mentioned earlier, we do not recommend to write parallel algorithms yourself due to the complexity of writing a parallel algorithm. However, in this case we will build the `parallel_for` algorithm using `std::for_each` as building block, thus leaving the complexity parallelism to `std::for_each`.

Combining std::for_each with linear range

What we can do instead is to combine `std::for_each()` with the `LinearRange` class described in `Chapter 5`, *A Deeper Look at Iterators*. To remind you, the `LinearRange` class is constructed via the function `make_linear_range()` which returns a range of numbers that can be iterated just like a regular container.

An index-based `for`-loop based on an STL algorithm can be created like this:

```
auto first_idx = size_t{0};
auto last_idx = mice.size();
auto indices = make_linear_range(first_idx, last_idx, last_idx);
std::for_each(indices.begin(), indices.end(), [&mice](size_t i){
  std::cout << i << " " << mice[i] << '\n';
});
```

This can then be further parallelized with an execution policy of choice:

```
auto p = std::execution::par;
std::for_each(p, indices.begin(), indices.end(), [&mice](size_t i){
  if (i == 0) mice[i] += " is first.";
  else if (i + 1 == mice.size()) mice[i] += " is last.";
});
for(const auto& m: mice) { std::cout << m << ', '; }

// Output: Mickey is first, Minnie, Jerry is last,
```

Simplifying construction via a wrapper

In order to iterate the indices with a neat syntax the previous code is wrapped into a utility function named `parallel_for()` as shown below:

```
template <typename Policy, typename Index, typename F>
auto parallel_for(Policy p, Index first, Index last, F f) {
  auto r = make_linear_range<Index>(first, last, last);
  std::for_each(std::move(p), r.begin(), r.end(), std::move(f));
}
```

The `parallel_for()` can then be used like this:

```
parallel_for(std::execution::par, size_t{0}, mice.size(), [&](size_t i){
  if (idx == 0) mice[i] += " is first.";
  else if (i + 1 == mice.size()) mice[i] += " is last.";
});
for(const auto& m: mice)
  std::cout << m << ', ';
// Output: Mickey is first, Minnie, Jerry is last,
```

As the `parallel_for` is built upon `std::for_each`, it accepts any policy that `std::for_each` accepts.

Executing STL algorithms on the GPU

Graphics processing units, or GPUs, were originally designed and used for processing points and pixels for computer graphics rendering. Briefly, what the GPUs did was to retrieve a buffer of pixel data or vertex data, perform a simple operation on each one of them individually, and store the result in a new buffer (to eventually be displayed).

GPU APIs and parallel operations

The main API for programming the GPU is OpenGL, although similar functionality is available in DirectX as well.

Here are some examples of simple, independent operations that could be executed on the GPU at an early stage:

- Transform a point from world coordinates to screen coordinates.
- Perform a lighting calculation at a specific point (by lighting calculation I refer to calculating the color of a specific pixel in an image).

As these operations could be performed in parallel, the GPUs were designed for executing small operations in parallel.

Technically, a CPU commonly consists of a few general-purpose cached cores, whereas a GPU consists of a huge number of highly specialized cores. This means that the better an algorithm scales when parallelized, the more suitable it is to execute on the GPU.

Programmable GPUs

Later on, these operations became programmable, although the programs were written in terms of computer graphics (that is, the memory reads were done in terms of reading colors from a texture, and the result was always written as a color to a texture). These programs are called *shaders*.

Shader programs

At the beginning, there were two types of shader programs, *vertex shaders* and *fragment shaders*.

Vertex shaders were used to transform world coordinates into screen space coordinates, and fragment shaders performed lighting calculations/texture lookups just before writing a pixel to the screen.

Over time, more shader-type programs were introduced and shaders gained more and more low-level options, such as reading/writing raw values from buffers instead of color values from textures.

STL algorithms and the GPU

In the future, the execution policies mentioned earlier in this chapter will hopefully be extended to support processing on the GPU, thus making all of the power available on a standard computer utilizable in C++. Nevertheless, there are already several libraries available that make GPU programming easily accessible.

As stressed earlier, if you have a code base built on algorithms rather than hand-crafted `for`-loops, moving it to take advantage of the GPU is far more accessible.

Boost Compute

In this book, we have chosen Boost Compute (written by Kyle Lutz) as the library for accessing the GPU. The reasons we picked Boost Compute are that it is very well written, vendor independent, and contains almost all STL algorithms. On top of that, it is a part of Boost, one of the most widely used C++ library.

Throughout this section we will keep a steady focus on the syntactic similarities between Boost Compute and STL algorithms, therefore many Boost Compute code examples will be presented side by side with its equivalent STL algorithm implementation.

Basic concepts of Boost Compute

Boost Compute has a few basic concepts, which are good to grasp before going further:

- Device, the equivalent of the actual GPU on which the operations will be executed
- Context, the context could be considered the gate to the device
- Queue, a command queue on which you push operations, which are then executed asynchronously via the GPU driver

On top of that, as GPUs in many cases have their own exclusive memory (although it often uses the standard RAM), all containers handled by Boost Compute must be copied to Boost Compute's designated containers before processing, and back to standard containers for further processing by the CPU.

OpenCL

We will not use OpenCL directly in this chapter. However, OpenCL is the underlying framework used by the Boost Compute library that we will use. OpenCL is maintained by the Khronos group, which also maintains OpenGL, and is available for a large number of platforms. Internally, the OpenCL program uses a C99 syntax that it executes on the GPU (just like the OpenGL shaders). The OpenCL shader is passed from your C++ application as a string containing its source code and compiled by the OpenCL when the application executes.

To use OpenCL, you would need to set up custom buffers through a quite complicated state machine, which we will not cover in this book. Instead, we will use Boost Compute to access OpenCL.

Initializing Boost Compute

Before you can use Boost Compute, we need to initialize a device, context, and a command queue. We will be passing the context and the command queue as mutable references to all our examples with Boost Compute.

The most simple way to initialize the context and the command queue is to use the system default device, like this:

```
#include <boost/compute.hpp>
auto main() -> int {
  // Initialize Boost Compute and OpenCL
  namespace bc = boost::compute;
  auto device = bc::system::default_device();
  auto context = bc::context(device);
  auto command_queue = bc::command_queue(context, device);
}
```

Transfer a simple transform-reduce algorithm to Boost Compute

Let's say we have a `std::vector` of circles, and we want to calculate the sum of all circle areas. The algorithm we will use is `std::transform()` to transform the vector of circles to a vector of areas, and then `std::reduce()` to summarize the areas.

The Circle struct is defined as shown below, where `x` and `y` denotes the position, and `r` denotes the radius.

```
struct Circle { float x, y, r; };
```

We will also use this function to generate a `std::vector` of random circles:

```
auto make_circles(size_t n) {
  auto cs = std::vector<Circle>{};
  cs.resize(n);
  std::generate(cs.begin(), cs.end(), [](){
    auto x = float(std::rand());
    auto y = float(std::rand());
    auto r = std::abs(float(std::rand()));
    return Circle{x, y, r};
  });
  return cs;
}
```

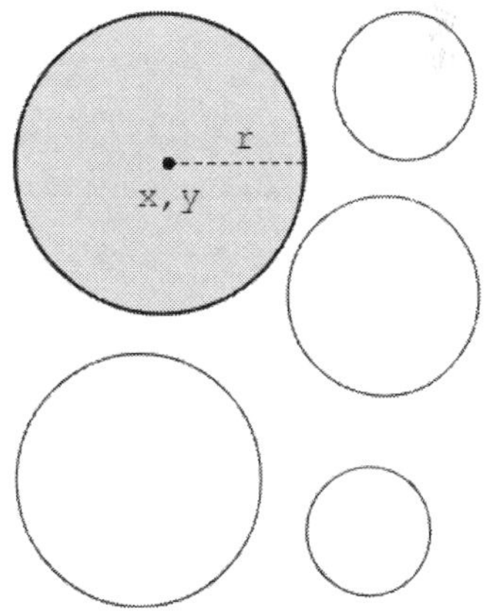

Circles of different size and position

The algorithm in standard C++

The formula for the area of a circle is, as you probably remember from middle-school; $area = r^2\pi$. In english, it's radius squared times pi. Here it is in code:

```
auto circle_area_cpu(const Circle& c) {
  const auto pi = 3.14f;
  return c.r * c.r * pi;
}
```

Using the `circle_area_cpu()` function, we can calculate the full area using `std::transform()` and `std::reduce()` in C++:

```
auto sum_circle_areas_cpu() {
  constexpr auto n = 1024;
  auto circles = make_circles(n);
  auto areas = std::vector<float>(n);
  std::transform(circles.begin(), circles.end(), areas.begin(),
    circle_area_cpu);
  auto plus = std::plus<float>{};
  auto area = std::reduce(areas.begin(), areas.end(), 0.0f, plus);
  std::cout << area << '\n';
}
```

Transforming the algorithm to Boost Compute

Let's see how the equivalent would be implemented using the GPU with Boost Compute. In order to implement it, we have to perform a few extra steps:

- Inform *Boost Compute* of the content of the `Circle` struct
- Implement an *OpenCL* equivalent of the `circle_area_cpu()` function
- Copy the data back and forth to the GPU

Note that `circle_area_gpu()` and `boost::compute::plus<float>` are compiled by the OpenCL driver at runtime, although the binary can be stored for future use.

Adapting the circle struct for use with Boost Compute

The first thing we have to do is to make Boost Compute know what the `Circle` struct looks like, in order to be able to use it on the GPU. This is achieved by using a macro where the first two parameters are the C++ name and the GPU name of the struct, and the third parameter is the list of members in the struct.

Only the members of the struct are exposed, member functions of the struct cannot be accessed from within Boost Compute.

Below is how we adapt the `Circle` for use with Boost Compute using the `BOOST_COMPUTE_ADAPT_STRUCT_MACRO`. The first parameter is the name of the C++ struct, and the second parameter is the name when accessed from inside Boost Compute.

```
BOOST_COMPUTE_ADAPT_STRUCT(Circle, Circle, (x, y, r));
```

This adaption is only necessary if we want to use a custom struct; standard data types such as floats, integers, and so on can be used directly.

All members of a struct adapted in Boost Compute **must** be aligned, that is, it may not contain any padding between members. For more information about alignment see `Chapter 4`, *Data Structures.*

Converting circle_area_cpu to Boost Compute

We now need to create an OpenCL function equivalent of the `circle_area_cpu()` function. The OpenCL programming language uses a standard C syntax, and is therefore quite similar to the C++ version. For further reference of the OpenCL language, we refer to its official documentation available at `https://www.khronos.org/opencl/`.

The source code of the function is passed as a `std::string` to `boost::compute::function`, where the first parameter is the name of the OpenCL function intended to be exposed, and the second parameter is the actual source code.

```
namespace bc = boost::compute;
auto src_code = std::string_view{
  "float circle_area_gpu(Circle c) { "
  "  float pi = 3.14f;               "
  "  return c.r * c.r * pi;          "
  "}                                 "
};

auto circle_area_gpu = bc::make_function_from_source<float(Circle)> (
  "circle_area_gpu", src_code.data()
);
```

The BOOST_COMPUTE_FUNCTION macro

As mentioned, we are using strings for the OpenCL source code. In order to get a little bit more readability, Boost Compute comes with a convenience macro called `BOOST_COMPUTE_FUNCTION`, which makes strings out of the source code parameter.

The following table shows a syntactical comparison of them:

<table>
<tr><th>Using <code>make_function_from_source</code>:</th><th>Using <code>BOOST_COMPUTE_FUNCTION</code> macro:</th></tr>
<tr><td><pre>
namespace bc = boost::compute;
auto circle_area_gpu =
 bc::make_function_from_source
  <float(Circle)> (
   "circle_area_gpu",
"float circle_area_gpu(Circle c){"
"   float pi = 3.14f;   "
"   return c.r * c.r * pi;   "
"}   "
);
</pre></td><td><pre>
BOOST_COMPUTE_FUNCTION(
  float, // Return type
  circle_area_gpu, // Name
  (Circle c), // Arg
  {
    float pi = 3.14f;
    return c.r * c.r * pi;
  }
);
</pre></td></tr>
</table>

As you can see, the return value, function name, and parameters have been stripped out of the string, and the source code does not need to be provided as a string.

Implementing the transform-reduction algorithm on the GPU

When implementing the actual transformation, we need to copy the data back and forth. The data structures housed at the GPU are prefixed with `gpu_`, and data structures housed at the CPU are prefixed with `cpu_`.

Note that Boost Compute has been nice enough to provide a `compute::plus<float>` functor equivalent of `std::plus`, which we use when the areas are reduced:

```
namespace bc = boost::compute;
auto circle_areas_gpu(bc::context& context, bc::command_queue& q) {
  // Create a bunch of random circles and copy to the GPU
  const auto n = 1024;
  auto cpu_circles = make_circles(n);
  auto gpu_circles = bc::vector<Circle>(n, context);
  bc::copy(cpu_circles.begin(), cpu_circles.end(), gpu_circles.begin(), q);
  // Transform the circles into their individual areas
  auto gpu_areas = bc::vector<float>(n, context);
  bc::transform(
    gpu_circles.begin(),
    gpu_circles.end(),
```

```
    gpu_areas.begin(),
    circle_area_gpu,
    q
  );
  // Accumulate the circle areas,
  // Note that we are writing to a GPU vector of size 1
  auto gpu_area = bc::vector<float>(1, context);
  bc::reduce(gpu_areas.begin(), gpu_areas.end(), gpu_area.begin(), q);
  // Copy the accumulated area back to the cpu
  auto cpu_area = float{};
  bc::copy(gpu_area.begin(), gpu_area.end(), &cpu_area, q);
  std::cout << cpu_area << '\n';
}
```

Using predicates with Boost Compute

If we would like to execute other algorithms, for example sort the circles by their radius, we provide predicates just like in STL.

Here is how you would use a predicate for sorting circles on the CPU and the corresponding predicate in Boost Compute/OpenCL.

Note that in this example, we use the Boost Computes capability to use a regular `std::vector` as input, although it does not operate on it. Internally, it still copies the `std::vector` back and forth to the GPU device before and after the algorithm is executed:

<table>
<tr><th>CPU predicate</th><th>GPU predicate</th></tr>
<tr><td><pre>auto less_r_cpu = [](Circle a,Circle b){
  return a.r < b.r;
};</pre></td><td><pre>BOOST_COMPUTE_FUNCTION(
  bool, // Return type
  less_r_gpu, // Function Name
  (Circle a, Circle b), // Args
  { return a.r < b.r; } // Code
);</pre></td></tr>
</table>

Sort the content on the GPU, and verify using the CPU:

```
namespace bc = boost::compute;
auto sort_by_r(bc::context& context, bc::command_queue& q) {
  auto n = 1024;
  auto circles = make_circles(n);
  // Sort on GPU
  bc::sort(circles.begin(), circles.end(), less_r_gpu, q);
  // Verify on the CPU using less_r_cpu
  assert(std::is_sorted(circles.begin(), circles.end(), less_r_cpu);
}
```

As you can see, modifying a standard STL function to execute on the GPU using Boost Compute only requires very few modifications.

Using a custom kernel in Boost Compute

As mentioned earlier, this is not intended as a course in OpenCL, but we will now have a look at how to move away from the algorithms and abstractions of Boost Compute and invoke regular `for`-loops where elements are read at random positions in an array. In other words, the following example is almost bare OpenCL, rather than Boost Compute.

As OpenCL evolves from a computer graphics background, it does contain a multitude of operations for handling textures and filtering, but in order to see the resemblance of regular C++ code, we will use traditional vectors to operate on.

Remember that a GPU is very good at executing many tasks in parallel, and OpenCL correspondingly needs to be informed of what exactly it can parallelize. When executing the kernel, we will therefore give it a number of ranges, just like a multidimensional `for`-loop of which it will apply the kernel in parallel.

Box filter

We are going to implement an algorithm, which applies a box filter of size **r** to a gray scale image. The box filter simply calculates the mean value of the surrounding floats, illustrated as follows, and the image itself is represented as a `std::vector<float>` and an integer representing its width. Note that we simplify the algorithm by avoiding the borders, which relieves us from out-of-bounds checks:

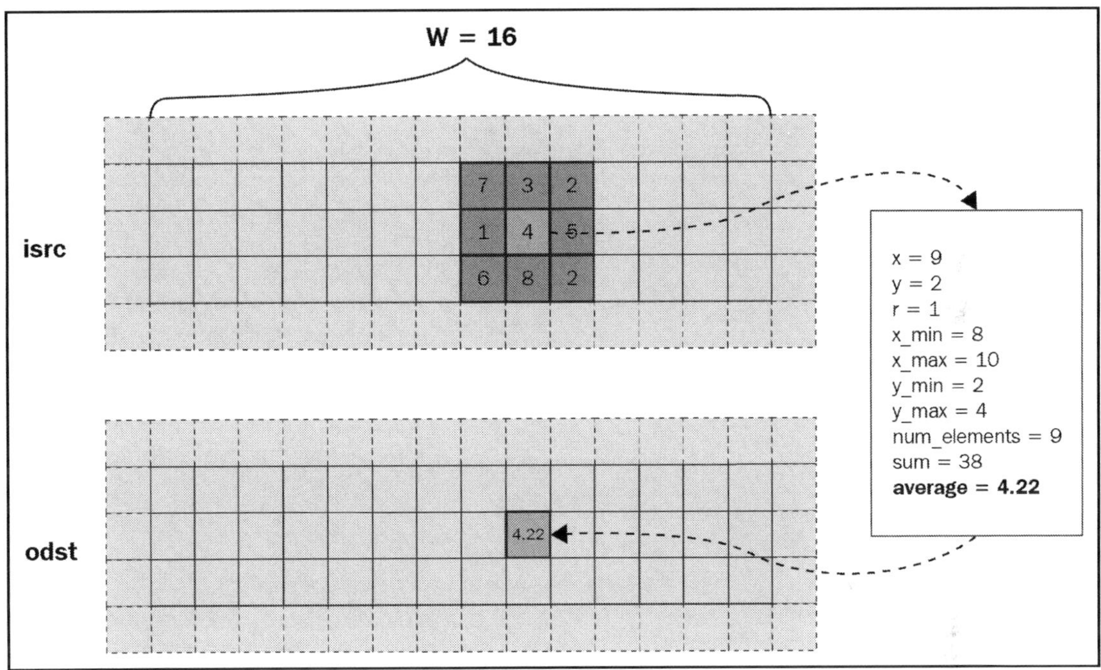

Box filter of an individual grid element

Implementing the kernel

We implement the per element box filter as a regular lambda function in C++, and the corresponding OpenCL kernel as a string. In order to see the resemblance, we've put them side by side:

<table>
<tr><th>C++ box filter kernel</th><th>OpenCL box filter kernel</th></tr>
<tr><td>
<pre>
auto box_filter = [](
  int x,
  int y,
  const auto& src,
  auto& odst,
  int w,
  int r
) {
 float sum = 0.0f;
 for (int yp=y-r; yp<=y+r; ++yp) {
  for (int xp=x-r; xp<=(x+r);++xp){
   sum += src[yp * w + xp];
  }
 }
 float n = ((r*2 + 1) * (r*2 + 1));
 float average = sum / n;
 odst[y*w + x] = average;
};
</pre>
</td><td>
<pre>
auto src_code = std::string_view{
"kernel void box_filter("
" global const float* src,   "
" global float* odst,   "
" int w,   "
" int r   "
") {   "
" int x = get_global_id(0);   "
" int y = get_global_id(1);   "
" float sum = 0.0f;   "
" for (int yp=y-r; yp<=y+r; ++yp){   "
"   for (int xp=x-r; xp<=x+r; ++xp){   "
"   sum += src[yp*w+xp];   "
"   }   "
" }   "
" float n=(float)((r*2+1)*(r*2+1));   "
" float average = sum / n;   "
" odst[y*w+x] = average;   "
"}   "
};
namespace bc = boost::compute;
auto p=bc::program::create_with_source(
  src_code.data(), context
);
p.build();
auto kernel = bc::kernel{
  p, "box_filter"
};
</pre>
</td></tr>
</table>

Parallelizing for two dimensions

Now, let's use the filters by applying them to the images. The arguments for the Boost Compute kernel are set using `set_arg` before execution, and when the execution is performed using `enqueue_nd_range_kernel()`, we apply the number of dimensions and the ranges of each dimension, which is the equivalent of how a double `for`-loop is used in the C++ code. The corresponding x and y variables in the kernel are then fetched using `get_global_id()` in OpenCL.

Take notice of the similarities between STL algorithms and the *Boost Compute* equivalents as shown in the table below:

<table>
<tr><th>Box filter on CPU</th><th>Box filter on GPU</th></tr>
<tr><td>

```
auto box_filter_test_cpu(
 int w,
 int h,
 int r
) {
 using array_t =
std::array<size_t,2>;
 // Create std vectors
 auto src = std::vector<float>(w*h);
std::iota(src.begin(),src.end(),0.f);
 auto dst = std::vector<float>(w*h);
std::fill(res.begin(),res.end(),0.f);
 // Make offset and elements
 auto offset = array_t{r,r};
 auto elems = array_t{w-r-r, h-r-r};
 // Invoke filter on CPU
 for (int x=0; x < elems[0]; ++x){
   for (int y=0; y < elems[1]; ++y){
     auto xp = x + offset[0];
     auto yp = y + offset[1];
     box_filter(xp,yp,src,dst,w,r);
   }
 }
 return dst;
}
```

</td><td>

```
namespace bc = boost::compute;
auto box_filter_test_gpu(
 int w,
 int h,
 int r,
 bc::context& ctx,
 bc::command_queue& q,
 bc::kernel& kernel
) {
 using array_t = std::array<size_t,
2>;
 // Create vectors for GPU
 auto src=bc::vector<float>(w*h, ctx);
bc::iota(src.begin(),src.end(),0.f,q);
 auto dst=bc::vector<float>(w*h, ctx);
bc::fill(dst.begin(),dst.end(),0.f,q);
 // Make offset and elements
 auto offset = array_t{r,r};
 auto elems = array_t{w-r-r, h-r-r};
 // Invoke filter on GPU
 kernel.set_arg(0, src);
 kernel.set_arg(1, dst);
 kernel.set_arg(2, w);
 kernel.set_arg(3, r);
 q.enqueue_nd_range_kernel(
    kernel,
    2,
    offset.data(),
    elems.data(),
    nullptr
 );
 // Copy back to cpu
 auto dst_cpu=std::vector<float>(w*h);
 bc::copy(
   dst.begin(),
   dst.end(),
   dst_cpu.begin(),
   q
 );
 return dst_cpu;
}
```

</td></tr>
</table>

Note that the `enqueue_nd_range_kernel()` function accepts any amount of dimensions to parallelize over, although we use two dimensions in this example.

Verify GPU computation on the CPU

As GPUs are generally harder to debug than a regular C++ program, verifying the results is utterly important. As we are dealing with floating-point math, the result might not be 100% accurate, therefore we use a `flt_eq()` function that accepts minor differences as equal:

```
auto test_kernel(bc::context& ctx, bc::command_queue& q, bc::kernel& k) {
  auto flt_eq = [](float a, float b) {
     auto epsilon = 0.00001f;
     return std::abs(a - b) <= epsilon;
  };
  auto cpu = box_filter_test_cpu(2000, 1000, 2);
  auto gpu = box_filter_test_gpu(2000, 1000, 2, ctx, q, k);
  auto is_equal = cpu == dst;
  auto is_almost_equal = std::equal(
    cpu.begin(), cpu.end(), gpu.begin(), flt_eq
  );
  std::cout
    << "is_equal: " << is_equal << '\n'
    << "is_almost_equal: " << is_float_equal << '\n'
}

// Possible output
is_equal: 0
is_almost_equal: 1
```

Note that `is_equal` might as well be one depending on the hardware. With this piece of code, we have successfully verified that our algorithm works on the GPU. We've intentionally not included any performance comparisons between the CPU and GPU in this book, as the GPU algorithms are often bottlenecked by transferring data back and forth to the GPU. But with that in mind, a computation time in the range of 30x faster on a standard GPU compared to a standard CPU is not uncommon.

In other words, a modern, computationally-heavy application will be written with GPU parallelization in mind in order to be competitive.

Summary

In this chapter, you have learned the complexity of handcrafting an algorithm to execute in parallel and how to use the parallel versions of the STL algorithms. On top of that, we've had a look at how to use *Boost Compute* in order to take advantage of the heavy processing power of modern GPU hardware.

Other Books You May Enjoy

If you enjoyed this book, you may be interested in these other books by Packt:

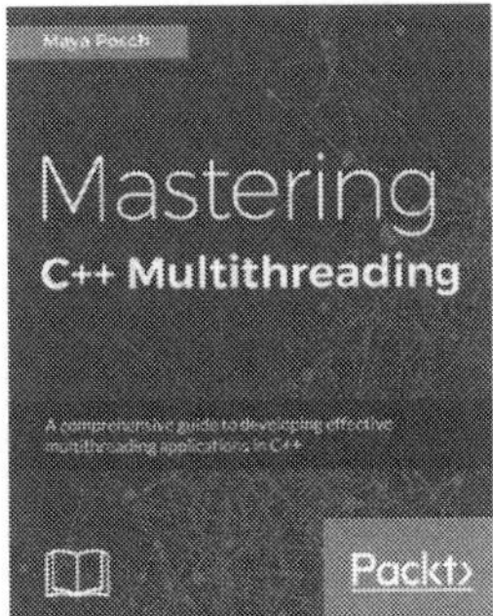

Mastering C++ Multithreading
Maya Posch

ISBN: 978-1-78712-170-6

- Deep dive into the details of the how various operating systems currently implement multithreading
- Choose the best multithreading APIs when designing a new application
- Explore the use of mutexes, spin-locks, and other synchronization concepts and see how to safely pass data between threads
- Understand the level of API support provided by various C++ toolchains
- Resolve common issues in multithreaded code and recognize common pitfalls using tools such as Memcheck, CacheGrind, DRD, Helgrind, and more
- Discover the nature of atomic operations and understand how they can be useful in optimizing code
- Implement a multithreaded application in a distributed computing environment
- Design a C++-based GPGPU application that employs multithreading

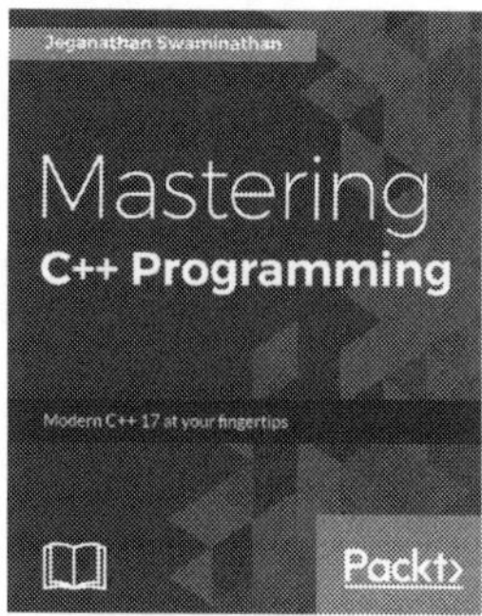

Mastering C++ Programming
Jeganathan Swaminathan

ISBN: 978-1-78646-162-9

- Write modular C++ applications in terms of the existing and newly introduced features
- Identify code-smells, clean up, and refactor legacy C++ applications
- Leverage the possibilities provided by Cucumber and Google Test/Mock to automate test cases
- Test frameworks with C++
- Get acquainted with the new C++17 features
- Develop GUI applications in C++
- Build portable cross-platform applications using standard C++ features

Leave a review - let other readers know what you think

Please share your thoughts on this book with others by leaving a review on the site that you bought it from. If you purchased the book from Amazon, please leave us an honest review on this book's Amazon page. This is vital so that other potential readers can see and use your unbiased opinion to make purchasing decisions, we can understand what our customers think about our products, and our authors can see your feedback on the title that they have worked with Packt to create. It will only take a few minutes of your time, but is valuable to other potential customers, our authors, and Packt. Thank you!

Index

A

B

C

D

E

F

G

H

I

L

M

R

S

T

U

V